BLUES GUITAR

THE MEN WHO MADE THE MUSIC

BLUES GUITAR

THE MEN WHO MADE THE MUSIC

From the Pages of Guitar Player Magazine

EDITED BY JAS OBRECHT

GPI BOOKS
San Francisco, Cupertino, Atlanta, Boston, Chicago, New York, Brussels

Dedicated to the men who made the magazine —
L.V. "Bud" Eastman, Jim Crockett,
Don Menn, and Tom Wheeler

GPI BOOKS
Miller Freeman Publications, 500 Howard Street, San Francisco, CA 94105

Library of Congress Catalog Card Number: 90-83119

ISBN 0-87930-188-0

Designed by Christian Ledgerwood
Printed in the United States of America

95 94 93 92 91 90   5 4 3 2 1

CONTENTS

INTRODUCTION

*"The blues is the first music that was here.
It was born with Eve and Adam in the Garden.
It is the one that tells the story."*
— John Lee Hooker

AND FROM THE BEGINNING, BLUES AND THE GUITAR have traveled side by side. W.C. Handy, hailed as the "Father Of The Blues," heard this music for the first time in 1903, when he was awakened in a Mississippi Delta train station by a ragged black musician. "As he played, he pressed a knife on the strings of the guitar in a manner popularized by the Hawaiian guitarists who used steel bars," Handy wrote. "The effect was unforgettable. His song, too, struck me instantly: 'Goin' where the Southern cross the Dog.' The singer repeated the line three times, accompanying himself on the guitar with the weirdest music I had ever heard." This description of a slide guitarist is also one of the earliest references to blues. Ever since then, blues guitarists have been pressing slides and fingers to strings, attempting to create the unforgettable. These articles profile some of the best.

The Country Roots section begins with the mysterious Robert Johnson — a direct descendent of the man Handy describes — and his pal Johnny Shines. Skip James and Rev. Gary Davis both recorded before Johnson and outlived him to become leading voices in the 1960s blues revival. Mance Lipscomb and Mississippi Fred McDowell soon joined them centerstage, while Son Thomas, R.L. Burnside, and John Cephas keep old-time country blues alive today. The Prime Movers chapters profile mighty Muddy Waters and a host of Chicago's finest — Willie Dixon, Jimmy Rogers, Hubert Sumlin, Buddy Guy, Otis Rush, and J.B. Hutto among them. You'll also meet John Lee Hooker, Jimmy Reed, Guitar Slim, Albert Collins, and the three Kings — Albert, B.B., and Freddie.

This is not a definitive history of blues guitar; no book without fat chapters on Blind Lemon Jefferson, Charley Patton, Lonnie Johnson, Tampa Red, T-Bone Walker, Lightnin' Hopkins, Earl Hooker, and many, many others could hope to be. Instead, it's a collection of the best blues articles published in *Guitar Player* magazine between 1974 and 1990. The focus is on players who've spent most or all of their careers as bluesmen (thus no chapters on Eric Clapton, Stevie Ray Vaughan, and dozens of other deserving practitioners). Several of the articles and discographies were updated during the editing. Enough said. Let's get to the "raw what's happening."

— Jas Obrecht
July 1990

COUNTRY ROOTS

Robert Johnson

September 1990

BY JAS OBRECHT

ROBERT JOHNSON WAS THE GREATEST country blues artist who ever lived. He mastered the Delta style as none had before, learning firsthand from men such as Willie Brown and Son House, and then expanded his music with outside influences from 78s by Lonnie Johnson, Kokomo Arnold, Leroy Carr, and many others. A slide guitarist without parallel, Johnson cast strikingly original lyrics with Shakespearean skill. He was truly standing at a musical crossroads when he made his 29 recordings, simultaneously looking back to old-time Delta blues while foretelling the future of electric blues, R&B, and rock and roll. For the first time, all of Johnson's 1936 and '37 Vocalion titles — including the various takes — have been gathered in one package, Columbia's *Robert Johnson: The Complete Recordings*.

Robert's spectacular talent, shrouded background, and unsolved murder gave rise to wild speculations: He was a fierce, driven man, it was whispered, who walked side by side with the devil himself and swapped his soul at a lonely crossroads for an ungodly talent. Slowed by stones in his passway, betrayed by evil-hearted women, dogged by hell hounds, he drifted shadow-like through the Mississippi Delta, never staying long in one place. When his number was up, he went out on his hands and knees, barking and snapping like a dog.

Fueling the mystery was the fact that no photograph of Robert Johnson was published before 1986. Today, thanks to the research of blues scholars such as Steve LaVere, Gayle Dean Wardlow, Robert Palmer, and David Evans, a new sense of the historical Robert Johnson has emerged. This article strives to separate facts from fiction.

The son of Noah Johnson and Julia Major, Robert Leroy Johnson was born in Hazelhurst, Mississippi, on May 8, 1911. Years earlier, his mother had been married to a successful wicker furniture maker, Charles Dodds, who fled to Memphis with a lynch mob at his heels. Julia's eighth child, Robert was born out of wedlock. The boy's earliest years were spent traveling with his mother around various plantations and labor camps, and for a few years he lived in Memphis with

Charles Dodds, who was then calling himself Charles Spencer. About 1918, Julia and her second husband, Willie "Dusty" Willis, moved to Commerce, a sharecroppers' settlement on Richard Leatherman's plantation near Robinsonville, 40 miles south of Memphis. Robert lived with the family until he was 18, although his relationship with Willis was fraught with friction. A hard-working fieldhand, Dusty had little tolerance for his stepson's lackadaisical ways, and on occasion Robert found it prudent to run away and stay with sympathetic neighbors. Robert went by the last name of Spencer until his teens, when his mother told him about Noah Johnson. It's been suggested that he used other names, as well: Robert Dodds, R.L. Spencer, Robert Saxton, or Sax. Johnny Temple, who traded licks with Johnson, knew him only as R.L. In several songs, Johnson referred to himself as Bob.

Like many Delta performers, Robert's first instruments were Jew's harp and harmonica. Son's wife, Evie House, remembered his displays of harmonica prowess during recesses at a one-room Methodist church near the Robert Coxer plantation. Around 1927, Robert acquired a guitar and began teaching himself to play blues. One of the first tunes he worked out was Leroy Carr's 1928 hit, "How Long — How Long Blues."

For many plantation blacks, blues was "devil's music" and strictly taboo. Robert Palmer described in *Deep Blues* [Viking]: "Blues in the Delta, which may or may not have been the first blues anywhere but is certainly the first blues we know about, was created not just by black people but by the poorest, most marginal black people. Most of the men and women who sang and played it could neither read nor write. They owned almost nothing and lived in virtual serfdom. They were not considered respectable enough to work as house servants for whites or to hold responsible positions within their own communities. Blues was so disreputable that even its staunchest devotees frequently found it prudent to disown it. If you asked a black preacher, schoolteacher, small landowner, or faithful church-goer what kind of people played and listened to

For many plantation blacks, blues was "devil's music" and strictly taboo.

blues, they would tell you, 'cornfield niggers.'" It was in this class that Robert found his heroes. Willie Brown, a much-admired guitarist living in Robinsonville, taught Robert some chords and fingering techniques, and introduced him to Charley Patton, the heaviest and best-known Delta guitarist. Robert followed Brown around to juke houses, picnics, and country stores, studying his techniques and arrangements. Years later, Johnson sang about "my friend-boy Willie Brown" in "Cross Road Blues."

Johnson married 15-year-old Virginia Travis in February 1929 and moved in with his half-sister on the Klein plantation. Palmer's research indicates that the author of "Me And The Devil Blues" was an attentive husband, but within 14 months Virginia and their baby died during childbirth. Robert found his greatest musical inspiration a few months later when Son House settled in Robinsonville. Cut in May 1930, House's 78s were among the most intense, anguished, and powerful blues yet recorded. Unlike Patton — a "clowning man" with a guitar — House took his music mighty seriously. Sitting on a straight-back chair, he'd suddenly whip his head back, roll his eyes inside his skull, and yank his bottleneck up to the 12th fret. Veins bulging in his forehead, he'd moan, thump a bass note, and sing with the deep conviction of a sinner on judgement day. His propulsive one-chord slide and frighteningly intense vocals in "My Black Mama" must have seemed apocryphal to the church-raised teenager:

> *Hey, it ain't no heaven now*
> *It ain't no burning hell*
> *Says where I'm going when I die*
> *Can't nobody tell*

Still a novice, Johnson sat at the feet of House and Brown (and probably Patton), who'd occasionally down too much moonshine and growl, "Beat it, kid — you'll get stepped on!" Robert picked up experience playing with Son's brother Frank House, appeared at barrelhouses with pianist Punk Taylor from nearby Lost Lake, and worked around Hughes,

Arkansas, with a second guitarist named Wash Hemp. Elizabeth Moore recalled seeing him sit in with Willie Brown at a juke joint just north of Robinsonville, where Brown played *backup* to Johnson. By then Robert had what was surely one of the loudest guitars around — a wood-bodied Stella with a metal resonator. It suited his style, which was soon to expand beyond his mentors'. "When Saxton'd be playin'," Willie Moore told Gayle Dean Wardlow, "he want to play lead all the time." Around this same time, Wardlow reports, "Willie Moore was arrested with Robert Johnson on the streets of Robinsonville, and they got put in the city jail for two or three hours. The reason was because they were singing about the local sheriff! Robert had been playing lead, while Willie played second guitar on the bass strings."

Rory Block, a superb guitarist who specializes in close covers of deep Delta blues, feels that Son House is the musician Robert most resembled: "He probably got his command of the popular open-G tuning heard in 'Cross Road Blues' and 'Walkin' Blues' from Son House and Willie Brown. Willie Brown had a great snapping bass-string style and was putting percussion and unbelievable rhythm to that tuning. He was also very clean and precision-oriented; you can hear it in 'M&O Blues' and 'Future Blues.' Charley Patton did all that pounding and strumming, and he was snapping the bass strings, too. But where Patton was using open G in a really smooth way, Johnson took it away from the flowing sound into this dimension of sophisticated rhythms and percussion. Son House was definitely from the same school, but nobody got it as incredibly sophisticated as Johnson. Robert's slide style was spectacular, too, especially with its separation of individual notes. Robert Johnson learned to combine it all into one style — the strumming, the slide, the percussion, the snapping, everything. He's it. He's the king."

A former playing partner of Charley Patton and Willie Brown, Willie Moore chanced upon Johnson in front of a Robinsonville grocery store in about 1930 and joined him in an impromptu jam. Decades later, Moore described Johnson's repertoire to Gayle

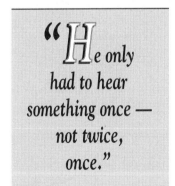

"He only had to hear something once — not twice, once."

Dean Wardlow and Stephen Calt for an account published in *78 Quarterly*: "He sing about: 'Captain George, Did Your Money Come.' Next thing he played about: 'Make Me Down,' but he never did say '*Make* me down a pallet,' he say: '*Flung* me down a pallet on your floor, an' make it so your man won't never know.'" Johnson then launched into "Black Gal, Whyn'cha Comb Your Head," "You Can Mistreat Me Here But You Can't When I Go Home," "President McKinley" (a slide song derived from "Frankie And Johnny"), "East St. Louis Blues," and a bottleneck "Casey Jones" renamed "A Thousand And Five On The Road Again." From this account, Wardlow speculates, "it would appear that the only one of Johnson's recordings that might have been typified by his early repertoire was 'Last Fair Deal Gone Down,' a 16-bar 'rag' ditty Henry Thomas had recorded as 'Red River Blues.'" By the time he returned to Robinsonville in 1932, Wardlow reports, Johnson was performing "Kind Hearted Woman Blues," "32-20 Blues," "Rambling On My Mind," "Cross Road Blues," and "Come On In My Kitchen," a slide take-off on the Mississippi Sheiks' popular "Sitting On Top Of The World."

Johnson quickly developed the best musical ear in the Delta. "He only had to hear something once — not twice, *once*," insists Johnny Shines, who began his celebrated rambles with Johnson in 1935. "Whatsoever you did on a horn or on a piano, he figured he could do on a guitar, and he did it. And he didn't look for it, either. I never seen him practice. I never seen him look for nothin'. He'd just sit down, tune a guitar, whatsoever you wanted him to play, he'd play it. Robert heard something on the radio he liked, he never stopped talking with you. Tonight or tomorrow, he'd pick up his guitar and play the song, note-for-note, chord-for-chord, word-for-word. He was way before his time. I know many chords he never heard of, because he couldn't read music, but he could just pick up a guitar and make them. He was a genius."

Much of Johnson's growth was due to his extraordinary ability to cop music from records. Lonnie Johnson's brilliant single-string solos inspired him to expand his dexterity and harmonic awareness, and Robert's "Malted Milk" and "Drunken Hearted Man" are patterned on Lonnie's tunes. Robert drew from pianists, too. Leroy Carr's lush chording and rolling rhythms and Roosevelt Sykes' rumbling bass may have been a source for his boogie bass lines. Johnson reworked Carr's "When The Sun Goes Down" as "Love In Vain." Carr's partner, Scrapper Blackwell clearly impacted Johnson's guitar playing.

Robert undoubtedly owned or heard Kokomo Arnold 78s, recasting Arnold's 1934 hit "Old Original Kokomo Blues" (along with its predecessor, Blackwell's 1929 "Kokomo Blues") as "Sweet Home Chicago." He mined the 78's flip side for the lyrics of "Milkcow's Calf Blues," which also borrowed from Son House's "My Black Mama." Arnold's "Sagefield Woman" provided the familiar lyrics of "I Believe I'll Dust My Broom." Johnny Temple, who learned the E minor tuning from Skip James, showed Robert the pattern for James' "Devil Got My Woman," which Robert transformed into "Hell Hound On My Trail." Skip's "22-20 Blues" was recast as "32-20 Blues," the frantic quality of which, notes David Evans, "seems to foreshadow the ascendency of jive and bebop music in the late 1930s and the 1940s." Inspired by Ishman Bracey's rapid vibrato and field holler phrasing, Peetie Wheatstraw's studied laziness, and the falsetto jumps and yodels of Tommy Johnson and Skip James, Johnson's singing developed an emotional range capable of extending from growls and howls to sly innuendos, passionate come-ons, and desperate pleas.

Robert Palmer describes in *Deep Blues* how Robert's musicianship may also have been helped by a fine, unrecorded guitarist steeped in East Coast styles: "After Johnson left Robinsonville, he returned to the vicinity of Hazelhurst, which he must have only dimly remembered from his earliest childhood, and married an older woman. She worked to support him while he developed his guitar playing under the tutelage of a musician named Ike Zinnerman, who was from Alabama and

claimed to have learned to play by visiting graveyards at midnight." By the time he returned to Robinsonville a year or so later — without a wife — Johnson had transformed himself into the Delta's most progressive bluesman. Palmer continues: "He made the instrument sound uncannily like a full band, furnishing a heavy beat with his feet, chording innovative shuffle rhythms, and picking out a high, treble-string lead with his slider, all at the same time. Fellow guitarists would watch him with unabashed, open-mouthed wonder. They were watching the Delta's first modern bluesman at work, and the experience must have induced more than a few cases of future shock." It also gave birth to the rumor that Johnson shook hands with Satan, exchanging his soul for musical skill.

"I've got ramblin', I've got ramblin' on my mind" could well be Johnson's most autobiographical lyric. Driven by incurable wanderlust, he spent his last five years drifting from town to town, woman to woman, never staying long enough to make deep friendships. While his records netted him several hundred dollars — big money during the Depression — most of the time he lived hand-to-mouth, playing for tips at plantations, levee camps, railroad stations, house parties, and streetcorners. After orbiting Jackson, Sunflower, and other Delta towns, he ventured to St. Louis and Memphis. Johnny Temple, who picked up his "Lead Pencil Blues" boogie-bass lick from Johnson, was interviewed by Gayle Dean Wardlow in 1967 and '68. Wardlow reveals: "Temple told me that R.L. was living in Hattiesburg, Mississippi, around 1932. He said that R.L. — and that's the name he knew Johnson by — would hop a freight train from Hattiesburg to Jackson on Friday afternoons, and then he and Temple would play together in Jackson on Friday nights. On Saturdays, he told me, R.L. would ride the freight to Sunflower County to play up there. Then he'd ride back home."

Robert's life on the road was littered with heartbreak women, empty whiskey bottles, Jim Crow laws, and scrapes with cops and railroad bulls.

> *Robert's life on the road was littered with heartbreak women, empty whiskey bottles, Jim Crow laws, and scrapes with cops and railroad bulls.*

As Shines describes it, after riding the rails or hitch-hiking to a town, they'd head straight for the black neighborhood: "All the towns was segregated then, whites on one side of the tracks, blacks on the other one. We'd play all day, if the money was still hoppin', because we didn't have no particular place to go. As long as there's nickels and dimes afloat. When they quit, then we'd just walk on."

What sort of traveling companion was Robert Johnson? Shines remembers him as a peaceable man who "wouldn't carry a gun huntin'" — until intoxicated: "He started drinking, he'd do any goddanged thing. Wasn't nothin' too good for him to do. We drank that fist-made liquor at that time. Corn liquor. And Ten High when the bonded liquor come in, Ten High and Dixie Dew."

While Shines and Johnson shared freight cars, meals, and boarding houses, they did not play together. Shines worked one side of the street, while Johnson worked the other: "He'd draw his gang; I'd draw mine." In those days, Johnson had a Kalamazoo arch-top, while Shines played a Regal. Neither man owned a case, and they traveled with guitars slung across their backs. "We used regular tuning, most time," Shines observes, "but we'd tune them in open G or open A for bottleneck. Open D, E. Open A was called vastapol." (A guitar in open G is tuned *D G D G B D*, low to high; open A is the same pattern a whole-step higher. Open D is *D A D F♯ A D*, and open E follows the same configuration two frets higher.) Johnson fashioned his own slides by breaking long-necked bottles and trimming them to size with a pair of pliers. "He used the slide on his little finger; it wasn't long enough to fret across the whole neck," Johnny remembers. "For certain tunes he liked using a knife. As far as picking, he'd play with a thumbpick, fingerpick, straight pick, and sometimes he'd ride bareback [*laughs*]. He'd play with his thumb and first finger mostly, though he'd sometimes use his thumb and two fingers." On occasion, Johnson blew through a harmonica attached to a rack on his guitar.

With his disfigured left eye and scarred cheek, Johnson was sometimes described as a seedy, low-life character, but this image is strikingly contradicted by a Memphis studio portrait taken in 1935: Smiling broadly, Robert wears a plastic thumbpick while fretting a fifth-position chord on a round-hole acoustic. With his perfect three-piece pinstripe suit, high-gloss wingtips, and jaunty fedora, he exudes the essence of 1930s cool; in this getup, one senses, he could easily be whisked into a swanky Harlem bijou. Shines says his language matched his image: "He talked really hip. Like, 'Yeah, man,' you know, or 'Look, daddy so-and-so' and 'Look, baby so-and-so' — like that."

Robert Johnson's first recording sessions were arranged by H.C. Speir, a white man who owned a music store at 111 N. Farrish in Jackson, Mississippi. Years before, Speir had proved his uncanny talent for recognizing blues talent, arranging sessions for many of the Delta's finest musicians — Charley Patton, Son House, Willie Brown, Tommy Johnson, and the Mississippi Sheiks among them. On occasion he cut demo acetates on the recording machine upstairs from his shop; Tommy Johnson and Ishman Bracey both recorded there in 1928. "Mr. Speir just loved old blues and fiddle music," reports Gayle Dean Wardlow, "and he started scouting to earn extra money. The way it worked was a guy would come in, and he'd listen to him, and then he'd go back out the door. As far as I know, his store was not a hangout for musicians. They'd come by and audition, but as far as sitting around playing goes, no.

"Robert Johnson auditioned in 1936 with 'Kind Hearted Woman Blues.' Mr. Speir had recorded in Hattiesburg in July of '36 — Blind Roosevelt Graves, people from south Mississippi — so Johnson missed that session by three or four months. The record company, ARC, hadn't paid Speir for that session. He was angry about it, but he must have thought Johnson had talent, so he sent his name to Ernie Oertle, ARC's sales rep for Louisiana and Mississippi. He trusted Oertle. When I interviewed him, Speir remembered Johnson playing 'Kind Hearted Woman,' but other than that, he thought he was just another musician. Remember, he'd heard a lot of great guitar players; he listened to guitar all the time." Steve LaVere believes that

On occasion, Johnson blew through a harmonica attached to a rack on his guitar.

Johnson, too, may have recorded at Speir's: "Robert cut a sample record and gave it to his sister. His sister told me that she had a disk of that nature until it wore out and she threw it away."

Ernie Oertle sought out Johnson, heard him play, and offered to take him to San Antonio to record. Robert was elated, going over to Georgia Street to share the good news with his sister Carrie. Blues researcher Mack McCormick has retraced the route Oertle and Johnson took to San Antonio, and claims to have found several witnesses who remembered the white salesman and his black companion. (This material is due to be published in McCormick's long-awaited book, which also reportedly contains eyewitness accounts of Johnson's murder.)

On Monday, November 23, 1936, Oertle brought Robert Johnson to the Gunter Hotel for his first recording session. (Lawrence Brown, a researcher in San Antonio, questions the location: "The notion of Johnson recording in a makeshift studio in a hotel room is a myth. Those sessions were held at the KONO radio station facilities at the Blue Bonnet Hotel, which was very near the Gunter. Vocalion cut records on the second floor there." But according to information provided by Don Law, ARC's Regional Branch Manager who oversaw the session, the location was the Gunter.) ARC's recording crew had already been on location for several days, and an item appearing in that afternoon's *The San Antonio Light* suggests that the scene may have been hectic: "Brunswick [ARC's sister company] recording crew here figures it set a record when it got under the wire with 105 recordings made in the first three days of its San Antonio set-up." LaVere's research through the file cards at CBS, though, indicates that Johnson was the only one who recorded on the 23rd, cutting eight masters. On the day before, six masters were cut by W. Lee O'Daniel And His Hillbilly Boys.

Robert began with two takes of his best-rehearsed number, "Kind Hearted Woman Blues." Each performance was a gem, with deliberately

Each performance was a gem, with deliberately paced, perfect guitar playing and falsettos cooler than Little Richard's.

paced, perfect guitar playing and falsettos cooler than Little Richard's. He followed with a pair of songs destined to become postwar standards: "I Believe I'll Dust My Broom" and "Sweet Home Chicago." By day's end, Johnson had completed two masters each of "Ramblin' On My Mind," "Phonograph Blues," and "Come On In My Kitchen," as well as two takes of "When You Got A Good Friend." The session also produced "Terraplane Blues," a sexy automobile blues that became Johnson's biggest-selling record. ("Robert didn't have one," Shines remembered, "but that was a hell of a car at that time — fast!") Johnson's lyrics gave layers of meaning:

I'm 'on' get deep down in this connection,
    keep on tangling with your wire
I'm 'on' get deep down in this connection,
    whoo ah, keep on tangling with your wire
And when I mash down on your little starter,
    then your spark plug will give me fire

Had Robert Johnson never recorded again, his place in blues history would still have been ensured.

What happened after the session? The big event in San Antonio that night was Paul Muni starring in *The Story Of Louis Pasteur* at the Lux Radio Theatre. But according to the liner notes for the first Robert Johnson anthology, 1961's *King Of The Delta Blues Singers*, Robert had another entertainment in mind: "A country boy in a moderately big town, Johnson found trouble within hours after he arrived. Don Law considered himself responsible for Johnson, found him a room in a boarding house, and told him to get some sleep so he would be ready to begin recording at ten the following morning. Law then joined his wife and some friends for dinner at the Gunter Hotel. He had scarcely begun dinner when he was summoned to the phone. A policeman was calling from the city jail. Johnson had been picked up on a vagrancy charge. Law rushed down to the jail, found Johnson beaten up, his guitar smashed; the cops had not only picked him up but had worked him over. With some difficulty, Law managed to get Johnson freed in his custody, whisked him back to the boarding house, gave him forty-five cents for breakfast, and told him to stay in the house and not to go out for the rest of the evening. Law returned to the hotel, only to be called to the phone again. This time it was Johnson. Fearing the worst, Law asked, 'What's the matter now?' Johnson replied, 'I'm lonesome.' Puzzled, Law said, 'You're lonesome? What do you mean, you're lonesome?' Johnson replied, 'I'm lonesome and there's a lady here. She wants fifty cents and I lacks a nickel.'" The vagrancy story can't be confirmed, since the San Antonio police records were destroyed by fire long ago.

Three days passed before Johnson recorded again. In the interim, masters were cut by a pair of guitar-playing Mexican sisters, the Hermanas Barraza, and by a fine white gospel group known as the Chuck Wagon Gang. On November 26, the Chuck Wagon Gang preceded Johnson with six masters, and then Robert cut one master of "32-20 Blues" while Mexican musicians Andres Berlanga and Francisco Montalvo awaited their turn. On the 27th, Johnson went first, followed by the Hermanas Barraza and pianist Daniel Palomo. This final session on Friday produced some of Robert's wildest and most memorable sides. Starting out with the hokumy "They're Red Hot" and "Dead Shrimp Blues," Johnson then bared his soul in two takes of "Cross Road Blues." He began with a mighty slide, followed by a patented turnaround. Voice charged with other-worldly passion, he sang:

> I went to the crossroads, fell down on my knee
> I went to the crossroads, fell down on my knee
> Asked the Lord above have mercy, save poor
> Bob if you please
>
> Mmm, standing at the crossroads, I tried to
> flag a ride
> Standing at the crossroads, I tried to flag a ride
> Didn't nobody seem to know me, everybody
> pass me by

This was the stuff legends were made of. Johnson's next selection, "Walkin' Blues" was a sophisticated 12-bar variation of Son House's "My Black Mama." (A cache of unissued Paramount test 78s discovered in 1985 contained a previously unknown version of "Walkin' Blues" cut by Son House in 1930. Much more country-sounding than Johnson's, it works smooth upper-register bottleneck against a primitive, deep-Delta bass pattern. One stanza presents a variation of the often-heard "Good morning blues, blues how do you do" lyric.) With its frantic *drive*, Robert's next song, "Last Fair Deal Gone Down," is a direct ancestor of rock and roll. He based "Preachin' Blues" on Son House's "Preachin' The Blues," and wound things up with "If I Had Possession Over Judgement Day," a hyper-charged reading of Hambone Willie Newbern's familiar "Roll And Tumble Blues" that climaxes with stratospheric slide. For songs in the key of B, such as "Walkin' Blues" and "Cross Road Blues," Robert's guitar was either tuned in open A and capoed at the 2nd fret, or tuned in open G and capoed at the 4th. (Some of Patton's best sides were also played in open G, capoed at the 4th.) "Preachin' Blues" was probably recorded without a capo in open E.

Don Law, the A&R man in charge of Johnson's session, was asked to recall the event a quarter-century later for *King Of The Delta Blues Singers*. Law remembered Robert as "slender, handsome, of medium height, with beautiful hands and a remarkable ability to project while he was singing or playing guitar." Law added this curious description: "Embarrassed and suffering from a bad case of stage fright, Johnson turned his face to the wall, his back to the Mexican musicians. Eventually he calmed down sufficiently to play, but he never faced his audience." This account was recently challenged by Ry Cooder in *Guitar Player*: "Listen to Johnson's singing and his forceful personality. This is a guy who was afraid of the audience? Hell, no! This is a 'chew them up and spit them out' kind of a guy. I'll tell you what he was doing. I think he was sitting in the corner to achieve a certain sound that he liked.

"Find yourself a plaster corner without wallpaper or curtains sometime — all those hotel rooms were plaster. Go and sit facing the corner with your guitar tight up against the corner, play, and see what it sounds like. What you get is something called 'corner loading.' It's an acoustic principle that eliminates most of the top end and most of the bottom end and amplifies the middle, the same thing that a metal guitar or an electric guitar does. The midrange is where that metallic, kind of piercing sound is. Robert Johnson sounds funny, let's face it. He doesn't sound like anybody playing an acoustic wood guitar, but it's not a metal guitar. If you stick your face up into that corner and listen, you'll hear that sound. It ties the notes together and compresses the sound, too. And his sound is very compressed.

"I'm sure he would have liked somebody to say, 'Robert, I'm going to boost the midrange' — because it's a dry sound, the acoustic guitar, finally. It's a boring sound for Robert. He wants to hear *wang!* He wants to hear the electric; he wants to hear that boosted midrange. I bet if you could have done that with equalizing and headphones in the modern era, he'd have been very glad. I'll bet you if you'd have given him a Marshall amp to play through, he would have been *extremely* glad. But sitting in the corner, he could achieve something like that."

Steve LaVere agrees that Johnson may have faced the wall for sonic reasons, but adds: "More than anything, Johnson was very protective of his playing because he was doing things on the guitar that nobody else was doing at the time. Rather than take a chance even with the Mexican musicians — especially musicians who were about to make records — he wasn't going to share what he knew."

While researching his liner notes for *King Of The Delta Blues Singers, Vol. 2*, Pete Welding observed that Johnson was a tireless perfectionist who had carefully prepared his arrangements: "Those musicians who knew and worked with him — Johnny Shines, Henry Townsend, and David Edwards, among others — have commented on this aspect of his music, remarking that once Johnson had developed a song to his satisfaction, he performed it exactly the same way every time he did it thereafter. This is supported by a comparison of the several takes of some of his recordings; in most cases where alternate versions of his songs exist, they are almost identical, even down to the smallest subtleties of accompaniment, to the originally issued takes. The few exceptions to this ('Ramblin' On My Mind' being the most notable) are probably the result of Johnson's not yet having brought the songs to the ultimate shape he desired. In these cases, the second take is usually much stronger, more tightly focused. That this attention to detail paid off handsomely is self-evident: Listen to the

performances, and you'll hear some of the most forcefully impassioned and starkly beautiful blues ever recorded." Welding's view is supported by the fact that each of Robert's recordings was carefully paced to fit within the 78's three-minute time limit, and few blues artists have ever ended songs with as much finesse as Johnson.

Seven months later Robert Johnson made his final 13 recordings at ARC's Dallas branch. "This took place in an office building, a distribution point for Brunswick Records," describes Steve LaVere. "Robert recorded on the third floor, which had an open area, like a warehouse storage area for records. They just set up some baffles and did the recording." He cut three disks on Saturday, June 19th — one master each of "Stones In My Passway," "I'm A Steady Rollin' Man," and "From Four Until Late," a show-bizzy tune that somehow seems better suited for someone like Blind Willie McTell. Robert returned the following day for his final and most productive session. He began with "Hell Hound On My Trail," described by Palmer as "pure, icy cold paranoia." His voice a wounded cry, Johnson infused the lyrics with what must be the most apocalyptic vision in all blues:

> I got to keep movin'
> I got to keep movin'
> Blues fallin' down like hail
> Blues fallin' down like hail
> Mmm, blues fallin' down like hail
> Blues fallin' down like hail
> And the days keeps on worryin' me
> There's a hell hound on my trail
> Hell hound on my trail
> Hell hound on my trail

While only one take of this monumental track survives, LaVere speculates that others were probably cut: "ARC's standard practice at that time was to record enough to get two acceptable masters. See, in San Antonio the masters were made on wax, so any alternates that might have been recorded were scraped clean and destroyed on the spot. The Dallas recordings were made on the first batch of the advanced new process of acetate recording. When they cut into acetate, any masters that were not acceptable or damaged were returned to the plant for replating. Aluminum discs were rather rare at that time, so they would strip the acetate off the disc and replate it. The only song he may not have done a second take of was 'Honeymoon Blues.'"

Robert then retuned his guitar from open E minor to standard for two masters of "Little Queen Of Spades" and one of "Malted Milk." His voice took on a very soulful quality in "Drunken Hearted Man," convincingly delivering its message of repentance. His next selection, "Me And The Devil Blues" echoed the harrowing theme that inaugurated the session:

> Early this morning, you knocked upon my
> door
> Early this morning, whoo, you knocked upon
> my door
> And I said, "Hello, Satan, I believe it's time
> to go"
>
> Me and the devil was walkin' side by side
> Me and the devil, whoo, was walkin' side by
> side
> I'm going to beat my woman until I get satis-
> fied

"Hell Hound On My Trail" and "Me And The Devil Blues" did much to promote tales of Johnson's pact with the devil. It's a tribute to his terrifying genius that neither song has been adequately covered. ("In these songs," says Rory Block, "the intensity of Robert Johnson's life came straight through his music. You don't just hear technique; you hear this *lonesome* man, this incredibly soulful, confused, powerful person. His soul is just beaming through the music. That mysterious presence is what makes his music so magnificent.") Johnson spent the rest of the session recording "Stop Breakin' Down," "Traveling Riverside Blues," "Honeymoon Blues," "Love In Vain," and "Milkcow's Calf Blues." Once again, the takes were very close: "Johnson was a very studied musician," LaVere says. "Comparing alternate takes, you might find an additional verse or the omission of a verse, but in some cases — and this includes most of the Dallas session — most of

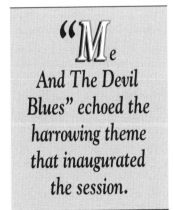

"Me And The Devil Blues" echoed the harrowing theme that inaugurated the session.

the duplicate versions are nearly identical."

When he stepped back out onto the streets of Dallas on June 20, 1937, Robert Johnson had less than 14 months to live. Shines says that they met up in Red Water, Texas, not long afterwards, and headed south to cotton country when cold weather set in. Shines went on to Hughes, Arkansas, to visit family, while Johnson spent some time with Robert Jr. Lockwood's mother in Helena, and then made several stops in the Delta. He came back for Shines, and they set out for St. Louis and Memphis. "St. Louis was a profitable town," Johnny explains, "and Memphis was always good. You never got to be too well known in Memphis. I'd go down to Handy's Park, play with the guys down there. Now, a guy over here have a big crowd, and we'd strike up over there and probably pull half his crowd or all of his crowd. If you pull all of his crowd, that's what we called 'headcuttin',' you know — we just cut his head! Yeah."

With his uncanny ability to mimic practically any music he heard, Robert was no doubt one of the baddest headhunters of all. Shines described in *Frets* magazine: "He could play anything — in the style of Lonnie Johnson, Blind Blake, Blind Boy Fuller, Blind Willie McTell, all those guys. And the country singer Jimmie Rodgers — me and Robert used to play a hell of a lot of his tunes, man. Robert was good at ragtime, pop tunes, waltz numbers, polkas. A whole lot of them things nobody else played with a slide, he played them with a slide. It was just natural to him."

In one journey, LaVere indicates, Johnny Shines and Robert Johnson made "a straightforward shot from Mississippi to St. Louis, up through Decatur, Illinois, where they played a square dance for white people, and then they went on to Chicago, into Detroit, and then to New York and then back home. When they got back South, Johnson said he was going to Mississippi, and Shines said, 'That's where he got rid of me.' Shortly thereafter, Johnson died."

While visiting Detroit, the men crossed over into Windsor, Ontario, to play a radio show: "It was called *The Elder Moten Hour*," Shines explains. "He was a preacher, and he broadcasted out of Canada.

Lots of people could pick him up back over there in Detroit and all over Canada. He was a sanctified preacher, and he wanted a lot of music with his outfit, you know. He had a pretty good-sized choir. Robert, Calvin, and myself, we go over there and play for him. Calvin Frazier was my first cousin." Were blues part of the broadcast? "No! No, no," Shines laughs. "I was playing gospel music. Regular old gospel songs, like 'Ship Of Zion,' 'Stand By Me,' 'When The Saints Go Marchin' In,' 'Just Over In Glory Land,' songs like that."

Robert Johnson lived long enough to hear his 78s, which were issued on the Vocalion label and ARC subsidiaries such as Melotone and Romeo. By 1938, even the Sears, Roebuck company carried Johnson 78s in its Conqueror line — "I Believe I'll Dust My Broom" backed with "Dead Shrimp Blues" was the first. Near the end, Robert was said to have visited some of his illegitimate children, giving each of them one of his 78s. It's also been rumored that he acquired an electric guitar in 1938 and was leading a small band that included a drummer.

Mystery shrouds the death of Robert Johnson on August 16, 1938. An early report indicated he was stabbed. The most probable account is that he drank too much at a house party near Greenwood, flirted with someone's wife, and was handed a glass of poisoned whiskey. Shines, who wasn't there, laid the blame on a jealous woman, adding: "Before he died, Robert was crawling along the ground on all fours, barking and snapping like a mad beast." Chances are, Johnson lingered between life and death for a few days: "He was playing on a Saturday night, and his date of death, August 16th, is a Tuesday," explains Wardlow. "When you're poisoned, you bleed internally, so that story about him barking was probably a description of him gagging or vomiting. He obviously died of internal bleeding." The death certificate filed with the State of Mississippi two days after the murder indicates that his body was taken by his family to Greenwood's Mt. Zion Church for burial. The certificate states that Robert L. Johnson was 26 years old and had been a musician for 10 years. In place of the cause of death is a handwritten "No doctor." His resting place near Highway 7 heeded his lyric from "Me And The Devil Blues":

You may bury my body down by the highway side
(Babe, I don't care where you bury my body when I'm dead and gone)
You may bury my body, whoo, down by the highway side
So my old evil spirit can get a Greyhound bus and ride

Robert's mother sent his guitar up to his brother, Charles Melvin Leroy Dodds, in Memphis.

Ironically, Johnson's death occurred at a time when, unbeknownst to him, his career could have taken off. Columbia's top talent scout, John Hammond was convinced that Robert Johnson was "the greatest primitive blues player of all time" and was anxious to book him for his 1938 presentation of American Negro music, the Spirituals To Swing Concert at Carnegie Hall. Had things gone as planned, Johnson would have been presented on the same stage with Count Basie and boogie woogie piano greats Meade Lux Lewis, Albert Ammons, and Pete Johnson, but by then Johnson had been dead four months. Hammond's program notes eulogized: "Robert Johnson was going to be the big surprise of the evening. I knew him only from his blues records and from the tall, exciting tales the recording engineers and supervisors used to bring about him from the improvised studios in Dallas and San Antonio. I don't believe that Johnson ever worked as a professional musician anywhere, and it still knocks me over when I think of how lucky it is that a talent like his ever found its way to phonograph records. At the concert we will have to be content with playing two of his records...." Hammond selected "Walkin' Blues" and "Preachin' Blues," and Big Bill Broonzy appeared onstage in Robert's place.

Robert Johnson made an immediate impact on other musicians. Muddy Waters was among the first to record in his style, when Alan Lomax and John Work, unaware of Robert's death, journeyed to the Delta in hopes of recording him for the Library of Congress. Their second choice, Elmore James, couldn't be found, either, but locals directed them to Waters, a tough young field hand who, they said, played in a manner remarkably similar to Robert's. With its deliberate pacing, dead-serious vocals, popping bass, and fierce slide chorus, Muddy's debut recording, 1941's "Country Blues," was unmistakably patterned after Johnson's "Walkin' Blues." While elements of Muddy's guitar tone and vocal style were drawn from Son House, his arrangement techniques and slide embellishments were closer to Johnson's records. "I was influenced by Son House and Robert Johnson," Waters explained. "Robert's records were out in 1937, like 'Terraplane Blues' and 'Walkin' Blues.' I never followed him around to hear him or anything like that, but Son House I did follow around and listen to. And I do believe that the way Robert played, you could hear some of Son House in him. Robert was putting in more notes. It was about three notes to one. Robert was one of the greatest of the slide players."

Muddy, Elmore James, Johnny Shines, Robert Jr. Lockwood, and scores of others electrified Robert's music in the '40s, making it a cornerstone of modern blues. The release of *King Of The Delta Blues Singers* and *King Of The Delta Blues Singers, Vol. 2* in the early '60s carried his music to a new generation. Eric Clapton, Taj Mahal, Johnny Winter, and the Rolling Stones helped transform Johnson's music into rock and roll, while artists such as John Hammond and Rory Block launched their careers with eerie, note-for-note acoustic reproductions of Johnson songs.

Robert Johnson's influence still reverberates through popular music. It's there in lyrics, cool turnarounds, boogie bass lines, and most important of all — *attitude*. "I know he played rock and roll," Shines insists. "It was the same beat, but it just wasn't called rock and roll. That's all." When one returns to the source — Columbia's *The Complete Recordings* — the emotion-charged voice, troubled lyrics, and superb guitar playing remain as fresh and potent as any music ever recorded.

Special thanks to Steve LaVere, Gayle Dean Wardlow, Pete Whelan, Rory Block, Ry Cooder, John Obrecht at The San Antonio Light, and the University of Texas' Institute of Texan Cultures for their generous assistance in preparing this article.

Johnny Shines

April 1989

BY JAS OBRECHT

J OHNNY SHINES AND ROBERT Johnson hoboed together through Depression-era America. They hopped freights, played on streetcorners, shared rooms and whiskey, and made it as far north as Canada. Johnson, the Mississippi Delta's most celebrated blues performer, was murdered more than a half-century ago, and yet his spirit still haunts the music of Johnny Shines. It's there in the turnarounds, the mournful bottleneck slides, the impassioned lyrics and falsetto moans. At clubs, concerts, house parties, or high schools, Johnny Shines is just as likely to play Robert's "Cross Roads Blues," "Terraplane Blues," and "Sweet Home Chicago" as he is his own "Evil-Hearted Woman Blues," "A Little Tenderness," and "Ain't Nobody's Fault But Mine."

Raised in Tennessee and Arkansas, Shines took up guitar in 1932, and within three years began his celebrated rambles with Johnson. He moved to Chicago in 1941, amplified his guitar, and staked Frost's Corner as his home turf. He played Tom's Tavern for many years with pianist Sunnyland Slim, and worked in nearby Robbins with the jazzy Dukes Of Swing. His first recordings, four 1946 sides on *OKeh Chicago Blues*, remained unissued for a quarter-century. In fact, bad luck seemed to dog Johnny's recording career the whole time he lived in Chicago. After two 1950 sides as Shoe Shine Johnny, a pair for Chess in '52, and a handful for J.O.B. with harmonicist Walter Horton in 1953, he pawned his guitar and quit music altogether. He wasn't persuaded back into the studios until 1965's *Chicago/The Blues/Today!* Shines eventually became a blues celebrity, touring America and Europe and recording albums for Biograph, Testament, Flyright, Blue Labor, Advent, Rounder, and other labels.

A kind, intelligent man with a subtle wit, Johnny has lived near Tuscaloosa, Alabama, since the late '60s. A stroke may have slowed his fretting hand, but his powerful voice is still remarkably similar to his earliest records, echoing the deep Delta blues of a bygone era. At 73, he was playing California clubs and house parties during the week of this interview. Back home, he says, he regularly

14

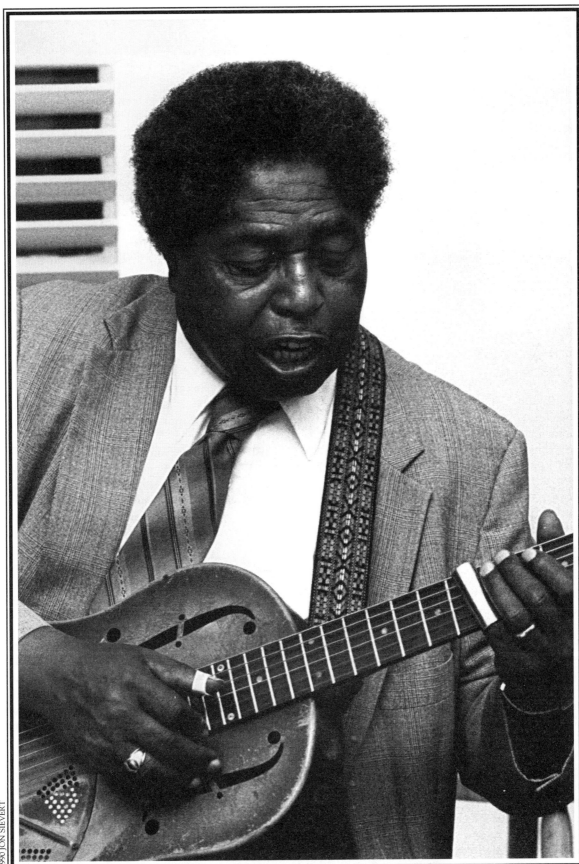

appears at "three joints — the Chucker, the Getaway, and the L&N."

Several years ago you were writing an autobiography.

Yeah. I never did anything with it so far. I been so busy going to upholstery school in Tuscaloosa every day, and doing different things. That will be my main line. See, I had a stroke back in '80, and my left hand is not very good. It affected my playing very badly. So the biggest playing I do now is slide, because I can't hold a chord down good. The chord is all muted out. So I've taken these trades as therapy as well as a position in life.

Where can someone hear your best guitar work?

I think they should look up *Hangin' On.* When I did that [in 1980], why, I was playing like hell. I was playing *good.* I like "Razzmadazz," "Big John," "Early In The Morning," and "Lonesome Whistle." Those songs was done acoustically — just Robert Jr. Lockwood and myself — and I was in the peak of my playing right then. See, on *Mister Blues Is Back To Stay*, I had had the stroke, and I didn't play at all on it.

Do you prefer acoustic guitar?

Well, yes. I prefer playing acoustic over electric, but since I've had the stroke, I have to play electric to really be heard, because I mutes the strings out so bad. Acoustic guitar is a wonderful instrument, if you're learning to use it effectively. Now, the one I traded off, I bought a home and fed 11 people and clothed them, just out of that little round hole there. That means a lots to me, that guitar does. I traded it off because I thought I'd get more action out of this Alvarez, but I'm gonna get it back. That was a Gibson B-25. Blind fellow let me have that guitar in '70, Jeff Butram. I went to England with it, come back, went to Germany with it, come back. I went to Sweden with it, come back. I fed 11 people out of it, so I think it's a hell of a guitar.

> "When I was a kid, a person heard you singing the blues and recognized your voice, you couldn't go down their house, around their daughters."

When did you start playing?

I really was 16 when I started playing, but I didn't turn professional until I was about 17. I played a little organ, as a kid. Gospel music, you know.

Did you ever hear people refer to blues as devil's music?

Yes, I did. When I was a kid, a person heard you singing the blues and recognized your voice, you couldn't go down their house, around their daughters.

Is that why bluesmen traveled around?

No, they was travelin' around to make paydays and things like that, with cash money being out.

Did you learn slide and fingerpicking at the same time?

Yes, I did. Most people think it's two guitars when I'm picking by myself. Well, that's because I learned to carry my own background by using two fingers and a thumb. I always used fingerpicks — metal ones. To make a slide, I'd find or buy a long-neck bottle and just break it off — get some pliers on there and break it off down where you could use it.

Guitar strings must have been pretty different back then.

I broke up a lot of guitar strings, because at that time I didn't know how to play in all the keys. And I had to use a capo to change keys lots of times, so that was hard on a guitar string — wrapping them down, tuning with the clamp on, and pullin' it. The guitar strings would rattle and break. You could make a capo yourself with a pencil and string. Put the pencil on the neck, wrap the string around it on the back side, pull it up tight. Just as good as any capo.

What were the first songs you learned?

"Jim String," "Bumblebee Blues," "Rollin' And Tumblin'." "Jim String" — that was a song about a pimp and his whore. He killed his whore: "Jim

String killed Lulu one Friday night." I learned those songs from my brother. See, my brother was a guitar player, too. He never played professionally. His name was Willie Reed. But when it come to the heavy stuff, I had to go to somebody else, like Willie B. Burnam or Willie Tango or Eddie Vann, some of those guys.

Did you know many bluesmen back then?

Well, Houston Stackhouse was about the only somebody until I met Robert Johnson through a piano player named M&O.

What kind of a musician was Robert Johnson?

To me, he was just as great as Charlie Parker. The man did everything. Whatsoever you did on a horn or on a piano, he figured he could do on a guitar, and he did it. And he didn't look for it, either. I never seen him practice. I never seen him look for nothin'. He'd just sit down, tune a guitar, whatsoever you wanted him to play, he'd play it. Just like we're sitting here talking now, the radio be playing. Robert heard something on the radio he liked, he never stopped talking with you. Tonight or tomorrow, he'd pick up his guitar and play the song, note-for-note, chord-for-chord, word-for-word. He was way before his time. I know he played rock and roll. It was the same beat, but it just wasn't called rock and roll. I know many chords he never heard of, because he couldn't read music, but he could just pick up a guitar and make them. He was a genius.

Did you do much two-guitar music together?

No, he didn't like that. He'd go one way, and I'd go the other. We'd work in the streets. I'd go over here and start playing, and he'd go over there and start playing. He'd draw his gang; I'd draw mine.

How did you travel?

If an empty boxcar was handy, we'd get in it. If it was not, we'd get *on* it. Ride it until it stops or somebody hit you upside the head [*laughs*].

What was the first thing you'd do when you hit town?

Just try to find out where the black neighborhood was. Walk up and down the railroad track and just watch to see the black kids. Whichever side we find the black kids on, that's the side we go, because that was the black side. All the towns was segregated then — whites on one side of the tracks, blacks on the other one. We'd play all day, if the money was still hoppin', because we didn't have no particular place to go. As long as there's nickels and dimes afloat. When they quit, then we'd just walk on.

Do you remember this as a good time of your life?

It was some of the best of the times, because I had to make my own way through my own skills. I felt more freer than at any other time. But now, if I got into a town like tonight — on a Monday night — by Thursday I'd have me a job somewhere. Because at that time the police was bad about picking you up for vagrancy. I always had a job to go to, because the police knew when you went there. Everybody knew everything you did in those small towns. I was dishwashing, busing dishes, doing something to keep the police off of me, but I was living off the guitar. I'd get off of work in the evening, come and get my guitar and walk down the street, be playing real slow. Somebody go, "Hey! Come over here!" I go, and that's where we pitched the party at. They'd slip me a dollar that night, and I wasn't getting that much for a week's work — $4.75 or something like that.

Were there any places where you did especially well?

St. Louis was a profitable town. Memphis was always good. You never got to be too well known in Memphis. I'd go down to Handy's Park, play with the guys down there. Now, a guy over here have a big crowd, and we'd strike up over there and probably pull half his crowd or all of his crowd. If you pull all of his crowd, that's what we called "headcuttin'," you know — we just cut his head! Yeah.

You've said that Robert Johnson played polka music on guitar.

Yeah. You had to do it. You see, when I come along playing guitar, lots of times you wake up in the morning and you didn't have no money at all. Somebody ask you to play a song, maybe they'd give you a dollar for that song. That meant about four meals off of a dollar, 'cause you could get a meal for a quarter or 30 cents. And if you couldn't play that song, you miss that money. So you had to learn to play some of everything you heard. If we passed a white dancing hall and the big bands was playing in there, whatsoever kind of music they was playing, we used to have to listen to. Hide around outside and listen. So we'd go home, and when we get ready, we'd play those same pieces.

So when you were working the streets with Johnson, you only played blues once in a while.

Lot of popular songs in between — whatsoever the people seemed like they enjoyed more. When we played for Polish people, we had to play Polish music. I learned "Beer Barrel Polka," "Too Fat Polka," as well as a few Jewish tunes. We had to learn them, too.

What were your favorite guitars back then?

I had a little black Regal guitar and then later on I had a Kalamazoo like Robert had. We both had them. The Kalamazoo was an f-hole Gibson with a flaw in it. He really liked that arch-top. Yeah, had more body to it. Then we bought a flat-top in Steele, Missouri, after we lost our guitars in a fire in West Memphis. Robert and I walked out to get some food, and on our way back we looked up and saw this place afire. I said, "Robert, that look like where we live at." He said, "Yeah, it sure do." Sure enough, got there, that's what it was. Hunts Hotel — this black fellow had a little place there, nothing but a rooming house. Paper walls and things like that. Rooming houses ain't worth a shit. You could fart in your room and deafen the fellow in the other room [*laughs*].

Would you keep your guitars in an open tuning?

Regular tuning, most time. We'd tune them in open G or open A for bottleneck. Open D, E. Open A was called vastapol.

Did you or Robert spend much time playing when no one else was listening?

No.

> "*I* had the habit when I went to bed, I had the habit when I woke up, I had the habit when I got up."

Was he a peaceable person?

Until he started drinking. He started drinking, he'd do any goddanged thing. Wasn't nothin' too good for him to do. At first, he drank corn liquor. When the bonded liquor come in, Ten High and Dixie Dew. Those cheap brands of whiskey. We drank that 'cause that's what we was able to buy. We'd buy a better brand once in a while, such as Old Taylor and Old Grand Dad.

Were you ever much of a drinker?

That's all I would do. Yeah. I had the habit when I went to bed, I had the habit when I woke up, I had the habit when I *got* up. This was pretty well all through my life, but younger some.

One of the guitarists you both admired was Lonnie Johnson. Was he one of the top players in those days?

Him? Was he one of the top ones? He *was* the top. I don't know why he didn't record that much, but I know he didn't. I remember one record of his was strictly jazz, and boy, he was so goddamned fast — *whoo!* With a straight pick. I've seen guitar players use three fingers wasn't as fast as him.

Did you play *The Elder Moten Hour* radio show with Robert Johnson?

Yeah. He was a sanctified preacher, and he broadcasted out of Canada. Lots of people could pick him up back over there in Detroit and all over Canada. He wanted a lot of music with his outfit, you know. He had a pretty good-sized choir. Robert, Calvin, and myself, we go over there and play for him. Calvin Frazier was my first cousin.

You played blues on a preacher's show?

No! No, no [*laughs*]. I was playing regular old gospel songs, like "Ship Of Zion," "Stand By Me," "When The Saints Go Marchin' In," "Just Over In Glory Land," songs like that. See, we had been hired to play somewhere in Illinois, and they paid us good money — Robert, Calvin, and me. Come to find the fellow was charging to see us and the people was coming just because we was black people! They'd never seen any before! We didn't like that, so we up and left. Went to Detroit. Then Robert left me in Detroit, and I went up to Chicago. Later I was in New Jersey and somebody told me about a guy who sounded just like me, and I knew it had to be Robert. Sure enough, it was. So we went back to Chicago, to St. Louis, Memphis, and then Helena, Arkansas, where we stayed a month. Robert said he was going to Mississippi, and I said, "I'll see you." Next thing I heard, he was dead.

Did you sense that he was going to have a short life?

No, I never did. It was very hard when I heard he was dead. I just couldn't believe it. Honeyboy Edwards was the one who confirmed it with me that he was dead. See, Sonny Boy [Rice Miller] said Robert died in his arms, but Sonny Boy was such a big liar. He speaked lying lies. Still couldn't believe that Robert was dead. Since I made my comeback, I look any day to walk up on Robert or Robert walk up on me. I feel his presence many times.

What was it like when you moved to Chicago in 1941?

A lot of guys was playing then — Big Bill Broonzy was playing, Arthur Crudup, Tampa Red. Dr. Clayton and Memphis Slim was singing somewhere. Memphis Minnie and Son Joe was playing somewhere. Everybody was playing, so pretty soon I got started. It wasn't bad. I played with a piano player. I didn't need no other guitar player. I bought another Kalamazoo, and I used a DeArmond pickup on it, which electrified it. That was in '41, '42. The first person I ever saw with an electric guitar was Big Bill or Memphis Minnie at a place called the White Elephant.

What were your impressions of Tampa Red and Big Bill?

Tampa Red was one of the best guys there ever was. Very good-natured. Kind person. Open-minded. He and his wife was close to each other.

> *"I'd been whupped around and screwed around, so I just said I wasn't going to record no more."*

Big Bill Broonzy was fun. He was a hell of a man, very helpful. Those two guys were mountain of men towards musicians.

Is it fair to say that Muddy Waters was the person most responsible for changing Chicago blues?

I think Muddy used his style, which was a Mississippi style, of singing. And he changed the style of music, through Willie Dixon. See, a lot of people don't give Willie Dixon no credit for things that happened. Willie Dixon was the man that changed the style of the blues in Chicago. As a songwriter and producer. That man is a genius. Yes, sir. You want a hit song, go to Willie Dixon. Play it like he say play it, and sing it like he say sing it — even Willie Dixon can't sing a lick, but just find out what he's talking about and do it — you damn near got a hit.

Why didn't you play slide on your earliest sessions?

I didn't want to. I was pickin' pretty good then.

What led you to quit recording after 1953?

I'd been whupped around and screwed around, so I just said I wasn't going to record no more. Matter of fact, I quit playing. I took all my stuff, about $3,000 worth of material, and carried it to a pawn shop and got $100 for it. I tore the ticket up and threw it on the floor, because I didn't want the stuff. I had some pretty shitty deals. I was playing about seven nights a week, but I was only turning in tax on three to the union. They caught up with me and fined me four hundred and some dollars, and I thought they should have said, "Fine suspended," or anything. Then, too, the union never got me a job in my life. I paid my dues, sit down there goddamned day in and day out, never got a job in my life. Boys just drive in town and get jobs. It overlooked me, so I felt pretty bad towards the union. Then I was trying to play progressive jazz, too, and I wasn't doing no good at that. Went home one night and the plug was in my door — I couldn't get in because I hadn't paid my rent. A lot of things happened to me, man. I just got disgusted. I didn't record again until '65, and I'm very unhappy with that record. That [Vanguard] session was done without any rehearsal whatsoever.

Do you ever regret becoming a bluesman?

No, not really. The experience has been worth it, yes. Like the crowd we had Saturday night [in Los Angeles] — I enjoys a crowd like that. Hell of a damn nice crowd — four hundred and some people. We sold a box of tapes. Now that's telling you something — people appreciate your music well enough to buy a whole box of tapes.

What are the songs you'd like to be remembered for?

"I Don't Know" — that's one. And "A Little Tenderness" — I'll probably be remembered for that one. "Ain't Nobody's Fault But Mine," which is a gospel song; people think it's a blues. "Evening Sun." Those are the songs the rest of the people learned, most of them.

What advice would you give someone who wants to learn slide?

Learn all the chords that go along with the slide, which is the accompaniment to the slide. Learn how to place the slide. And then you go from there. Wear it on the finger you're most comfortable with. I'm most comfortable wearing it on my little finger. If you want to heel [damp], why then you heel behind the slide. If you don't, why then you just let the slide ring.

Do you consider yourself a Delta bluesman?

That's what I am, a Delta bluesman. And now I'm considered the king of the Delta blues. But what we call the Delta blues is not blues. It's storytelling music. It's something that has happened in some-

> *"Whatsoever touches the heart is where the blues come from."*

body's life that they're telling a story about. For instance, I walk up to you as you was fixing to catch a bus and go to work. I tell you, "My house burned down last night and burnt up three of my children." You say, "Yes, I'll listen to you later. Say, here comes my bus. I'll see you." You get on your bus and go. But now tonight, when I put music to it, you pay $10 to hear me tell the same story I tried to tell you for free over there at the bus stop. Same story!

You see, blues don't have no race. Blues don't have no level. The blues is just like death. Everybody is going to have the blues. If they haven't already had 'em, they're gonna have 'em. Because everybody is going to have some bad luck in their life. They are going to be confronted with fortunes unexpected—one way or the other. The blues is only a thought, anyway. You see, whatsoever touches the heart is where the blues come from. Say a man wins $15,000 or $20,000 at the racetrack. Well, he'll have a happy blues, because he's happy from the heart on out. And the man go out there and lose all his money — his wife has told him she gonna quit him if he lose his money again — he got a different blues. [Laughs.]

What kind of blues do you have?

Right now I got the I wanna go home blues [laughs]. But I knew that was coming before I left home.

At 73, do you have any thoughts of retiring?

No, not yet. I got too much to do. I really wants to get myself together and buy me a nice small farm someplace. I love to garden. Preferably a 10-acre farm, where I can put a nice catfish lake on it and a trout lake on it. Let people come and fish, have fun. I like to see people enjoy themselves.

A SELECTED
JOHNNY SHINES DISCOGRAPHY

Solo albums: *Dust My Broom* (complete J.O.B. sessions), Flyright; *The Johnny Shines Band* ('66), Testament; *Johnny Shines With Big Walter Horton* ('66/'69), Testament; *Standing At The Crossroads* (solo, '70), Testament; *Sitting On Top Of The World*, Biograph; *Johnny Shines And Co.*, Biograph; *Nobody's Fault But Mine*, Black And Blue; *Johnny Shines*, Advent; *Recorded Live, 1974*, Wolf; *Too Wet To Plow* ('75), Tomato; *Country Blues* (live in '78 with acoustic group), JSP; *Hey Ba-Ba-Re-Bop*, Rounder; *Johnny Shines And Friends* ('88 cassette with Bart Pate on guitar), PTP.

With Robert Jr. Lockwood: *Robert Jr. Lockwood & Johnny Shines*, Rounder; *Hangin' On*, Rounder; *Mister Blues Is Back To Stay*, Rounder.

Anthologies: *Okeh Chicago Blues*, Epic; *Chicago Blues: The Beginning*, Testamant; *Chicago/The Blues/Today*, Vanguard; *Drop Down Mama*, Chess; *Atlantic Blues: Guitar*, Atlantic; *Chicago Slickers 1948-1953*, Nighthawk; *Chicago Slickers, Vol. 2* ('53), Nighthawk; *Windy City Blues*, Nighthawk; *The Story Of The Blues*, Columbia; *The Great Blues Men*, Vanguard; *Ann Arbor Blues & Jazz Festival 1972*, Atlantic; *Country Blues Classics, Volume 2*, Blues Classics.

Soundtracks: *The Velvet Vampire*.

On film: *Johnny Shines On And On* ('89 PBS documentary); *Roots Of American Music* (produced by the University of Washington School of Music, '71); *Good Mornin' Blues* (a brief appearance, '78).

Skip
James

August 1974

BY STEFAN GROSSMAN

O NE OF THE MOST FASCINATING guitar styles to come out of the Mississippi Delta was that of Nehemiah Skip James. Before 1964 this style was a mystery, and could only be heard on a handful of rare old Paramount 78s. Tunes such as "I'm So Glad," "Devil Got My Woman," and "Hard Time Killin' Floor" were performances that seemed unique, and in many ways far from the blues traditions of the Delta.

In 1964 John Fahey and Bill Barth rediscovered Skip in Mississippi. Skip performed at that year's Newport Folk Festival, and subsequently started touring all over America and Europe. His songs became better known, and bands such as Cream began featuring his numbers, the most popular being "I'm So Glad."

Skip had a definite view of life and music, and was at ease to express these feelings. James' comments that follow were taken from a long discussion that covered many aspects of his music, life, and times. In talking with Skip, I discovered that his playing style was influenced by guitarists in his hometown, Henry Stuckey being foremost on the list. Skip was not only a guitarist, but he also had an impressive piano style that was just as interesting as his guitar sounds. Skip passed away in 1971, but he left several excellent LPs and a legacy of wonderfully expressive and highly individualistic blues playing. Here is Skip's account in his own words:

I can sit right here with a guitar in each hand, and I can show you day in and day out. But if you're not musically inclined, you'll never get no further than when you first started. But if you *are* musically inclined, you can just go on. You might hear some song, and that sound will stay within until you get someplace where you can try it yourself. You say, "Yeah, I'm gonna change this thing; play it this-a-way." May not be but one verse of a song, and you can hold it until you get home. That way you can practice on it. You can still add onto it, rearrange it, and change it anyway you want, or use his ideas

about it. I likes to rearrange songs, if I be interested enough in it to learn some of it. But mostly I sings and plays in my own words and my own composin' and music.

I come in contact with lots of musicians — some older than me, some younger. They have their version of playin' music, and I have mine. It seems like mine is kind of complicated to most people, but I often wondered why. They got 10 fingers just like myself. And they got a head just like me. And a vocabulary. And they also got ideas just like me. I can play most some of everything I hear, but still, I don't like to make it a practice. I like to play somethin' from *Skip*. Why? So it'll be strange to people, to the rest of musicians.

It's complicated to some of them when you mix the minor with the major — some people don't know minor from major. Most of the people I heard played in common C, natural guitar tuning; some few in Spanish [open G].

I don't start that way, never did. After my teacher learnt me — the rudiment guy [Stuckey] — then I jumped through that; I wanted it different all the way. Contrary to the rest, so I'd have somethin' they couldn't grasp at. So I just fished around findin' those minor chords. I played minor even before I started playin' pretty good. And minor music is the most difficult music to play of anything.

When I play, sometimes I'll have four different instruments: a piano, and then three different guitars in three different tunings. Of those guitars, one may be tuned in natural, one in Spanish, and one in cross-note [E minor]. You can comangle all your music together, if you understand. Your major and minor, too.

The best thing I've learned to do is this: Whatever I do, I try to do it right. Decently, and in order, regardless to what it is. And I guess that's why I'm so precautious along the line of musical errors. I can get a guitar, and if it's not substantially in tune, I wouldn't hit the stage with it.

When I play I don't have no assistance. Nothin' to float on, and nothin' to depend on, but Skip. Skip's fingers and his motion and his music and his art. No one to have a lendin' hand out in

> **"I** like to play somethin' from Skip. Why? So it'll be strange to people, to the rest of musicians."

case I should slip or fall. That's why it plays me so hard, 'cause I have to show up everything for Skip, and to carry it; everything direct and correct, properly and in order. If not, well, there's a failin' on Skip.

Suppose I get onstage with another guitarist or two or more. Then there'd be maybe a badly discord made. They [the audience] wouldn't impersonate [point out] the one individual that did that, they'd say he was "they." *I'd* be involved in it as well as the one that did it. And the first thing you'd see, "You know, Skip made a flunk-out. Made that discord." And so rather than that, I always had the idea that if I made a failure in life, it'd be me on it. So there's why Skip would like to play and act by himself, because if I get out in deep water I don't expect to have two paddles — I'd be pullin' this side and you'd be pullin' that side. And then if I sink, I cannot pull the boat for you and myself, too. I tote nobody else but Skip. That fair? If I don't drift, I'll sink.

When I play I never use a pick, because my nails grow strong; that's why I can touch my strings without hittin' the flesh of my finger. There's lots of people use picks, because they can't finger very well. And they use those picks in frailin' and rappin' [strumming] where they're not active enough in the fingers to pick things enough to keep their music in harmony. Mostly people raps with picks; mighty few you see pick with a pick. Mighty seldom do you see me rap with a pick unlessn' it is to harmonize my major with my other notes. I don't believe in no rappin' and frailin' — never did.

And when I started tryin' to learn, I always did want to pick my music clear, where I could understand it. And you know, if I can understand it, quite naturally the people will.

But I can't tell about my music. I try to satisfy the listeners. When I satisfy them and my manager, I'm perfectly satisfied. I like to hear him be satisfied first. I hate to hear him go, "Skip, the listeners aren't satisfied." But if he says, "I'm satisfied, and the listeners are satisfied," that's quite an encouragement — that'll get you through and goin' on further the next time. Is that right?

A SELECTED
SKIP JAMES DISCOGRAPHY

1931 sides: *The Complete 1931 Session*, Yazoo; *Skip James, 1931*, Matchbox; *Early Blues Recording, 1931* (includes a couple of 1960s cuts), Biograph. Various Paramount 78s also appear on *Mississippi Blues 1927-1941*, Yazoo; *Lonesome Road Blues*, Yazoo; *The Roots Of Robert Johnson*, Yazoo; *Really! The Country Blues*, Origin Jazz Library; *The Mississippi Blues, 1927-1940*, Origin Jazz Library; *The Mississippi Blues, No. 3*, Origin Jazz Library; *In The Spirit, No. 1*, Origin Jazz Library.

1960s solo albums: *A Tribute To Skip James*, Biograph; *Skip James Today*, Vanguard; *Devil Got My Woman*, Vanguard; *Greatest Of The Delta Blues Singers*, Melodeon; *Live At The 2nd Fret*, Document.

Anthologies: *Three Shades Of Blue* (three tracks from '64), Biograph; *The Great Blues Men*, Vanguard; *The Great Bluesmen/Newport*, Vanguard; *Living Legends*, Verve/Folkways.

Rev. Gary Davis

February 1974

BY STEFAN GROSSMAN

EV. GARY DAVIS WAS UNIQUE AMONG blues and ragtime guitarists for many reasons. Whereas most guitarists usually perfected one style or perhaps two, Rev. Davis worked on perfecting a dozen. He combined the alternating bass idea with Blind Blake's syncopation, and then added hundreds of his own ideas and methods. An outstanding teacher, he was always eager to help his students. Today, looking back on his influence, one is amazed at how many musicians have been affected by this man's music. Black bluesmen such as Blind Boy Fuller and Brownie McGhee learned directly from him. Ry Cooder, David Bromberg, Jerry Garcia, Bob Dylan, and a host of other modern-day guitarists also learned his music first-hand, either at his home in the Bronx or while he was touring the country.

Rev. Davis' songs have become part of the mainstream of today's pop culture. "Samson And Delilah," "Candy Man," "Cocaine Blues," and "Death Don't Have No Mercy" have been recorded by a wide variety of artists, including Peter, Paul & Mary, Hot Tuna, and Bob Dylan.

Rev. Gary Davis was born in Larens, South Carolina, on April 30, 1896, and died in New York City on May 5, 1972. He was born blind and started to play the guitar at an early age. Moving throughout the South, he played on street corners, and during the 1930s he settled for several years in Durham, North Carolina, where he taught and played with Blind Boy Fuller. In July 1935, Davis and Fuller traveled to New York to record for the ARC Company. Davis joined Fuller on a couple of cuts, and recorded 15 blues and gospel sides on his own, including "I Saw The Light," "I Am The Light Of The World," and "You Got To Go Down." Settling in New York during the 1940s, Davis recorded for many labels in the ensuing years — Stinson and Folkways in the mid 1950s, and Bluesville, Prestige, Vanguard, and Kicking Mule in the '60s, among others. Of all the ragtime-oriented bluesmen, Rev. Davis was perhaps the most widely recorded. With so many styles and techniques, he was truly a master of the guitar.

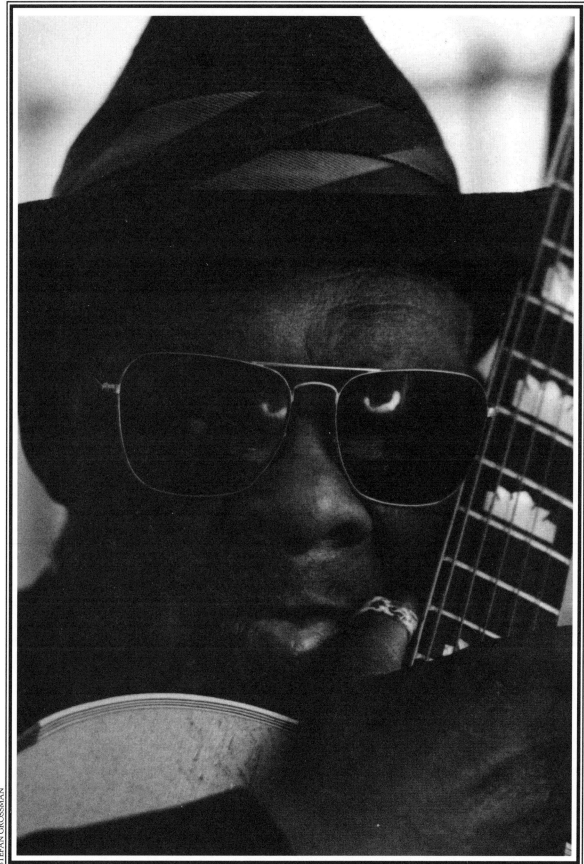

Could you tell us about your way of playing the guitar?

Well, you see, you've got three hands to play a guitar and only two for a piano. Your forefinger and your thumb — that's the striking hand, and your left hand is your leading hand. Your left hand tells your right hand what strings to touch, what changes to make. That's the greatest help! You see, one hand can't do without the other.

I always thought that your guitar styles tend to imitate the piano.

Well, that's the way I always play the guitar. It's supposed to be played just like you're playing a piano.

Why do you use only two fingers to pick?

Because that's all you need.

Do you think guitar students should use only two fingers also?

That's what I use. I teach them the same as me.

Does using two fingers give you a certain sound?

It is a certain sound. You're going to talk about it, you see. You don't give the rest of your hand time to do nothing if you play with all of your fingers.

Were you using fingerpicks when you started playing the guitar?

Oh, no, I started using them about 25 years ago — or longer.

Were you using fingerpicks when you recorded in 1935?

Yes.

Do you think it's better to use fingerpicks?

It saves your fingers!

When do you think a guitarist should practice?

Well, to love for anything to come to you — you practice early in the morning, at seven o'clock until eight, and then put down your guitar. At eight o'clock in the evening until nine, you practice again. After that you should concentrate.

> "My motto's always been to bring out something somebody else hadn't heard before."

Why so early in the morning?

That's because when music comes to you early in the morning your [re]members are alright. There's nothing to stir you, to disturb you. By eight o'clock everything is going on. At eight o'clock at night everything is once again pretty still. By nine you can call it bedtime — something like that.

What type of guitar do you like?

Any types that's good to play. Don't make any difference what type of guitar, as long as it is a good one. I like a guitar that I can just slip down onto — with a good action. A hard-playing guitar will make your fingers sore. You know something about that, don't you?

Where did you learn how to play?

Well, I was in the South when I learned the guitar. I practically picked it up myself. I made my first guitar out of a tin can. I was a boy about 10 years old. I drove me a hole in each end of the pie pan, run me up a stick through there; that's the way I made it.

Did anybody show you how to play?

No, I learned all by myself. My motto's always been to bring out something somebody else hadn't heard before. I always loved to do things different than anybody else did.

Did you ever put down the guitar?

Well, for three years I didn't have no guitar; that's when I was a boy. There was a time also when I broke my wrist. That was in North Carolina. I was carrying on a revival, and I slipped down. I was going along one night, and there was snow on the ground. When I stepped up on a bank of snow, my foot slipped, and to keep from falling, I was shuffling around. I struck my hand on an iron water-dog. I didn't know it was broken until I went to the doctor the next morning. He told me it was broke. He put me up on a table and put me asleep. When I woke up he had a cast slammed up to my elbow. I lost the use of that hand a long time. I thought I was never going to be able to play no more — but I did! [*Author's note: Rev. Davis' left-hand wrist seemed to* have been set out of position — a little to the left of its axis — which enabled him to play many unusual chord positions.]

Did you ever play 12-string guitar?

First 12-string guitar I run across was in 1920. Never heard tell of one before. I went to the store and asked the man to show it to me, and I found out how it was tuned. I played it just like I played a 6-string guitar.

Were a lot of guitarists playing 12-string back in those days?

Yeah! But them guitars didn't have much of a good action. They were mostly old Stellas.

When is the right time for a guitar player to perform in public?

God never called anybody to preach when he didn't have any words to say. It's no use offering yourself to somebody. If they want you, they'll call you. You can go find a lot of puppies, you understand. They all belong to the same dog. When you lay eyes on those puppies you can tell which one is going to be on top. You can pick that one out. You can see something in that one you don't see in the rest. Don't you go picking yourself out to the people. It's them that pick you out.

Do you find it hard to perform?

Ain't no easy job to sit down and play guitar, no how! Some of the people that look at it think it's easy, because it looks easy to them.

How do you approach the guitar?

I sit down and study how to take advantage of a guitar, you see.

What advice would you give to guitar students?

You know, you can't give a two-week-old baby peas and corn bread. You've got to give it what it's able to eat. Lot of people come here wanting me to teach them things, but they're not able to stand up to it. I'm subject to mistakes. All of us are. Sometimes you're going East, and you're actually going West. That's the way it happens with all of us sometimes. Mistakes is the best start in life. You know too much, you understand, then you done made a mistake already. You be too perfect, then the mistake's been already made. But you go try to do a thing and make a mistake to start off with, then that's the best start in life. It gives somebody a chance to correct you.

A SELECTED
GARY DAVIS DISCOGRAPHY

Solo albums: *Reverend Gary Davis* (1935 and '40 recordings), Yazoo; *The Singing Reverend* (1950s), Stinson; *American Street Song* ('56 gospel recordings), Riverside; *When I Die I'll Live Again* (two-record reissue of 1960's *Harlem Street Singer* and 1961's *A Little More Faith*), Fantasy; *Reverend Gary Davis* ('62-'70), Flyright; *Ragtime Guitar* (instrumentals, '62-'70), Kicking Mule; *Children of Zion* (in concert, '62), Kicking Mule; *Lo' I Be With You Always*, Kicking Mule; *Let Us Get Together*, Kicking Mule; *I Am The True Vine* (recorded at home, '62-'63), Heritage; *Pure Religion And Bad Company*, 77 Records; *The Sun Is Going Down*, Folkways; *The Guitar & Banjo Of Rev. Gary Davis* (instrumentals, '64), Prestige; *Pure Religion*, Prestige; *At Allegheny College* ('64), Document; *At Al Matthes', Toronto* (private acetates, '66), Document; *At the Newport Folk Festival* ('66), Vanguard; *New Blues And Gospel* ('71), Biograph; *Blues & Gospel, Vol. 2* ('71), Biograph.

Anthologies: *Blues Rediscoveries*, RBF/Folkways; *The Great Blues Men*, Vanguard; *The Great Bluesmen/Newport*, Vanguard.

On film: *Blind Gary Davis* (11-minute B&W study by Harold Becker, '64, includes "Death Don't Have No Mercy"); *Reverend Gary Davis* (26-minute film, '67, featuring "Candy Man," "Twelve Gates To The City," and "Stove Pipe Rag"); *Black Roots* ('70).

Mance Lipscomb

March 1974

BY JIM CROCKETT

RITISH HISTORIAN PAUL OLIVER has put it best: "Mance Lipscomb's music is first and foremost entertainment, to be enjoyed with the heart and the body rather than be subjected to academic analysis." Mance was a real original. No influences, no teachers, no books — just the music he heard around him, filtered through a life of hardship and joy. As Paul Oliver also said, he was "one of the last great exponents of the Southern Negro folk song forms, before the blues and the mass media which popularized it swept them aside."

Born in Navasota, Texas, in 1895, Mance wasn't raised on the blues, because the music he heard around him came from the pre-blues era — circus tunes, jigs and reels, church songs, breakdowns, and rags. He learned to play guitar while accompanying his father, a fiddler who was born into slavery. As Mance grew older, the blues became a part of his musical life, but in concert he always interspersed them with religious hymns, children's rhymes, ballads, slow drags, and old-time pop songs such as "Polly Wolly Doodle," "It's A Long Way From Tipperary," and "Alabama Jubilee." His fine fingerpicking style underscored his soft, expressive voice, and he used a pocket knife to play slide.

Mance Lipscomb was 66 years old when he made his first major public performance. Previous to that, he would augment his meager sharecropper earnings (as little as $100 per year) by playing for local parties and church meetings in his hometown. In the summer of 1960, Arhoolie Records' Chris Strachwitz and a friend were driving along Texas' Brazos River "blues country," inquiring about singers in the area. The name Mance Lipscomb came up. The two men searched until they found him cutting grass, the "boss" of a three-man highway maintenance team. In Lipscomb's tiny home, they made a few informal tapes that later became *Texas Sharecropper And Songster*, the Arhoolie label's — and Mance's — first record.

The following year Barry Olivier brought the "songster" (Mance's own term for people who use songs of all types to entertain) to the Berkeley Folk Festival. It was Lipscomb's first concert and his first

30

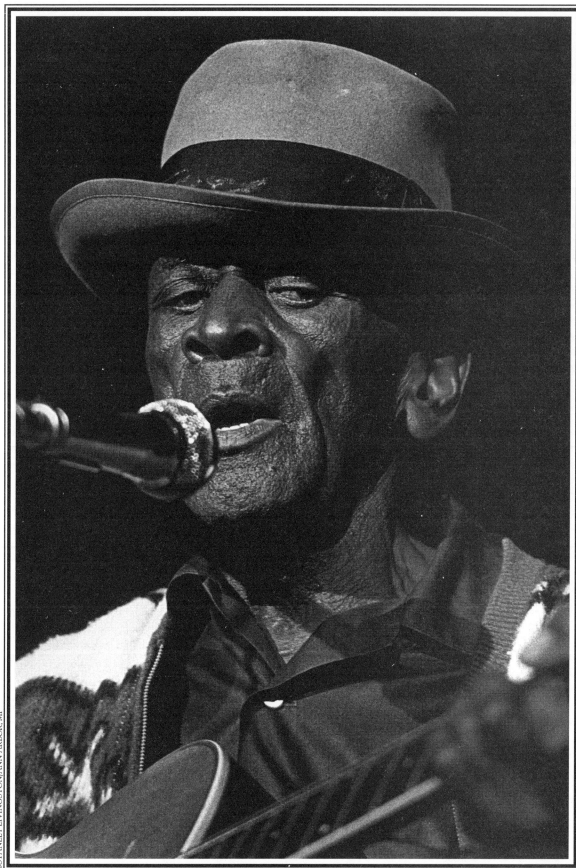

trip outside Texas. More recordings followed, as did additional bookings at colleges, festivals, and clubs. Having enough material was never a problem, since Lipscomb had a repertoire of nearly 1,000 songs.

We met Mance at the 1973 Monterey Jazz Festival, where we sat outside the arena in the grassy area, shaded from the afternoon sun by giant oaks. Mance had his guitar with him, and as soon as we sat at one of the picnic tables, people began gathering around. Inside the arena, Bo Diddley was knocking out fans with his rough, double-entendre blues. But there on the lawn outside, away from the screaming, dancing crowd, Mance gave one of his best, low-keyed performances for a tiny, smiling, spellbound group of students, musicians, middle-aged jazz fans, and newspaper journalists from around the country. After about a half-hour of friendly anecdotes, startling guitar licks, and delightful songs, Mance apologized to the growing audience, put his Gibson J-200 in the case, and began talking about his life in music. Three years later, Mance Lipscomb passed away at the age of 80, leaving behind a legacy of several wonderful albums. Here are Mance's words, just as he spoke them that sunny afternoon in Monterey.

"No one plays like me. Oh, they can play maybe three or four notes of mine. They can start it, but they can't finish it."

───────────

My daddy was a fiddler, and I heard music all the time. Like, it's in my blood. And blood is your life, right? You can learn music easy if it's in your blood.

My mother used to sing all the time. We'd be working the cotton fields together, and she'd be singing. Then one day when I was about 13, a gambler came by where we were working. He was broke and needed some money. He had a little pine guitar with him, and all the time he and my momma were talking, I was staring at it. It only had about three or four strings on it, but it was beautiful to me. He wanted $1.50 for it, and momma bought it for me.

I couldn't play anything, though. My two older brothers played good guitar for parties around town, but they thought I'd break their guitars, so they

wouldn't let me near them. When I got my own, it was really a thrill to pluck it.

I'd give my mother my cotton-picking money, then she'd give me 25¢. I'd head for town, buy some bread and sausage, and have 15¢ left for the carnival or Barnum & Bailey circus. The clowns would do their buckdancing, and people would toss coins. I'd stay as long as I could, watching the circus musicians real close. Then I'd go home and try the songs out on my guitar. I didn't think about singing then; I just wanted to make music on that guitar of mine.

I was learning everything by ear, of course, but by the time I was 15 I could accompany my father in his little shows. I did that for years. During the week I'd try playing by myself a little here and there. I figured how to play double-time by myself. Fingerpicking, too. I use my thumb and two fingers. I use a thumbpick now, but I didn't back then. I never heard of picks until many years later. When I was around 16, I started working what they called "breakdown suppers" for my father. He was getting on by then, and people seemed to like my guitar playing, so I started taking over from him.

I never got to hear many players when I was growing up. We were on a farm so there weren't many others, just myself. Oh, maybe I heard three or four guitar players who came through town, but that was about all. I knew one old man who could play two songs, and I'd sit outside his door listening to him play them over and over.

I learned to tune the guitar on my own. I just tune by chords to the sound I like. The two E's are usually in tune, then I tune the rest to them and just wham away on it. I play in three tunings, mostly: E; triple E, where I also tune the D up to E; and one where I tune the A up three tones and the D up two. I just keep tuning until it sounds right.

Nowadays I use a Gibson J-200 [acoustic guitar outfitted with a soundhole pickup]. Someone gave it to me backstage in Minneapolis. I didn't know Gibson from anyone else at the time. People like a good clear sound, so I don't use it as an electric very often. The electric guitar is a fraud; the sound rings because of the electricity, not because of the player. People can't remember electric songs very well, either, because the music's too fast and too loud.

It's not that I don't like today's music — I like portions of *all* music — but if it's stuff in these later years, I don't understand it. I don't catch up to it.

From the time I was 14 until 1961 I was on my own. Then Chris found me sharecropping. By then I had all that music going around in my head. White folks didn't get to hear me, because I wasn't allowed to play the white dances. That Berkeley Folk Festival was my first white crowd. Man, talk about a scared boy!

I'm playing more today than I ever have. I used to play only one day a week, but now I'm working six or seven months out of the year. The phone keeps ringing for jobs all over the nation. And I don't get tired, either. I can play all night; you can't hurt me. But the thing that's wrong with festivals is that you don't have any time when you're performing. No one can do something in a minute — it takes time. I know 350 songs, but I can only do two or three in a show, so I have to cut out the instrumentals, which I hate to do. I got to have at least 40 minutes.

No one plays like me. Oh, they can play maybe three or four notes of mine. They can start it, but they can't finish it.

A SELECTED
MANCE LIPSCOMB DISCOGRAPHY

Solo albums (on Arhoolie): *Texas Sharecropper And Songster* (1960 recordings); *Texas Songster Volume 2* ('64); *Texas Songster Vol. 3* (onstage in Berkeley, '66); *Mance Lipscomb Vol. 4* ('64 and '66); *Mance Lipscomb Vol. 5* ('68 and '69); *Mance Lipscomb Vol. 6* ('73); *You'll Never Find Another Man Like Mance* (onstage in Berkeley, '64); *Texas Songster* (a 22-cut CD of material from *Texas Sharecropper And Songster* and *Texas Songster Vol. 3*, with substantial liner notes).

Anthologies (on Arhoolie, except as indicated): *Blues 'N Trouble*; *Texas Blues Vol. 2*; *Blues Festival: Concert & Dance*; *The Roots Of America's Music*; *The Great Blues Men*, Vanguard.

On film: *A Well-Spent Life* (the best Lipscomb study, this 44-minute profile was filmed in Texas by Les Blank, '71); *The Blues Accordin' To Lightnin' Hopkins* (Blank's excellent documentary features scenes of Mance backing Lightnin', '68); *En Remontant Le Mississippi/Out Of The Blacks, Into The Blues* ('71 West German/French film featuring Mance's "All Night Long"); *Roots Of American Music* (produced by the University of Washington School of Music, '71).

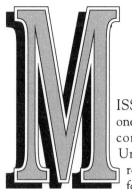

Mississippi Fred McDowell

November 1977

BY TOM POMPOSELLO

ISSISSIPPI FRED McDOWELL WAS one of the most important rural guitarists to come out of the 1960s blues revival. Undiscovered until 1959, Fred was first recorded by Alan Lomax on one of the folklorist's many field trips to the South.

McDowell's specialty was bottleneck slide, with an eerie, vocal-like tone. In '69 the blues singer switched from acoustic to electric, which, if anything, only added intensity to that subtle, whining quality. McDowell's playing influenced numerous rock and blues slide guitarists, including Keith Richards and Bonnie Raitt. Bonnie remembers: "He thought it was really funny, meeting this 18-year-old girl playing guitar, but he was flattered at my interest, and he taught me."

Fred would take the time to show his music to anyone who would ask, flattered that they were interested. Unlike so many artists who are reluctant to explain the intricacies of their styles for fear (often with good reason) of being ripped off and receiving no recognition, McDowell's philosophy was, "Well, that might be true; that's just what they may do. But I do know that in their hearts, after I'm dead and buried, they're always gonna remember that I was the one that showed it to them, even if they don't tell nobody else."

McDowell was born somewhere between 1903 and 1906. No one seems certain, because back then if you were black and living on a plantation, no one kept accurate documentation of such things. He was born in Rossville, Tennessee — a fact that always used to bemuse him: "They call me Mississippi Fred, but really my home is in Rossville, Tennessee."

"When I was a boy," he continues, "I think the first blues record I ever heard was Blind Lemon Jefferson singing 'Black Snake Moan.' 'O-oh, ain't got no mama now.' Man! I tell you, I thought that was the prettiest little thing I'd ever heard." He became interested in guitar when he was in his late teens. By this time, music was all around Fred. His uncle Gene Shields was a guitarist and the leader of a trio. He credits Shields with being the first person he saw play in the bottleneck style, using a smoothed beef rib bone on his little finger.

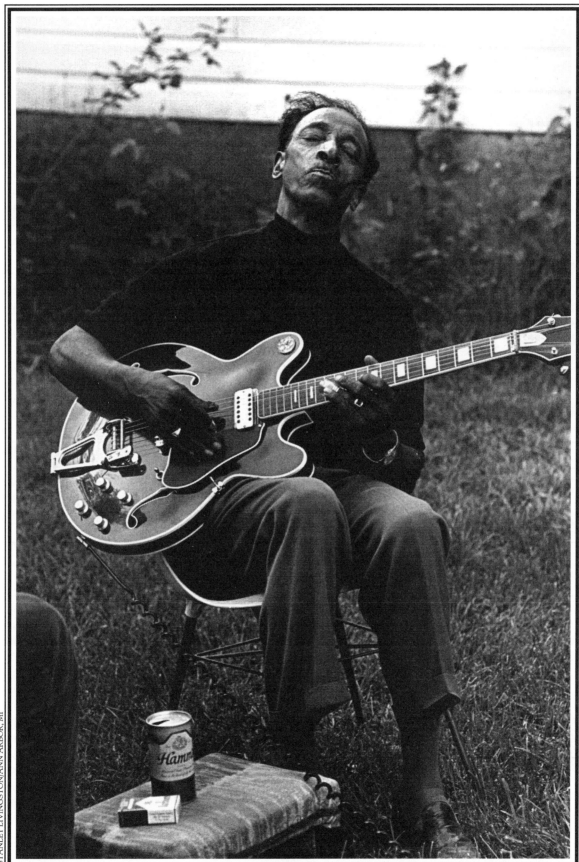

The harmonica player in Gene's trio, Cal Payne, showed Fred "John Henry." Cal's son Raymond, who was about the same age as Fred, recalls, "He was a real good guitar player — regular style, not bottleneck." But Raymond would never show anyone anything. "If you'd walk into the room when Raymond was playing," Fred recalled, "he'd right away put the guitar down so you couldn't see what he was doing. Then he'd make some kind of excuse — 'I'm tired now' or 'My fingers hurt.' No one could show me nothing anyway. Everyone could play 'cept me. All the boys. But I had to learn things my own way. Even if you'd be showing me, I'd have to go off on my own and get it my way. They'd all be playing ball or something, and I'd be practicing on Booster Green's guitar." (An older friend, Eli "Booster" Green taught McDowell his celebrated tune "Write Me A Few Lines." In 1966 the musicians were reunited for a couple of tracks on Arhoolie's *Fred McDowell, Vol. II*.)

The first song Fred ever learned was Tommy Johnson's "Big Fat Mama (With The Meat Shakin' On Your Bones)." "I learned it on one string," he explained, "then two, note by note. Man, I about worried that first string to death trying to learn that song." This note-by-note method became an intricate part of Fred's later-day technical approach. While McDowell experienced his share of obstacles on guitar, he was always sought after as a vocalist. He would sing along with other guitarists at old-time Saturday night suppers, and then take over on guitar when they got tired.

Tired of plowing fields with a mule, Fred left Rossville when he was about 21. During a trip to Cleveland, Mississippi, in the late 1920s, he heard the legendary Charley Patton perform at a juke joint. He was quite impressed, and consciously adapted several of Patton's tunes to his own style. His "Gravel Road," for instance, was adapted from Patton's "Down The Dirt Road Blues." McDowell lived in Memphis during the 1930s, working as a laborer. He tried to master the guitar, but was hampered by not owning his own instrument. Finally, a white man from Texas named Mr. Taylor (whom Fred remembered quite fondly) presented

him with one. This was 1941, and soon afterwards Fred decided to move south to Mississippi and settle down near his sister. While living in Como, Fred McDowell refined the style that would lead to his becoming one of the greatest postwar country bluesmen.

In 1959 folklorist Alan Lomax came to Como and asked if there were any local bluesmen that he should hear. Among the first names given was Fred McDowell's. Lomax found Fred at home that evening and proceeded to record him. Fred played well into the night — from 8:00 P.M. until almost 7:00 A.M., as he recalls it. Before departing, Lomax promised that these recordings would bring McDowell fame and fortune. Well, he was half-right. Despite the fact that the payment was nominal, the recordings were met by much enthusiasm in folk and blues circles. They established the 55-year-old as one of the great "new discoveries" in the blues world. Fred had the opportunity to play and record for a whole new audience.

At 55, Fred became one of the great "new discoveries" of the blues world.

Arhoolie and Testament issued solo albums, and Fred was a sensation at the 1964 Newport Folk Festival. He toured Europe with the American Folk Blues Festival in 1965 and '69, going over especially well in Germany and Great Britain. Keith Richards heard Fred's version of the spiritual "You Got To Move" and rearranged it for the Rolling Stones' *Sticky Fingers*.

In 1969 Fred recorded a solo album for the Transatlantic label, using an *electric* guitar. It seems odd today, but the reaction at the time among purists was mixed. Everyone was used to Chicago blues played electrically, but Delta blues? One critic observed that much of the subtlety, especially in McDowell's fills, was lost, but nothing could have been further from the truth. One listen to "Amazing Grace" performed on the electric instrument, and you were a believer. The instrument proved very appropriate for the spirituals Fred loved to perform, intensifying his shimmering tone and sophisticated vibrato. His blues numbers, particularly the percussive, driving rhythmic patterns of songs such as "Shake 'Em On Down" and "Drop Down Mama," were also greatly enhanced. And the electric instrument undoubtedly made Fred's music more accessible to a new generation of blues enthusiasts. He was well aware of this, and used to caution his admirers: "I do not play no rock 'n' roll, y'all. Just the straight and natch'l *blue*."

Prior to 1968, the majority of McDowell's recordings were performed on his old wood-bodied National or his acoustic Hofner. His first electric was a red, dual-pickup imitation of a Gibson ES-335. He then found a good deal on a mid-'60s Gibson Trini Lopez Standard, which he used until his death. His only modification was to slightly raise the action by installing a small metal shim just above the nut. He used light-gauge Black Diamond Electric Strings, but didn't care much about the brand or the gauge, so long as the set included an unwound G string. (Whenever purchasing a new set, he'd always check for that unwound string before laying down his money.) To get the necessary clarity on acoustic, Fred would pick with his bare right-hand thumb and index finger. For electric guitar, he used a standard plastic thumbpick and a plastic fingerpick on his index finger. His style of picking ranged from simple note-to-note to highly complex rhythmic and heavily syncopated brush strokes, or any combination of the two.

Most of McDowell's touring during the late '60s and early '70s was done by Greyhound bus. He hated to fly unless it was absolutely necessary. Consequently, he carried only a small practice amp with him, hoping that when he arrived at a club or festival, he could plug into whatever better equipment was available. Sometimes a well-meaning producer would want to record the bluesman through his own amp, insisting that it would be inaccurate to record a blues artist using someone else's equipment, or a club would close-mike his amp through the PA system. Unless this was done absolutely right, the result was a very muddy sound, which is why many of Fred's recordings leave the listener with a false impression of his tone. Judging from his reaction to good amps, he was after a clean, clear sound with a good amount of top end.

The first time Fred tried to play bottleneck guitar, he used a pocket knife to emulate Uncle Gene's style. But it didn't take long for him to realize that in order to get the volume and clarity he wanted, he had to switch to a glass bottleneck. Since his style did not utilize full chords barred with a bottleneck, he chose to use a short slide (about 1" long) made from a Gordon's Gin bottle. First, he scribed the bottle with a sharp object along the lines where he wanted it to break. Then he ran it under hot water in a bathtub, then under cold water while he gently tapped it along the scribed seams. It worked on the first try. (It's funny how a musician can get attached to something like a bottleneck. One evening I saw Fred nervously rummaging through his guitar case, and then breathing a sigh of relief upon finding his treasured Gordon's bottleneck. "Tom, if I'd have lost that," he said, "I might as well turned around and went back home.")

Where he wore his bottleneck depended on his tuning — standard, open A, or open E. On his earlier acoustic records, he often used the open-A tuning, wearing the bottleneck on his little finger. In standard tuning, he'd usually play in the key of E and wear the bottleneck on his little finger. For open E, Fred wore the bottleneck on his ring finger. He preferred to use his bottleneck more often in the E tuning, because it lends itself more toward melodic playing. (It's important to note that Fred's tuning were relative, since he tuned to his voice — rather than a piano or tuner — before performing.)

Most of Fred's playing was based in the tonic. He would often thumb the open bass strings while picking slide melody lines with his fingerpick. In songs such as "You Got To Move," he might depart from that procedure and simply play the melody line on the bass strings alone. His guitar part often echoed his vocal phrasing almost exactly, such as in "Baby, Please Don't Go," where his voice would trail off while his bottleneck finished the vocal line: "When you hear me play, if you listen real close, you'll hear the guitar say the same thing I'm saying, too." He was very flattered one time by a perceptive fan who said, "You know, that's the first time I ever heard a talking guitar."

"When you hear me play, if you listen real close, you'll hear the guitar say the same thing I'm saying, too."

Fred returned home during the winter of 1971, cancelling his tour because of severe stomach pains. Undergoing an operation, he was not to leave his home again. I visited him in Mississippi the following spring, and found him in good spirits as he showed me the time of my life. A few days later, he was back in the hospital. He never complained, but it was obvious he was in great pain. In July 1973 Fred McDowell died from abdominal cancer.

I have never heard anybody play or sing like Mississippi Fred McDowell, and I am convinced that what made Fred great as a musician was what made him great as a man. That "Mississippi mystique" of his, that undefinable something, is the spirit of the real blues.

A SELECTED
MISSISSIPPI FRED McDOWELL DISCOGRAPHY

Solo albums: *Shake 'Em On Down*, 1959 (first recordings), KC; *Mississippi Fred McDowell* ('62), Heritage; *Fred McDowell* ('62), Flyright; *Fred McDowell* ('63-'64), Testament; *Delta Blues* ('64), Arhoolie; *Fred McDowell, Vol. 2*, Arhoolie; *Mississippi Delta Blues* (a CD combining *Delta Blues, Vol. 1* and 2), Arhoolie; *Fred McDowell And His Blues Boys*, Arhoolie; *Keep Your Lamp Trimmed And Burning*, Arhoolie; *Somebody Keeps Calling Me*, Antilles; *My Home Is In The Delta*, Testament; *Fred McDowell & Johnny Woods*, Rounder; *When I Lay My Burden Down*, Biograph; *This Old World's In A Hell Of A Fix*, Biograph; *I Do Not Play No Rock And Roll*, Capitol; *Mississippi Fred McDowell*, Archive Of Folk; *Long Way From Home*, Milestone; *Levee Camp Blues*, Origin Jazz Library; *Mississippi Delta Blues* (issued in England on Black Lion, '65), Vogue; *Standing At The Burying Ground* (live in London, '69), Red Lightnin'; *Shake Em On Down* ('71), Tomato; *Amazing Grace* (with the Hunter's Chapel Singers), Testament; *Mississippi Fred McDowell In London*, Sire/Warner Bros.; *Mississippi Fred McDowell In London, Vol. II*, Transatlantic; *Mississippi Fred McDowell Live In New York*, Oblivion; *Mississippi Fred McDowell, 1904-1972*, Just Sunshine.

With others: *Big Mama Thornton In Europe*, Arhoolie; *Honest Tom Pomposello*, Oblivion.

Anthologies: *Atlantic Blues: Guitar* ('59), Atlantic; *The Great Blues Men*, Vanguard; *The Great Bluesmen/Newport*, Vanguard; *The Roots Of America's Music*, Arhoolie; *Kings Of Country Blues, Vol. 2*, Arhoolie; *Bad Luck 'N Trouble*, Arhoolie; *A Double Dose Of Dynamite* (one side only, live in '69), Red Lightnin'.

On film: *Newport Festival* (appearance from mid '60s); *Blues Maker* (14 minutes of outstanding B&W footage, '69, made by the University of Mississippi); *Fred McDowell* (15 minutes, '69, produced by Seattle Folklore Society); *Roots Of American Music* (produced by University of Washington School Of Music, '71).

James "Son" Thomas

April 1990

BY DAN FORTE

JAMES "SON" THOMAS IS A FOLK artist in the truest sense of the term — in more ways than one. Although he looks considerably older, he is 63, and the Delta blues he has been playing for close to 53 of those years has scarcely changed since he first started. He also sculpts: From Mississippi River clay mud, he molds birds, rodents, fish, human heads and skulls, and scenes depicting death, such as his open-casket figures complete with coat-hanger-wire handles. As a boy, Son earned his other nickname, "Ford," thanks to the clay trucks he made.

Thomas grew up in Yazoo County, and his high, ghost-like singing is reminiscent of another Yazoo blues legend, the late Skip James. Tommy McClennan, from Yazoo City, was among the first bluesmen Son heard on records — songs like "Bottle Up And Go" and "Whiskey Headed Woman" — along with Son House, Tommy Johnson, and Robert Johnson. "I heard their records, but I never did meet them," he points out. "The only guy from way back that I met who probably knowed them was Big Joe Williams. Now he's dead, Muddy Waters is dead — I got to meet him, James Brown, Mrs. Reagan." Mrs. Reagan? "I was in Washington, at the Corcoran Gallery up there in '81, with my art," he explains. "She came by to see my sculptures, and we had a picture made," he says, pointing to a framed 8x10 on his bedroom wall showing Thomas with the former First Lady.

"I play a little country music, but mostly blues," says Son. "That's mostly what I like to play. I learned from my uncle, Joe Cooper, and other people who used to be around the house playing. When I got large enough to go out, I used to go listen to Elmo James and Arthur 'Big Boy' Crudup. They played in clubs around Yazoo. I had to wait till they stopped charging at the door, because I wasn't able to pay 50 cents to go in. Elmo would let me plug in his guitar when he'd take a break. He was real nice. Sonny Boy [Williamson] would get really mad because Elmo would let me play. That was Rice Miller, not the real Sonny Boy; he and Elmo used to play a lot together. Elmo played an acoustic, but he had a silver pickup in it."

His initial exposure to artists like James and Sonny Boy Williamson was via radio. "I heard them on the radio before I saw them," he clarifies. "They played in Helena, Arkansas. Back in them times on the radio, they had 15 minutes of blues, and you wouldn't hear no more blues. I used to quit out in the field to go and listen to that 15 minutes of blues. Mostly you'd hear country music, and I like some of that, too. But the music they're playing now, this disco, I just don't like it. I can't get nothing out of it."

Son's first local performances were with his uncle: "I'd make a dollar a night; he wasn't gettin' but about three dollars. It was what you call house parties; they used to call them country jukes. People didn't have a way to travel around long-distance. If you're gonna have something in Memphis, now they can jump in their car and go up there. But people didn't travel as fast then as they can now; they didn't have transportation. There was mighty few blacks that had cars, and they used them for taking people to the doctor and stuff like that. After I quit playing with my uncle, it was mostly by myself. Then I started making three or four dollars. My uncle could have left during the time when Tommy McClennan would go and record, but he wouldn't do it."

The first guitar Son owned was a Gene Autry model he bought from a Sears, Roebuck catalog for $8.50. "I picked cotton to make enough money to get that guitar," he remembers, "and then I played on the post office steps and made my money back. Later on, I played an electric for a while — I forget the name. It had three pickups and six dials, but it got stolen. I have a Martin now, with a pickup in the bridge. I tune it standard, but when I play slide I change to a cross tuning, about like Spanish [open G]. I use a steel slide now, on my little finger. I keep my fingernails cut off when I'm playing. They make me make mistakes. I play with my bare fingers."

In 1961 Thomas moved to Leland, Mississippi, and continued to play strictly around Mississippi until blues scholar William Ferris discovered him in 1967. "I stayed right in this area because I was doing

"*I* do some of Elmo's, Arthur 'Big Boy' Crudup, and I like Li'l Son Jackson. I play a little country music, too, but I change it up."

work, and you had to be where your job was. I worked in funeral homes, furniture stores, yard work. Just something to keep the house goin'. Never made no big money — what I call big money — until I started playing. My first trip overseas was in '81. I went to Norway to play for 30 minutes on a television show. I've been overseas about six times."

Besides recording Thomas, Bill Ferris took pictures of his artwork to Yale, resulting in Son's first exhibit, in 1969. "I've been doing that ever since I was a little bitty boy in school," Son recounts. "My uncle used to try to make mules, so I started trying to make mules and other things. I made a skull once to scare my grandfather. I made this skull and put it on the shelf, and he come in and had to light a match to light the lamp, and I put that skull up where he could see it when he'd light that lamp. He made me take it out of the house. Then I tied a string to his bed springs — those old coil springs — and ran it through a crack in the wall to my room. When him and my grandmother went to bed, I would lay in my bed in the next room and shake 'em up. He accused my grandmother of shakin' the bed, so she got up out of bed to show him she wasn't shakin' the bed. I really shook it then. He said, 'I know what it is. You're bringing these white folks clothes in here. Some of 'em are dead, and they're coming back for 'em.' From then on, he always believed there was a ghost in the house; he didn't know it was me."

In addition to his own songs, Son still relies on his original favorites for inspiration. "Some of them are mine, and some I record other people's," he says, "but I play it different, you know. I do some of Elmo's, Arthur 'Big Boy' Crudup, and I like Li'l Son Jackson. He lived in Texas, and I thought I'd go to see him, but he was dead. I saw a film once of Lightnin' Hopkins fishing, catching some white perch out in a boat. I never did meet him, but I loved his records." On electric, Thomas sometimes gives Muddy Waters or even B.B. King a run for their money.

Son reaches for his decal-stickered Martin and

slides a metal tube onto his little finger. But instead of playing some Lightnin' Hopkins or Elmore James, some Big Boy Crudup or Li'l Son Jackson, he begins the familiar strains of "Steel Guitar Rag" by Bob Wills & The Texas Playboys. "See, I play a little country music," he smiles, "but I change it up a little bit."

A SELECTED
SON THOMAS DISCOGRAPHY

Solo albums: *Highway 61 Blues*, Southern Culture; *Son Down On The Delta*, Flying High; *Good Morning School Girl*, Black And Blue (France); *The James "Son" Thomas Album*, L+R; *Delta Blues Classics*, Swingmaster (Holland).

Anthologies: *Mississippi Blues Festival 86*, Black And Blue; *Mississippi Folk Voices*, Southern Culture; *Bothered All The Time*, Southern Culture.

On film: *Mississippi Delta Blues* ('69); *James "Son Ford" Thomas: Delta Blues Singer* ('70); *Give My Poor Heart Ease* ('75); *I Ain't Lying* (folk tales, '75); *Made In Mississippi* (folk art, '75). All of the preceding fims were made by William Ferris and are available through the Center for the Study of Southern Culture in University, Mississippi. In addition, Son performs two songs in 1977's *Got Something To Tell You: Sounds Of The Delta Blues.*

R.L. Burnside

April 1990

BY DAN FORTE

E'S THE DIRECT LINK FROM Robert Johnson to Mississippi Fred McDowell, for that style of slide," says bluesman Joe Louis Walker of R.L. Burnside. But Burnside is not merely a bottleneck specialist; playing solo, his acoustic country blues encompasses the styles of Li'l Son Jackson, Bukka White, Big Bill Broonzy, Muddy Waters, Son House, Lightnin' Hopkins, John Lee Hooker, and many others.

"With a band, he don't sound like himself now," Burnside says of Hooker. "He sounds a whole lot better by himself — that's the way I look at it." R.L. also plays with a band, however, which includes his sons Duane, Daniel, and Joseph, on guitar, bass, and drums, and extends his blues repertoire to B.B. and Albert King, Little Milton, and Bobby Blue Bland. The family band members are just three of the 63-year-old's 12 children, who range in age from 13 to 39.

Four generations of Burnsides, including R.L.'s 82-year-old mother, live in a four-room wooden house near Holly Springs, Mississippi. "I was born five or six miles outside of Oxford," R.L. details, "and I grew up in Coldwater, 10 or 12 miles from Holly Springs, down on 55. We moved from Oxford to Coldwater when I was 7, and I was around there until I was 18." He then moved to Chicago for three years, and after brief stays back in Mississippi, Memphis, and Chicago again, he settled in Holly Springs.

When he was younger, he explains, the centers of blues activity in Mississippi were towns like Clarksdale, Crenshaw, and Holly Springs. "Coldwater was a dry county. Stonewall Mays, he's 80-something now, still plays blues there — and was playing blues before I could play. So he played juke joints up around here."

R.L.'s father played guitar, but, in Burnside's words, "he never was good with it. I guess I just learned from sitting down and watching Fred [McDowell] and then Muddy, when I got to Chicago. He married my cousin, so I used to go to his house back when he was just playing at the Zanzibar every Friday night for whatever they took in at the door. I'd try to play like him, but it

44

wouldn't sound right. My second wife, the one I got now, said, 'Why don't you put that thing down?' I'd fool with it when she wasn't around. Finally, I got pretty good. So one night, maybe a year later, there was this house party, a country supper. They were shootin' craps, drinking whiskey, gambling. Son Hibler was playing, but he got tired and took a rest — laid his guitar down. I asked if I could play his guitar; my old lady said, 'You gonna make a fool out of yourself in front of all these people?' I started to play 'Boogie Chillun' and 'Hobo Blues' from John Lee Hooker. Man, people came out going, 'Who's that guy with the guitar?'"

In addition to hearing Joe Hill Louis, Robert Nighthawk, and Sonny Boy Williamson over the radio from Helena, Arkansas, Burnside listened to records by Tommy McClennan, Washboard Sam, Li'l Son Jackson, and Big Bill Broonzy. "I liked Robert Johnson's type of music, too," he adds. "I played with Robert Jr. Lockwood, his stepson, in Montreal, Canada, in '71. I always liked Lightnin' Hopkins and Muddy Waters and Li'l Son Jackson's playing, and Elmo James. Man, I loved his type of music. Never got to meet him, but I play stuff behind his songs. When I lived in Chicago in the '50s, I saw Little Walter and Big Walter Horton, Chuck Berry, and Sonny Boy Williamson was playing then. Maxwell Street Jimmy [Davis] was there, John Lee Granderson, Robert Nighthawk. I used to live one street over from Maxwell Street. But I couldn't play guitar then. Since then, of course, I've played in Chicago 30 or 40 times."

Burnside's mentor, Fred McDowell, was from Como, Mississippi, and R.L. points out, "I knew him all my life. When I was too little to even play, I knew him. He was 10 or 12 years older than me. I sort of watched him and caught on to what he was doing. I like a lot of things he was doing. I like those old-time blues.

"In that time, when Fred was playing, it was just one guy. Fred McDowell, Dennis Gardner, or a guy called Son Hibler. Just one guy playing, and maybe a harmonica player, like Johnny Woods. Me

and him and Fred all played together, and Ranie Burnette. I'm younger than all of them guys, by 8 or 10 years. See, at that time, when I was 17 and just started to running around, there wasn't no such thing as big clubs. You'd go to some house party. People would dance and carry on — just Fred playing his guitar. Man, I saw the floor break in!"

Playing solo guitar for dancers probably accounts for the strong rhythmic feel in Burnside's music. "That's right," he agrees. "That's where I got that from." In songs like "Skinny Woman" and "Poor Black Mattie," his approach is close to McDowell's or Bukka White's, beating on the guitar almost like a drum.

In songs like "Skinny Woman" and "Poor Black Mattie," his approach is close to McDowell's or Bukka White's, beating on the guitar almost like a drum.

His tunings also derive from Mississippi Fred. "In one way I tune mine like Fred, and in one way I don't," he says. "The same thing he plays in one tuning, I can tune it another way and play the same thing. It's easy to do that. I got 'cross-note' and 'Spanish.' Spanish is like G, and cross-note is something like a D. Can't use a pick. I just use bare fingers."

His main acoustic is an Epiphone, and his electric is an old Aria Les Paul copy, neither of which is played very often when R.L.'s not performing. "In my way of thinking, I believe you can do a lot of things by thinking about it. If you try, you're trying too hard. Just wait till it comes into your mind, and you'll do it. Part of that album, *Hill Country Blues*, was recorded in Holland in the hotel room. We didn't have enough songs, so I laid down and took a nap, slept a couple of hours, and when I woke up a song came to my mind. Then four or five songs that I didn't know nothing about, I just got up and made them up out of my head right there. Made the whole album the next day. Then I do stuff behind old records I heard — change the lyrics a little, maybe change the type of music with it."

Like Son Thomas, Burnside continued to play local functions until, in his forties, he was discovered and recorded by a blues enthusiast — in R.L.'s case, George Mitchell, author of *Blow My Blues Away*. "George Mitchell was out recording Other

Turner — the fife and drum band — in '68," he recounts. "And they knew about me. He asked about anybody else that played blues, and came here. At that time I was living on the plantation, working a sharecrop, and all that stuff. So George and his wife Kathy came and lived at my house there for a whole week, and every night when I'd get out of the field, he'd run the tape recorder, and I'd play some blues. That's what came out on the record [*Mississippi Delta Blues, Vol. 2*]. He was dealing with [Arhoolie Records'] Chris Strachwitz and gave him the record. First album. I never recorded before that. One side of the album was me, and one side was Joe Callicott."

R.L. had played electric guitar, but never in a band context until Tom Boyd, manager and agent for the Mississippi Delta Blues Band, sought him out. "I was living about 15 miles from where I am now. I was working on a plantation, renting my house, but driving a cotton-picking combine. I was making $15 a day, and this guy came up to the house. He had never seen me, but he got the Arhoolie record and had been looking for me. I was in the house, and the kids said, 'Who is this coming to the house?' He knocked on the door and said he was Tom Boyd. I don't know no Tom Boyd. I said, 'Let him in' — because I had an automatic shotgun, a pistol in my pocket and one under the pillow. He said he had that album and was trying to put a band together, and said, 'Do you know a harmonica player out of Jackson called Sam Myers?' I'd heard of him but never met him. Sam was in the band, and they wanted some Muddy Waters-style slide guitar. I said, 'What kind of money you talking about?' And like I said, making $15 a day, $200 a week — playing four nights a week — sounded pretty good. We went to Europe for 10 weeks."

"I don't like to go for that long anymore," he continues. "With my family, I can't do that. I'm a poor man; I ain't got nothing. And what's gonna happen while I'm over there? That's what I got to think of. The first time I went overseas in '71, with the Mississippi Delta Blues Band, I told the guys the first week, 'I'll just rock along with what you're doing. And you follow me on what I'm doing.' I can do some slide along with anybody. I'd do 10 or 15 minutes by myself, so the promoter in Holland asked me if I'd come over by myself. With the band I went to Denmark, Norway, Switzerland, Sweden, Holland, Germany, and France — for 10 weeks. Came back with about $400. Then I went back to Holland by myself for a week or 10 days, and I got back with $2,100!"

He has since been overseas 29 times. But when he's home in Holly Springs, it's business as usual. "A friend and I do a little commercial fishing when the weather's right," he says. "But the weather like it is this winter, we ain't doing no work at all. In the summer, when the weather's right, I make three or four hundred dollars a month. He don't pay me no salary; he owns the boat. But if we catch some fish, we just split what we catch. You sell your part, I sell mine. We haven't caught anything in two or three weeks, but sometimes we'll catch 1,800 pounds in a morning. We catch catfish, buffalo, carp. If you catch crappie and bass, you have to throw them back because we're commercial fishing, and those are sports fish."

R.L. is humble but proud of his music, as is his family. "Back when I was about 10, we'd listen to spiritual records," he points out. "Me and my sister started out singing spirituals when I was 12. And that's the first thing I played on guitar — spiritual music. My mom made us go to church every Sunday. I'm religious, but I don't believe you have to go to church every Sunday to be right. I think if you're right, you're right. At that time my mother didn't approve of the blues, but you ought to see her now [*laughs*]. I'll be playing the blues, and she goes, 'That's my boy.' Gets up and starts twisting. She's 82 years old, trying to do the twist."

A SELECTED
R.L. BURNSIDE DISCOGRAPHY

Solo albums: *Hill Country Blues*, Swingmaster (Holland); *R.L. Burnside*, Swingmaster; *Mississippi Blues* (live in France, '83), Arion; *Mississippi Delta Blues, Vol. 2* (one side each by Burnside and Joe Callicott), Arhoolie; *Sound Machine Groove* (Burnside and sons), Vogue.

John Cephas

March 1987

BY JAS OBRECHT

EXQUISITE AND HEARTFELT, BOWLing Green John Cephas' acoustic blues hearken back to Blind Boy Fuller, Rev. Gary Davis, Skip James, and other country blues greats of decades past. His rich, resonant voice projects a confidence that rivals Leadbelly's, and he's one of the few musicians on earth who can do a credible Skip James impersonation, complete down to eerie falsetto phrasings. "I play this music because I don't want it to die," says the native Virginian. "The blues is such good music, and it really has something to say. It's not like some of the rock and roll and punk rock and heavy metal and all that repetitious, noisy stuff. The blues is the backbone of all of that other music. It's the grassroots, and that's what people really love."

While his covers of Skip James' "Cherryball" and "Hard Time Killing Floor Blues" echo the Delta originals, Cephas draws another side of his guitar playing from the more sophisticated, ragtime-influenced Piedmont tradition. "The two styles are easily distinguished," he points out. "Mississippi Delta blues has more single-string, harsh progressions, whereas the Piedmont style has a richer, more fullbodied, melodious sound. It features a multitude of strings, just a ringing out of the guitar. Blind Boy Fuller and Rev. Gary Davis are absolutely the essence and the very tops, as far as the Piedmont is concerned. They have had the greatest influence on guitar players. Blind Boy Fuller is a little simpler to catch onto than Rev. Gary Davis. Gary Davis did some stuff that was so fancy that even I can't get it on the guitar. Buddy Moss was another important player."

By trade, John works as a carpenter for the Army National Guard in Washington, D.C. During the past few years, though, his blues have taken him on many European tours, as well as to Africa, Central America, South America, and the Caribbean. He performs the major American folk festivals, conducts seminars, and teaches at Seattle's Puget Sound Guitar Workshop and the Blues Workshop in Elkins, West Virginia. On most gigs, he's accompanied by his partner, Harmonica Phil Wiggins. John made the cover of *Living Blues* maga-

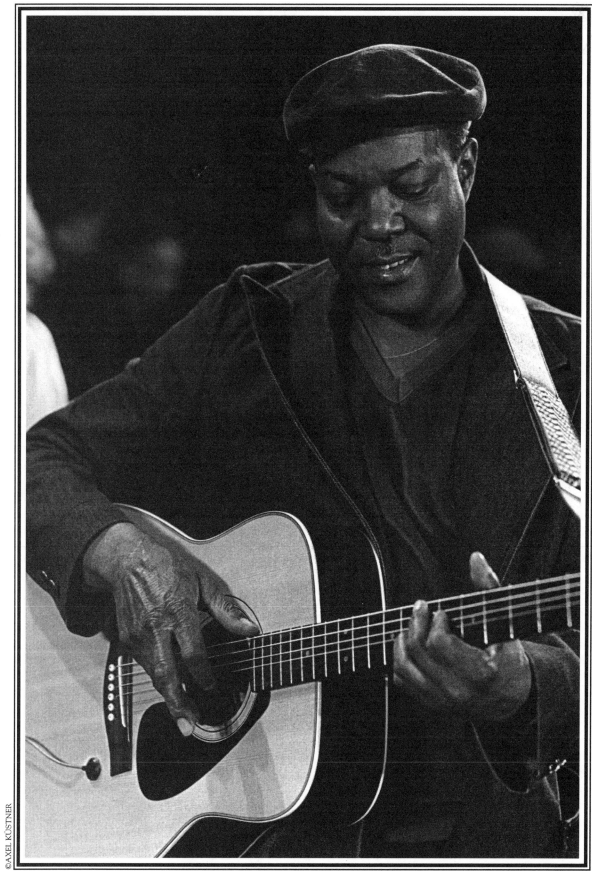

zine in January '85, and five years later he was extensively profiled in Barry Lee Pearson's *Virginia Piedmont Blues*, published by University of Pennsylvania Press.

Born in 1930, Cephas heard his first blues early in life. "I was reared mostly in Washington, D.C.," he says, "but my mother and father use to bring me back and forth to Virginia 'cause that was where most of my mother's family was from. Even when I was at a very early age, I was touched by the blues. There used to be a lot of blues musicians in the black community — not people that were really known, but it was like a way of life. My aunt used to play, and her boyfriend, Haley Dorsey, used to come around all the time and play. I heard that sound, and that's what got me started off. But even though my family liked the blues, they would always discourage me from pursuing it rather than religious music. They told me it was more like serving the devil." The son of a Baptist minister, the youngster was coached by his mother to sing gospel duets in church with his brother.

At age nine, John made his first attempts to learn guitar: "My father forbade me to play his guitar, because he feared that I would break it up. But when he would leave home, I used to get his guitar and play it. I started in open keys. He used to catch me all the time, just about — he would remember how he put it down, or I might break a string, and boy, I'd get a good lickin' behind that. But that didn't never stop me 'cause I would continue on to play the guitar every chance I got." John's aunt taught him his first chords. In his teens, he played blues and country breakdowns at house parties with his cousin David Talliaferro.

Cephas remembers Talliaferro as an excellent guitarist and credits him with teaching him the three-fingered Piedmont picking style: "I never use a flatpick. I always use a thumbpick and a fingerpick on my index finger. Sometimes I use one on my middle finger, too, but I usually play that without a pick. If I want to do a roll, I'll use my other fingers, but mostly it's just the thumb and two fingers." In his early years, he played slide with a knife, laying

> "*Even though my family liked the blues, they would always discourage me from pursuing it rather than religious music.*"

the guitar flat on his lap.

John's first acoustic guitars of note were Gibsons. Trashed in house-party fights, these were replaced with Yamahas. "I bought three or four of those and wore them out," he says. "Then a few years ago, Fender came out with their [F-270SCE] cutaway acoustic/electric, which I was very fascinated with after playing it. The guy at the music store let me borrow one and take it on tour, and I was so impressed with it that I bought three of them. That's what I'm playing now."

To this day, the influence of John's earliest recording heroes resounds in his playing: "I listened to a lot of Blind Boy Fuller, Rev. Gary Davis, Blind Blake, Buddy Moss, Mississippi John Hurt, and guys like that on one of them old wind-up record players. I guess Blind Boy Fuller and Gary Davis were my real, real heroes. I used to just love playing along to their records, and that's how I learned a whole lot of stuff. I also loved Skip James. I was so enchanted and fascinated with his sound that I practiced and listened to him for hours on end, just trying to figure out what he was doing. Practicing came real easy because I could remember sounds. And, experimenting with the guitar, I would hear sounds myself, or I might concoct them in my own head and just fool with the guitar until I got them out of there." John has fond memories of hanging around outside of Gary Davis and Blind Boy Fuller shows while still a grade-schooler in Virginia. Years later, he played gigs with Buddy Moss.

It wasn't until the '60s that Cephas began turning his blues into cash. "Before that," he remembers, "we played at house parties and a lot of juke joints, where guys used to gather up on weekends. We wouldn't get paid for jobs like that. As we got older, we played for drinks and food and to get high. We were like a band, but we didn't consider ourselves professional musicians." His first recognition came through blues pianist Wilbert "Big Chief" Ellis, who had been a busy New York City sideman during the '40s and early '50s. "I first met him at a house party," John recalls. "We didn't get a penny for it, but the house rocked all night 'til broad daylight.

He played barrelhouse piano in the style of Walter Davis and Otis Spann. I started doing some festivals with Big Chief, and that's when I finally got started getting a little recognition as a pretty good professional player. We never made a lot of money at that time, though — $25 or $50, and we thought we was really getting a whole lot." John worked as Big Chief's accompanist from the late '60s until the pianist's death in 1977. His debut recording — "John Henry" — was done solo in 1973 for the Library of Congress' collection of work songs. His first commercial sessions, though, were with Big Chief Ellis — a 45 of "Fallin' Rain" and the album *Big Chief*, which also featured Brownie McGhee and Tarheel Slim on guitar.

John met Phil Wiggins during a jam session at the 1976 American Folklife Festival in Washington, D.C. At the time, Wiggins was backing street singer Flora Molton. "Chief and I was impressed with his playing," Cephas says, "so we asked him to come on and play with us. We formed a group called the Barrelhouse Rockers. That was Chief, Phil, me, and a guy named James Bellamy on bass. We performed together until Chief died in 1977, which temporarily disbanded the group because he was the leader. People kept calling me to do jobs, though, because they was interested in my guitar playing. So I asked Phil if he wanted to try to go out and do some gigs together because the sound that we had was pretty good. We started to practice, and we've been playing together ever since." While their exchanges have often been compared to those of Sonny Terry and Brownie McGhee, Cephas and Wiggins project a distinct personality all their own.

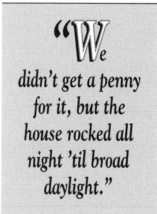

"*We didn't get a penny for it, but the house rocked all night 'til broad daylight.*"

After appearing at the National Folk Festival and the Down Home Blues Festival, the duo participated in the late-'70s Travelling Blues Workshop with John Jackson, Mother Scott, Flora Molton, and Archie Edwards. They cut an album in 1981 for West Germany's L+R label, *Living Country Blues, Vol. 1 — Bowling Green John Cephas & Harmonica Phil Wiggins From Virginia, U.S.A.*, and toured Europe several times during the decade. Billed as the Bowling Green Blues Trio, Cephas, Wiggins, and guitarist Barry Pearson also worked as blues ambassadors under the auspices of the U.S. State Department. Their 1982 African journey included concerts in Botswana, Zimbabwe, Ghana, Madagascar, Mali, Mauritania, and the Ivory Coast. The following year, the trio traveled through Central and South America.

Cephas and Wiggins recorded their second LP, *Sweet Bitter Blues*, on April 9, 1983, in Falls Church, Virginia. While less polished than later works, the album contains an outstanding arrangement of "St. James Infirmary," John's "Tribute To Skip James," a couple of fingerpicked instrumentals, and the deep blues "Highway 301" and "Sweet Bitter Blues." 1986's *Dog Days Of August*, cut in a single night at John's home near Bowling Green, has superior sound and performances — so much so that it won that year's W.C. Handy Award for Best Traditional Album. "They brought all the equipment down and set it up in my living room, which just happens to have good acoustics for recording," Cephas reports. "After they set up, we just went for it. I just started playing the guitar, they mixed it, and that beautiful sound came out of it. Most of the songs were done in one shot. There was no rerecording or dubbing-in on any of the songs on the album. The cassette version has an extra cut, Rev. Gary Davis' 'Will Do My Last Singing In The Land,' which was dubbed twice so I could sing a two-part harmony with myself. We did almost 20 songs during that session, so we have enough for maybe two albums."

Although the bluesman holds a Yamaha in the cover photo, a Fender was used for every track: "That Fender cutaway is a very good-sounding guitar. It has a large body and a good, booming bass. What you hear on that album is actually that guitar without amplification." In concert with Wiggins, Cephas often uses one guitar in standard tuning, plus another tuned to open *Dm* for Skip James material. He routes these to a small Peavey amp, finding that "this gives me mobility where I don't have to sit and hold the guitar at a mike that's aimed a special way. I can move around and get the spirit, you know." Like his hero Blind Boy Fuller, he favors an early-'30s steel-bodied National Duolian, open-tuned to G or E for slide. (He featured this instrument and a Martin D-28 during the 1990 Masters Of The Steel String Guitar tour.)

While he's known as an acoustic player, Cephas has experimented with electrics. "I had plenty of 'em," he laughs, "and I still have an Ibanez. But the acoustical guitar has more of a musical sound. It's more natural and sensible than electrified guitars. I just got disenchanted with that loud, repetitive music with that squealing and a-hollerin'. The acoustic music is more down to earth — *real* listening music. It's really saying something. Electric guitar is mostly a whole lot of noise, as far as I am concerned." Although he never uses it onstage, Cephas bought a steel guitar and took lessons for four years from Bud Charlton, former sideman for Ernest Tubb.

On occasion, John ventures outside of the blues: "I can play some of that upbeat stuff, like a few of those old torch songs — 'When I Grow Too Old To Dream,' 'Just An Old Shanty' — and some ragtime numbers. Man, I can't even take a stab at telling you how many numbers I know [*laughs*]." Cephas and Wiggins have written many songs together, including "Roberta" and the title track for *Dog Days Of August*. "Phil's more talented as a song-

> "If you want to play country blues, shut out all of that punk rock, funk rock, and even jazz."

writer than I am," John insists. "I've done some songs, but they haven't been very impressive. I think Phil takes the honors there." While the pair includes a few vocal duets in its repertoire, John does most of the singing.

Cephas' ultimate goal is the preservation of traditional blues: "More than anything else, I would like to see a revival of country blues by more young people learning to play this good music rather than going into all this electrified, loud noise that they're doing. I would like to see them supporting traditional artists — going to concerts, taking workshops and seminars so that they can find the backbone of all American music. That is why I stay in the field of traditional music and why I won't change and go over into the rock and roll and the upbeat stuff. I don't want it to die.

"If you want to play country blues, you should shut out all the other stuff that is appealing to the younger generations, like all of that punk rock, funk rock, and even jazz, which is wonderful. Get some old records and listen to the old guys. Apply yourself and practice diligently. And don't lose sight of your goal. If your goal is to play music, then stick with it. Don't change or get discouraged. If you're sincere about it, then you will reach that end."

A SELECTED
JOHN CEPHAS DISCOGRAPHY

With Phil Wiggins: *Living Country Blues, Vol. 1 — Bowling Green John Cephas & Harmonica Phil Wiggins From Virginia, U.S.A.* ('81), L+R; *Sweet Bitter Blues* ('83), L+R; *Let It Roll* ('85), Marimac; *Dog Days Of August* ('86), Flying Fish; *Walking Blues* ('88), Marimac; *Guitar Man* ('89), Flying Fish.

With others: Big Chief Ellis, *Big Chief Ellis* (three cuts, '76), Trix; John Woolfork, *Virginia Traditions: Tidewater Blues* ('82), Blue Ridge Institute.

Anthologies: *Virginia Traditions: Non-Blues Secular Black Music* ("John Henry," '73), Library Of Congress; *Songs Of Death And Tragedy* ('78), Library Of Congress; *American Folk Blues Festival '81*, L+R; *East Coast Blues* (two cuts, '83), L+R; *Blues Roots*, World Music Institute.

Prime Movers

Muddy Waters

August 1983

BY JAS OBRECHT

ROLLING HIS EYES TOWARD HEAVEN and shaking his head like a man possessed, Muddy Waters cast a powerful spell. His high cheekbones and Oriental eyes gave him a certain Eastern, inscrutable quality, and at times his face even became angelic. He could easily work audiences into a frenzy, marrying the unmistakable sexual urgency of his lyrics to the vocal slide statements that for 40 years were as much a part of his signature as his voice, which many claim was the best in electric blues.

A native Mississippi Delta bluesman, Muddy instinctively understood the unpretentious beauty and power in simplicity. Time and again, he transformed basic patterns into blues masterpieces. Decades after their introduction, hypnotic stop-time songs such as "Mannish Boy" still electrify audiences. Like the superstitions and voodoo images prominent in Waters' best-known lyrics, the primal earthiness of his rhythms contain a deep, almost subconscious appeal.

As a vocalist, Muddy Waters had few parallels. As a blues bandleader, he had none. More than any other performer, he was responsible for forging Delta acoustic music into the electrified, band-oriented urban blues of today. And some of his own bands were the stuff legends are made of. In the '50s alone, he employed Jimmy Rogers, Pat Hare, Willie Dixon, pianists Otis Spann and Memphis Slim, and the top names in blues harmonica — Little Walter, Walter Horton, Sonny Boy Williamson II (Rice Miller), Junior Wells, and James Cotton. British groups copied his songs in the early '60s, one naming themselves after his "Rollin' Stone." Guitarists such as Buddy Guy, Mike Bloomfield, Eric Clapton, and Johnny Winter came to share his stage. By the end of his life, Muddy Waters was hailed as "Father Of Electric Blues." Through the years and various sidemen, Muddy's music remained intensely his own. His vocals and playing patterns have often been imitated, but no one has ever quite captured his touch.

Old-time bluesmen would insist that to really have an instinctive feel like Muddy's, you'd have to be raised in the Mississippi Delta. A flat plain of

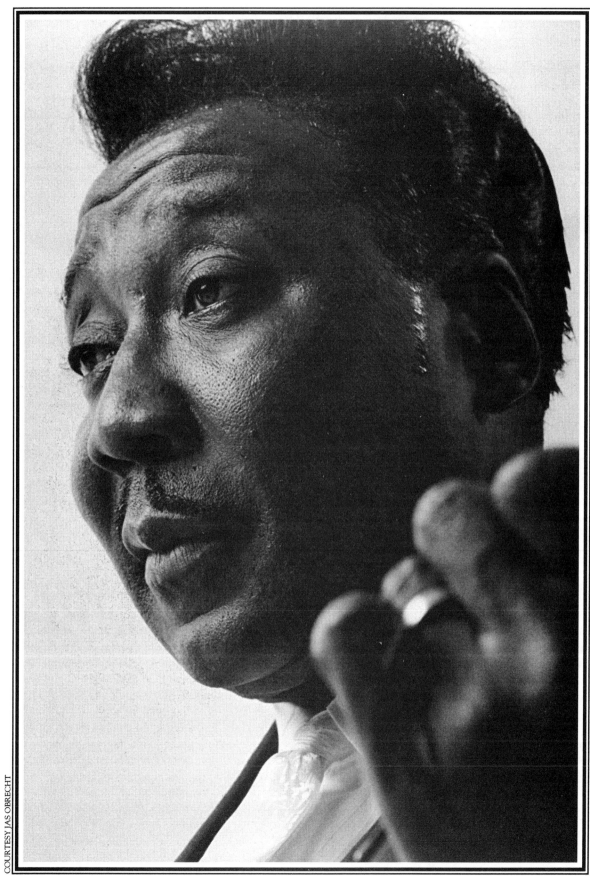

former swampland bordered on the west by the Mississippi River from Memphis to Vicksburg and on the east by the Yazoo River, the Delta has been predominantly black since it was first drained and cleared in the early 1800s. After the Civil War, most of its land was worked by cotton sharecroppers who lived on tenant farms or plantations. Many found solace from their physical hardships and low social status in the church's promise of salvation and a joyous afterlife. Others turned to earthier remedies, such as drinking, gambling, and listening to "devil's music" or, as it was more commonly known, the blues.

Bandleader W.C. Handy, the so-called "Father Of The Blues," heard this form of music for the first time in 1903, when he was awakened in the Delta's Tutwiler train station by a ragged black man playing guitar. "As he played, he pressed a knife on the strings of the guitar in a manner popularized by the Hawaiian guitarists who used steel bars," Handy wrote in his autobiography [*W.C. Handy*, Collier]. "The effect was unforgettable. His song, too, struck me instantly: 'Goin' where the Southern cross the Dog.' The singer repeated the line three times, accompanying himself on the guitar with the weirdest music I had ever heard." This description of a slide guitarist is one of the earliest known references to blues.

Charley Patton, the most famous progenitor of the Delta style, cradled his guitar on his lap and played knife-style. The rough-voiced singer moved to Dockery Plantation in the heart of the Delta before World War I, and performed at house parties and local juke joints with two other influential guitarists, Willie Brown and Tommy Johnson. A convicted murderer and failed preacher, Son House developed his ferocious slide style in the late 1920s, and he sometimes played with Willie Brown. Skip James, Garfield Akers, and Ishman Bracey were also among those who contributed to the Delta blues guitar style. Most of these men knew each other, and all had issued 78s by 1930.

For sheer finesse, though, Delta blues guitar reached its peak in the 1936 and '37 recordings of Robert Johnson, who was deeply influenced by Son House and Willie Brown. Johnson epitomized the Delta bottleneck style, executing poignant slide phrases or short fills against a steady, damped bass. Several of the 29 songs he recorded became postwar

blues standards: "Walkin' Blues," "Kind Hearted Woman Blues," "I Believe I'll Dust My Broom," and "Rambling On My Mind" among them. Of all the Delta bluesmen, Robert Johnson and Son House would have the most profound effect on young Muddy Waters.

Well, my mother told my father
On the day I was born
Gotta boy child coming
Gonna be a son of a gun
　　　　　　　　　—"Rollin' Stone"

The second son of sharecropper Ollie Morganfield and Bertha Jones, McKinley Morganfield began his Mississippi odyssey in the plantation town of Rolling Fork on April 4, 1915. The toddler loved to crawl in Deer Creek behind his father's two-room shack, so his grandmother nicknamed him Muddy. His sisters added Waters. Ollie Morganfield played blues guitar, but Muddy wasn't around long enough to remember it. With the death of his mother, the three-year-old was bundled off 100 miles north to be raised by his maternal grandmother, Della Jones, who lived three miles northwest of Clarksdale on Stovall's Plantation. Here Muddy grew up in a battered one-room cabin, less than a day's walk from where W.C. Handy first heard the blues.

The boy's earliest attempt at music consisted of banging on a kerosene can and singing. He failed at accordion, then took up Jew's harp. At seven, Muddy received his Christmas wish — a "French harp," or harmonica — and by thirteen he had fairly mastered the instrument. After minimal schooling, the boy was sent out to plow and chop cotton for 50¢ a day. Years later he described aspects of his field worker days in Paul Oliver's *Conversation With The Blues*, published by Horizon: "I do remember I was always singin', 'I cain't be satisfied, I be all troubled in mind.' Seems to me like I was always singin' that, because I was always singin' jest the way I felt. And maybe I didn't exactly *know* it, but I jest didn't like the way things were down there in Mississippi."

In 1932, the same year he married his first wife, Muddy fashioned a wooden box and some sticks into a rough guitar. He watched his friend Scott

Bohannon (sometimes spelled Bowhandle or Bohanna) finger chords, and taught himself to pick out little lead patterns. Within a year Muddy surpassed Bohannon on guitar, and the men formed an act patterned after the popular Mississippi Sheiks. Muddy played lead and harmonica, while Bohannon supplied the rhythm and Henry "Son" Simms, a former Patton sideman, doubled on guitar and violin. The trio appeared at fish fries and dances around Clarksdale, earning a sandwich and 50¢ apiece for playing blues and hillbilly tunes until sunrise. Muddy spent some of his money on 78s by Blind Blake, Blind Lemon Jefferson, Blind Boy Fuller, and Charley Patton.

Son House frequented Clarksdale and provided young Muddy with considerable inspiration. Waters explained to *down beat* editor Don DeMicheal: "Son House played this same place for about four weeks in a row, and I was there every night. You couldn't get me out of that corner, listening to what he's doing." While elements of Muddy's guitar tone and vocal style were drawn from House, his arrangement techniques and slide embellishments were closer to Robert Johnson records. "I consider myself to be what you might call a mixture of all three," Muddy continued. "I had part of my own, part of Son House, and a little part of Robert Johnson. I seen him at a distance a couple of times, but never actually seen him to play. I regret that very much, because I liked his style. I thought he was real great from his records, beautiful. Really, though, it was Son House who influenced me to play. I was really behind Son House all the way."

Son reportedly taught Muddy how to play the riff he had used in "My Black Mama," which Robert Johnson had repatterned into "Walkin' Blues." He also demonstrated how to smooth a bottleneck by holding its jagged end over a hot flame. Muddy learned that by loosening his strings to a "Sevastopol" tuning (also called open *D*) he could play multi-string slide patterns. He spent $2.40 of his profits from a horse sale for his first commercially made acoustic, a Stella, and earned 50¢ with it the day it arrived. His next instrument, a Sears Silvertone ordered from a catalog, cost

> **"I** had part of my own, part of Son House, and a little part of Robert Johnson."

$11.00. "I had a beautiful box then," he beamed.

Whenever possible, Muddy supplemented his tractor driver income by providing musical performances and, in a way, "community services." "I did it all, man," he confided to interviewers Robert Neff and Anthony Connor in *Blues*, published by Godine. "I tried to gamble, and I made and sold whiskey. I didn't stick nobody up, but I was successful with my whiskey. I used to make that jive out on the Stovall plantation. Had me a little still back out in the bushes, man. I never did believe I would get over working, though, and I probably never would have but for music. I'd have worked to 105 years old and saved $10,000 — *maybe!* Because they wasn't paying nothing. I made just as much as the guy who worked five days, 75¢ a day. I used to make $2.50 on Saturday night at a frolic or supper with my guitar, and you couldn't make but $3.75 for five days' work. So I laid back and hid from the bossman and made just as much as everyone, and was just as rested as I wanted to be. You got to use your brain." Eventually Muddy converted a cabin into a juke joint, where he peddled moonshine, reigned over marathon gambling sessions, and sang the blues.

During the summer of 1941, Alan Lomax and John Work, both members of the Library of Congress' field recording team, journeyed to the Delta to find Robert Johnson. By then Johnson was dead, and their second choice, Elmore James, couldn't be found. Locals directed them to a tough young field hand who, they said, played in a manner remarkably similar to Robert Johnson's. He worked under the name of McKinley Morganfield, but everyone called him Muddy Waters.

Muddy had wanted to record since he first heard Robert Nighthawk and Son House 78s on the jukebox, but he was disappointed to learn that Lomax' sides were for a library. After Lomax promised to send him a copy, Muddy sat down in front of the primitive aluminum recording disks with his bottleneck and Stella. His first song, "Country Blues" was based on Robert Johnson's "Walkin' Blues," with its deliberate pacing, dead-serious vocals, popping bass, and fierce slide chorus. While more of a standard country tune, "I Be's Troubled" provided a better indication of Muddy's mental framework at the time:

If I'm feelin' tomorrow
Like I feel today
I'm gonna pack my suitcase
And make my getaway
'Cause I'm troubled
I'm all worried in mind
And I never been satisfied
And I just can't keep from crying

Lomax kept his word and sent down a copy of the 78, which was enshrined in Muddy's jukebox. The following summer the researcher visited Stovall's Plantation again. On July 24, 1942, he recorded four tunes in Muddy's house with the Son Simms Four, a raucous back-country string band made up of guitarist Percy Thomas, mandolinist Louis Ford, Muddy, and Son. Exuberant and raw, these cuts may seem a little out of tune to modern ears, but the peculiar tonalities created by playing in unconventional tunings on homemade instruments were exciting. For decades to come, Muddy would use microtonal excursions outside of the standard blues scale to create emotional tension.

Muddy and Simms both played guitars on "Burr Clover Blues" and the country swing tune "Take A Walk With Me." Slide guitarist Charles Berry was brought in for a duet with Muddy on "I Be Bound To Write You," which melodically was the same as "I Be's Troubled." Waters once again displayed Johnson's unmistakable influence in his unaccompanied performance of "You're Gonna Miss Me When I'm Dead And Gone." Lomax' final session with Muddy that summer produced "You Got To Take Sick And Die Some Of These Days," "Why Don't You Live Right So God Can Use You," and a recutting of a tune from the summer before, "Country Blues, No. 2." A half-century later, these tracks still sound fresh and vital, and nowhere are Waters' roots better preserved.

After the Lomax sessions, Muddy drove the tractor for another season, but his heart was far from farming. "I always thought of myself as a musician," he explained to Pete Welding in American Folk Music Occasional. "The jobs I had back in Clarksdale, they were just temporary things. If I wasn't a good musician then, I felt that sooner or later I would be a good musician. I felt it in me." More than anything, Muddy repeated time and again, he wanted to be a "known person."

His ticket out of town came via Silas Green From New Orleans, the most famous of the Southern vaudeville carnivals still in operation. Muddy played harmonica behind the show's blues singers for only a few weeks. Returning to Clarksdale, he grew more restless than ever. He was well liked by the plantation hands who came to toss dice or drink whiskey in his juke joint, and his rocking blues performances had already made him a local legend. But his sense of what lay beyond the Delta troubled him. Many of the men he knew — including his uncle, Joe Bryant — had been lured to the North by the abundance of good-paying jobs. He soon made up his mind: "I wanted out of Mississippi in the worst way. I figured if anyone else was living in the city, I could make it there, too."

Carrying only a suitcase and guitar, Muddy Waters pulled out of the Clarksdale train station on a hot afternoon in May 1943. He changed over to the Illinois Central in Memphis, and arrived in Chicago at 9:30 the next morning. It was a Saturday, but within hours he was hired to unload trucks on the afternoon shift at the Joanna Western Mills paper factory. Muddy stayed with childhood friends on the South Side for a couple of weeks, then moved in with his cousin. Within six months, he had his own apartment a few doors down at 1851 West 13th.

The most popular radio shows of the day broadcast big bands fronted by Tommy Dorsey, Harry James, Glenn Miller, and Kay Kyser. Bebop was making inroads among record buyers, and the rage in Chicago was love ballads by Nat King Cole, Billy Eckstine, and Johnny Moore's Three Blazers. The city boasted a healthy blues community headed by pianists Big Maceo Merriweather and Memphis Slim, harmonica great Sonny Boy Williamson, and guitarists Big Bill Broonzy, Lonnie Johnson, and Tampa Red. The guitarists, some of whom already owned electrics, favored a smoother, more urbane style than Muddy's "deep bottom Mississippi blues."

Still, it was Broonzy who gave Muddy his start by introducing him around Sylvio's club as "a pretty good blues singer from Mississippi." Invitations to play house rent parties for whiskey and tips trickled in. Muddy soon found work with Sonny Boy

Williamson at the Plantation Club. Fingerpicking an acoustic guitar, he could scarcely cut through the din. He tried using metal fingerpicks, but that wasn't enough. Finally in 1944 Joe Bryant gave his nephew a cheap off-brand electric. Muddy's new instrument expanded his tone, but his style stayed the same.

Muddy journeyed back to Clarksdale in 1945 for his grandmother's funeral. Meanwhile, another young Mississippi guitarist/harmonicist took a job at a radio cabinet company with Muddy's cousin, Jesse Jones. Upon his return from Mississippi, Muddy was invited over to jam with the new guy, Jimmy Rogers, and one of the most important partnerships in Chicago blues history was born.

Rogers and Waters played a few house rent parties, then got a West Side gig at David & Mason's club. Rogers blew harmonica, while Muddy and Claude "Blue Smitty" Smith played guitars. Muddy stuck mainly to thumping bass notes or playing slide, although Blue Smitty did teach him how to fret some solo lines. The trio moved on to another "five dollar a night" club, and then, as the backing band for pianist Eddie Boyd, took a five-week stint at the Flame Club for a weekly salary of $52.00 apiece. When Boyd split for another full-time job, Sunnyland Slim took over on piano. Sonny Boy Williamson, who apparently liked Muddy's car as much as his playing, hired Waters for out-of-town dates, such as his weekly gig at the Spot in Gary, Indiana. The harmonicist would often get drunk and leave his accompanists to finish his sets, which gave them a chance to build their own reputations.

Muddy's first Chicago recordings occurred in September 1946, when producer Lester Melrose hired him to record three sides — sans bottleneck — for Columbia. None of these tracks were issued until 1971. In 1947, Sunnyland Slim requested that Muddy be the guitarist on his Aristocrat recording session. "Johnson Machine Gun" and "Fly Right Little Girl" were recorded under Sunnyland's name, while "Gypsy Woman" and "Little Anna Mae" were

Amplification added sustain to his searing, whining slide, and Muddy intensified his declamatory vocal style by emphasizing vibrato and running words together into quick phrases.

credited to Muddy. Ernest "Big" Crawford, Memphis Slim's subtle sideman, played string bass on the session. Amplification added new smoothness to Muddy's licks, and perhaps a little of Blue Smitty's coaching can be detected in the single lines of "Gypsy Woman."

Len Chess, co-owner of Aristocrat, was unimpressed by Muddy's first sides and shelved them for several months. After all, who was interested in old-time Delta blues? Encouraged by a female business partner, Len finally agreed to let Muddy record the following year. With Big Crawford thumping behind him, Muddy cut "I Can't Be Satisfied" and "Feel Like Going Home." Both were old-fashioned blues, essentially reworkings of his seven-year-old Library of Congress sides. But amplification added sustain to his searing, whining slide, and Muddy intensified his declamatory vocal style by emphasizing vibrato and running words together into quick phrases. Vastly different from the sax jumps and smoky ballads dominating the R&B charts, Muddy's surging Delta rhythms would soon redirect the course of urban blues.

"I Can't Be Satisfied" was released early on a Saturday morning in April 1948. Distributed from car trunks to record stores, beauty salons, barber shops, conductors, and train porters, the initial pressing sold out by 2:00 that afternoon. Muddy enjoyed recounting how he went to the Maxwell Radio Record Company to buy a couple of copies the following day and found they were charging $1.10 for the 79¢ record and limiting sales to one per customer. Even after exclaiming "But I'm the man who made it," he left clutching only a single copy. The release of "I Can't Be Satisfied" signaled the beginning of the greatest creative era of Chicago blues. Muddy explained to James Rooney in *Bossmen*: "To get a name, you had to get a record. People lived right up under me, they didn't know who I was until I got a record out. Then they say, 'He live right there!' — got to get a record. I got a hit thing the first one I got. I calls it luck. It was a big blues seller amongst the black peoples." With just a handshake, Muddy and Leonard Chess sealed their contract.

"I Can't Be Satisfied" sold well in Chicago and the South through the summer of 1948. The hit's immediate result was to land Muddy and his band — Jimmy Rogers on guitar and harmonica, "Baby Face" Leroy Foster on drums and guitar — prestigious gigs at the Du Drop Lounge and Boogie Woogie Inn. A superb Alabama-born, Delta-bred harmonicist named Little Walter Jacobs joined later in the year, permanently moving Rogers to guitar and Foster to drums. "There were four of us, and that's when we began hitting heavy," Muddy confided.

The band didn't limit themselves to any special blues turfs, as Muddy told *down beat*: "Little Walter, Jimmy Rogers, and myself, we would go around looking for bands that were playing. We called ourselves 'the Headhunters,' 'cause we'd go in and if we got the chance we were gonna burn 'em. Sometimes we'd come in and win the contest — they'd have an amateur contest with a prize — but the guy would come up to me after he found out who I was and say, 'Uh, uh, Muddy — you'se *too heavy*. You can work for me if you wants, but you'se too heavy to be in the contest.' Of course, I ain't like that no more. I know different now. 'Cause you can't be the best. You can just be a good 'un."

But Muddy's lineup was close to — if not *the* — best electric blues band ever. Their music was raw and physical, each song a taut, emotional plea with Muddy's voice and slide guitar at its heart. They seldom strayed from the structure of traditional 12-bar blues — outside of occasionally stretching out the count — and Muddy was unafraid to sing behind the beat. "You don't count it out," Waters would tell his men. "You *feel* it."

For transplanted Southerners, Muddy's sets conjured the joy and anguish of their own Delta days. He was the downhome blues shouter amplified, a commanding presence who could transfix the rowdiest tavern crowd with a patented bottleneck slide to the tonic and fifth, and a few words sung in

dark baritone. He took chances, and his tone had more bite than a scolding shrew. His greatest appeal? "It was sex," Marshall Chess, son of Leonard Chess, insisted. "If you had ever seen Muddy then, the effect he had on women. Blues, you know, has always been a women's market. On Saturday they'd be lined up 10 deep."

As tight as Muddy's band were, they were not allowed to accompany him in the studio. "Chess wouldn't upset things," Waters explained to Pete Welding. "He wouldn't mess with the harp or the extra guitar. He wanted to keep the combination that had made a hit record — just Big Crawford's bass and my guitar. It was amplified, but I was playing old-style blues." Muddy's final 1948 session produced the slow blues "Train Fare Home," followed by a slightly out-of-tune "Sittin' Here And Drinkin' (Whiskey Blues)." "Down South Blues" linked the popular "Rollin' And Tumblin'" Delta theme to different lyrics, and "Kind Hearted Woman" was closely patterned after Robert Johnson's recording.

> "*There were four of us, and that's when we began hitting heavy.*"

Baby Face Foster came in on second guitar for four of Muddy's 1949 Aristocrat sides, while the ever-present Crawford played bass. Of special interest, though, were two highly amplified cuts Muddy made with just Crawford: "Little Geneva" blended unusual slide licks into a theme based on Robert Johnson's "Love In Vain," while the bottleneck in "Canary Bird" buzzed around like a bumblebee. Muddy took his band on a tour of the South afterwards, centering on the Delta areas around Clarksdale and Helena.

On his return to Chicago, Muddy stepped outside of his leader's role to record behind his sidemen. With Big Crawford, he played on a couple of Chess cuts credited to Jimmy Rogers & His Trio. He also clandestinely met Leroy Foster and Little Walter over at the Parkway studios to be part of the Little Walter Trio and the Baby Face Leroy Trio. Muddy laid back on most tunes, but couldn't resist tearing loose with slide on Foster's wild "Rollin' And Tumblin'." Upset at hearing his most prominent artist on another label's release, Chess firmly advised Muddy not to appear on slide for any more records by Foster or other artists.

Johnny Jones came in on piano and Baby Face Foster played drums on Muddy's first 78 of the '50s under his own name. "Screamin' And Cryin'" was notable for its extended single-string slide solo. Muddy was then paired with Big Crawford for two takes of "Rollin' And Tumblin'" designed to compete with the Parkway issue. Snappy drums and bass lifted the song into the new decade, while Muddy's verse of moans paid homage to its Delta roots. After its release, brothers Len and Phil Chess bought out their remaining partner at Aristocrat and formed Chess Records.

Muddy provided the first hit for the newly organized label, "Rollin' Stone" backed by "Walkin' Blues." With guitar in the forefront of a barebones arrangement, "Rollin' Stone" became one of Waters' best-known songs. Despite the distorted electric guitar, "Walkin' Blues" retained the flavor of Robert Johnson's version. The 78 sold exceptionally well in the triangle covering St. Louis, Memphis, and Chicago, and ranks high among Muddy's strongest performances.

Muddy's band consistently packed the house at the Du Drop Lounge, where they were often double-billed in blues contests with Big Bill Broonzy or Memphis Minnie. Encouraged by audience response, Chess finally let Little Walter back Muddy in the studio. That they could lock so tightly together on the earliest effort, 1950's "You're Gonna Need My Help I Said," portended good things to come. Pushed by Little Walter's harp swoops and wails and the drummer's easy rim shots, Muddy's slide stung even harder on the session's remaining cuts, "Sad Letter Blues," "Early Morning Blues," and "Appealing Blues." The final taping of the year produced Muddy's first nationwide hit: "Louisiana Blues," which climbed into the R&B Top 10. A variation of the voodoo "mojo hand" theme with a nice guitar-harmonica unison, this side was backed by "Evans Shuffle," a showcase for harp gymnastics set to a boogie beat. In sessions that followed, Waters and Walter further forged their instruments into a seamless voice or created stunning call-and-response dialogs. Once Little Walter expanded his presence on record by using a good studio amp, he took over as the band's main soloist.

Jimmy Rogers, whose supple bass runs and unerring fills were essential to the stage act, was finally brought in to record with Muddy in 1951. Before the year was over, Muddy had racked up another Top-10 hit with "Long Distance Call." Two other steady sellers, "Honey Bee" (with its brilliant microtonal slidework) and "Still A Fool," featured Little Walter's downhome guitar. Pete Welding explains: "For all his strengths as a supporting guitarist, Rogers was never comfortable with such mixed-meter, Delta-derived pieces as these two; Walter, on the other hand, understood them perfectly. This fact is nowhere more evident than on 'Honey Bee' and 'Still A Fool,' where his second guitar part seems almost an extension of Muddy's lead. It's a pity Walter didn't record more on guitar, for his work on these two selections is flawless. This is not to take anything away from Rogers — his accomplishments are solid and well-documented on numerous records, both with Muddy and on his own." "She Moves Me," cut in '51 with Leonard Chess himself playing bass drum, became Muddy's biggest hit the following year.

With gigs nearly every night and widespread black radio play, Muddy reigned supreme on Chicago's South Side. His amplified Delta music had come to define Chicago blues, and imitators sprung up in the Delta, Memphis, Detroit, and on both coasts. Tours took him to the East and South. Understandably, the potential of success on their own began to attract his sidemen. After all, Muddy's men were all fine soloists, and he let them prove it. "I give everybody a chance to play," he told them. "I'm not going to hold you back. *I* love you, but I can't make the people do that. *You* do that." Mary Katherine Aldin wrote in her liner notes for *The Chess Box*, the comprehensive Waters collection released in 1989: "Some made it on their own and some didn't, but after you'd been in Muddy's band, you were *professional*. He tolerated no excessive drinking or drug use; he carried himself with enormous dignity always, and his band had to be on time, dressed well, sober and ready to play, and those who couldn't or wouldn't toe the line didn't last long."

Little Walter was the first to leave. He scored a huge 1952 hit on Checker with "Juke" (essentially the Waters band's instrumental signature) and quit to take over Junior Wells' position in the Four Aces. For a while, Walter's popularity eclipsed that of his former band leader. Naturally enough, Muddy hired

63

Junior Wells until the harmonica player's induction notice arrived. At Chess' insistence, Little Walter continued to back Muddy in the studio until 1957.

Walter Horton, a harmonicist with a wide, sweeping style, was brought into the band in 1953 and participated in the session that produced "Hoochie Coochie Man." With its voodoo imagery and commanding vocals, this was one of Muddy's finest efforts. The 78 sold 4,000 copies the first week and became his biggest seller. "Muddy Waters crashes through with his strongest sales gatherer in many, many releases," wrote a reviewer for *Cash Box.* "Waters, always a solid salesman, waxes a strong piece of material that should push its way close to the top, if not all the way. The cantor throws every one of his tricks into his job, and receives backing that is certainly not the least important part of the disc's success." It spent weeks in the R&B Top 10. A few months after joining Waters, Horton took a gig under his own name and sent Henry Strong in to substitute. A strict leader, Muddy fired Horton and hired Strong, whose style was close to Little Walter's. Walter himself blew the swinging harp lines in 1953's "Baby Please Don't Go."

Muddy finally actualized his dream of a blues "big band" when pianist Otis Spann joined him later in the year. Spann, whom Muddy lovingly referred to as his half-brother, was an unobtrusive sideman who could accommodate styles ranging from subtle fills to thunderous boogies. His admission into the band completed Muddy's move away from the intimate Delta-inspired sound epitomized by the Big Crawford-Little Walter trio sessions to a smoother, more uptempo style. The Waters lineup of two guitars, harmonica, bass, drums, and piano created a standard for blues bands that would endure for years to come.

With the added support of Spann, Muddy began concentrating on vocals and quit playing slide guitar. "The band sounded so good to me," he would later say, "I didn't think I had to play." Traditional 12-bar blues gave way to groove-oriented arrangements, and the work of Jimmy Rogers moved into the background with the new emphasis on harp, drums, and piano. For a while, the formula worked: 1953 and '54 proved to be the heydays of Muddy's commercial success. Following in the wake of "Hoochie Coochie Man," "I Just

Want To Make Love To You" reached #4 in the nationwide R&B charts and remained Top 10 for 13 weeks. The band ventured out of Chicago for one-nighters in St. Louis and Nashville, dates on both coasts, and a full-scale Southern tour with Sarah Vaughan and Nappy Brown.

Just as the Muddy Waters band was riding high on the successes of 1954, tragedy struck mid-summer: Stabbed by a girlfriend, Henry Strong bled to death in the back seat of Muddy's car on the way to the hospital. The incident deeply affected Muddy, who eventually hired West Memphis harmonicist James Cotton for Strong's position.

Bassist Luther Johnson and drummer Fred Below appeared on Muddy's final 1954 Top-10 entry, "I'm Ready," which spotlighted superb chromatic harp riffs and added to the lyrical mystique spun in "Hoochie Coochie Man." "Muddy swings out," is how the single was described in *Cash Box.* "Lyrics are pretty potent, and Waters' delivery is Grade A. Beat is solid, and ork-ing [backing] is torrid. A great bet to make it." And make it, it did: right into the Top 10. It was Muddy's last big hit.

Chicago blues record sales started out strongly in 1954, then dropped 25% in the summer. Some South Side execs blamed the depressed economy. Television was also drawing evening listeners away from the radio, the most important medium for blues promotion. But something more urgent was starting to come over the airways, a primal blend of R&B, blues, and country that was destined to eclipse the blues and every other popular style. Kids called it rock and roll.

In Memphis, Elvis Presley paired the country tune "Blue Moon Of Kentucky" with a pulsating R&B version of "That's All Right" and sold over 7,000 copies in one week. Bill Haley & The Comets scored million-sellers with "Shake, Rattle, And Roll" and "Rock Around The Clock." Alerted to the vast, new white teenager audience, A&R men from black-oriented independent record labels scrambled for rock acts. For many, Elvis' appearance on TV sealed the fate of older bluesmen: After all, how could 40-year-olds hope to compete with the hip-shaking gyrations of a teenage idol? Chess Records jumped on the bandwagon and signed artists recommended by Muddy Waters. Charles Edward Berry shortened his first name to Chuck, changed his country-style "Ida Red" to "Maybelline," and shot to #1 in August 1955. Berry became as popular as Little Richard and Bill Haley. Soon another new Chess artist could smile down from the top of the charts: Bo Diddley.

Muddy landed an occasional song on the R&B charts — "Mannish Boy" in 1956, "Nineteen Years Old" two years later — but his single sales would never approach those of the rock and rollers. He held onto his audience, though, working six nights a week in Chicago at Smitty's Corner and other clubs, and Wednesday night dances in Gary, Indiana. He toured the East and South. Willie Dixon began working with the band, as did guitarist Pat Hare. Muddy's first album, Chess' *The Best Of Muddy Waters*, was released in 1958.

More and more, Muddy came to rely on songs written by Dixon and others, causing a sameness to permeate his music. With dismay, he saw the new generation of city-born blacks abandon blues as low-class gutter music. "Young Negro kids now, they're so used to what they hear on the radio, they just turn away from the old blues," he told Pete Welding. "It's not the music of today; it's the music of yesterday." Muddy still lived comfortably in his house on Lake Park Avenue, but gigs were dwindling. Unbeknownst to him, across the Atlantic he was selling records and becoming a legend.

American blues discs had begun appearing in England at the close of World War II. Some were left behind by soldiers; others were U.S. releases repackaged on British labels. Impressed by the vital earthiness of Chess blues, youngsters such as Keith Richards and Mick Jagger sent away to Chicago for releases. By the mid '50s, trad jazz — a recreation of dixieland and Chicago styles of the '20s — and a folk-blues hybrid known as skiffle were the major British musical trends. Chris Barber, a leading exponent of trad jazz, arranged passage for Big Bill Broonzy, Josh White, and Brownie McGhee to come over and perform traditional acoustic blues in little clubs.

Before his death in August 1958, Big Bill recommended that Barber bring Muddy over. Just back from a tour of the South, Muddy flew to England with only his pianist, Otis Spann. Expecting to hear folk blues, British audiences were shocked by Muddy's tavern-shattering sound. One staid critic at the first show found himself retreating from the volume row-by-row until he was finally forced to seek refuge in the men's room. "I didn't have no idea what was going on," Muddy confided to James Rooney. "I was touring with Chris Barber — a dixieland band. They thought I was a Big Bill Broonzy, which I wasn't. I had my amplifier, and Spann and I was going to do a Chicago thing. We opened up in Leeds, England. I was definitely too loud for them. The next morning we were in the headlines of the paper — 'Screaming Guitar And Howling Piano.' That was when they were into the folk thing before the Rolling Stones." Muddy lowered his settings for the rest of the tour, which reportedly went well.

Much to his surprise, the English tour gained Muddy the attention of American folk and jazz fans. In April 1959 he appeared onstage at Carnegie Recital Hall with James Cotton and Memphis Slim. To capitalize on his newfound audience, he was encouraged by Chess to record *Muddy Waters Sings Big Bill*, an undistinguished album of Broonzy material. Muddy's first European release, the French Vogue label's *Mississippi Blues*, took a harder stance, packaging cuts such as "I Can't Be Satisfied," "Evans Shuffle," and "Louisiana Blues."

Meanwhile, the savage power of Muddy's stage presentation remained undiminished. Paul Oliver attended a 1959 show at the F&J Lounge, a blue-collar black club in Gary, Indiana. "His band was his instrument," wrote Oliver in *Jazz Monthly*, "and he sang unhampered, stamping, hollering, his whole body jerking in sheer physical expression of his blues. He would double up, clench his fists, straighten with a spring like a flickknife, leap in the air, arch his back, and literally punch out his words whilst the perspiration poured down his face and soaked through his clothing." Muddy was in a near-trance when he came offstage at 4:00 in the morning, Oliver added in his report, and spent most of the next day lying in a dark room with an icepack

> "*The next morning we were in the headlines of the paper — 'Screaming Guitar And Howling Piano.'*"

applied to his forehead.

The Newport Jazz Festival booked the full Waters band to headline its 1960 Fourth of July blues program. Muddy was a sensation, earning standing ovations and being called back to sing "Got My Mojo Working" a second time. Along with Otis Spann and John Lee Hooker, he was filmed at the event for *Jazz USA*, a series of programs by the U.S. Information Agency. Chess issued the performance as *Muddy Waters At Newport*. Muddy returned to England in 1962, once again misjudging his audience. He told James Rooney: "I went back — took my acoustic with me — and everybody's hollering, 'Where's your amplifier?' I said, 'When I was here before, they didn't like my stuff.' But those English groups had picked up on my stuff and went wild with it. I said, 'I never know what's going on.' A bunch of those young kids came around. They could play. They'd pick up my guitar and fool with it. Then the Rolling Stones came out named after my song, you know, and recorded 'Just Make Love To You,' and the next thing I knew they were out there. And that's how people in the States really got to know who Muddy Waters was."

Back in Chicago, Waters hired Matt Murphy and Earl Hooker to play guitar on sessions. In 1963 he contributed tracks to Chess' high-energy *Blues From Big Bill's Copa Cabana*, with Buddy Guy handling electric guitar. He appeared coast-to-coast on CBS' *International Hour*, and was filmed in England by Granada TV for *Blues And Gospel Train*. Encouraged by Otis Spann, Muddy took up guitar again, using his red, late-'50s Fender Telecaster for a session in Bremen, West Germany. Buddy Guy added second guitar on the unadorned, all-acoustic *Folk Singer*, issued in January 1964. Muddy's unaccompanied "Feel Like Going Home" harkened back to his Stovall days, while "My Home Is In The Delta" featured his unmistakable slide.

When British groups began arriving in America circa 1964, they proclaimed Muddy and other black bluesmen their sources of inspiration. Bruce Cook reports in *Listen To The Blues* [Scribners] that the Beatles announced their desire to see Muddy Waters and Bo Diddley soon after they landed. "Muddy Waters," asked one reporter, "where's that?" An incredulous Paul McCartney answered, "Don't you know who your own famous people are here?"

Many British blues-rock guitarists paid Muddy homage through imitation, notably John Mayall, Eric Clapton, Jeff Beck, Jimmy Page, and Alvin Lee. Their praise awakened still more white American youths to the fact that the songs credited to one "M. Morganfield" on their favorite albums were indeed by an active performer. "That's a funny damn thing," Waters told Rooney. "Had to get somebody from out of another country to let my white kids over here know where we stand. They're crying for bread and got it in their backyard. They got some of the best blues singers that ever lived right here in the United States [*laughs*] — there's nobody else, you know. They sure ain't got no real good blues singers in England. But they got some heck of a players there — guitars, every other thing."

Young white musicians in the U.S. followed suit. Students from the University of Chicago made pilgrimages to nearby South Side clubs and began duplicating what they heard. Foremost among these were a young harmonica student named Paul Butterfield and his guitar-playing pal, Mike Bloomfield. They formed the Butterfield Blues Band, stole the show at Newport, and paved the way for other white Chicago blues acts fronted by Charlie Musselwhite and Steve Miller. Jimi Hendrix unabashedly admitted his debt to Muddy and worked the bluesman's motifs into his repertoire. As rock and blues became more closely integrated, traditional performers such as Howlin' Wolf, Buddy Guy, and Junior Wells found bookings in East Coast coffeehouses and clubs.

For the first time, Muddy himself was welcomed full-scale onto the turntables and stages of young white America. And with the possible exception of

> "*That's a funny damn thing. Had to get somebody from out of another country to let my white kids over here know where we stand. They're crying for bread and got it in their backyard.*"

B.B. King, no other bluesman made the transition so easily and gracefully. His new fans found him confident, articulate, and proud: "I wasn't a cat to come in with a big bottle of wine in my pocket and talking loud." Billed as "The Living Legend," Muddy discovered his new audience was appreciative of his original style, which enabled him to drop some of the newer songs he tended to dismiss as "commercial gimmicks." With the exception of rare stints at black venues such as Harlem's Apollo Theater, Muddy found himself performing before predominantly white audiences at clubs, colleges, and festivals in Monterey, Newport, and Europe. Even New York's Museum of Modern Art and the Illinois Governor's Ball provided him venues.

Chess issued Muddy's *The Real Folk Blues* — a compilation of hits — in January 1966, and then attempted to "update" his sound by casting him a soul singer on *Brass And The Blues*. Competing with heavy organ and honking horns, Muddy was painfully out of character. Otis Spann's 1966 Bluesway album *The Blues Is Where It's At* contained more satisfying Waters work in the train-like slide effects of "Chicago Blues" and the slide signature in "My Home Is On The Delta." More early Chess sides were reissued on 1967's *More Real Folk Blues*.

For his next appearance on vinyl, Cadet's *Electric Mud*, Waters was submerged in psychedelic fuzztones, wah-wahs, and overbearing drums. It troubled him that the tracks couldn't be reproduced onstage: "If you've got to have big amplifiers and wah-wahs and equipment to make your guitar say different things, well, hell, you can't play no blues." A far more satisfying project from this period was *Fathers And Sons*, a pure blues collaboration with Otis Spann, Paul Butterfield, Mike Bloomfield, drummer Sam Lay, and bassist Duck Dunn. Butterfield and Bloomfield shone on the project, providing smooth, urbane accompaniment, especially on a memorable concert version of "Long Distance Call."

Muddy's popularity with rockers peaked in the late '60s. His 1969 appearance at Chicago's Auditorium Theater almost brought the house down — literally. "For nearly 10 minutes after he left the stage," wrote Don DeMicheal in *Rolling Stone*, "the audience roared its delight. They stomped, shouted, clapped, whistled, screamed, jumped up and down the aisles and seats. Pleadings from the stage to calm down were to little avail." Muddy and his band then undertook a tough series of one-nighters at colleges and clubs. On their way home in October, Muddy was injured in a high-speed freeway accident that killed his driver. It was rumored he would never perform again.

After nearly a year, Waters was able to discard his crutches and play guitar as well as before. He organized a stage band with guitarists Sammy Lawhorn and James "Pee Wee" Madison, pianist Pinetop Perkins (Otis Spann passed away in 1970), and drummer Little Willie Smith. The group stayed active on the college and European circuits and made occasional forays into Chicago clubs, where Muddy Waters was invariably revered as the city's statesman of the blues.

Muddy's kinetic home-turf performances of "Hoochie Coochie Man" and "Nineteen Years Old" were captured in Harley Cokliss' 1970 film *Chicago Blues*. Waters found himself back in front of a camera in 1971, singing "Long Distance Call" and "Got My Mojo Working" in *Black, White And Blues*. A collection of Chess sides from 1951 through '67, *They Call Me Muddy Waters* won a 1971 Grammy for Best Ethnic/Traditional recording. Muddy flew to London to record his follow-up album with a mixture of Chicago bluesmen and white English rockers such as guitarist Rory Gallagher and bassist Rick Grech. *The London Muddy Waters Sessions* won high praise and another Grammy, and Muddy landed a starring role at the 1972 Montreux Jazz Festival. His slide playing was improving, taking on a vocal, almost conversational quality in "Honey Bee" from *Ann Arbor Blues & Jazz Festival 1972*. Muddy's next studio album, *Can't Get No Grindin'*, was followed in '74 by *London Revisited*, which presented unissued tracks from the *The London Muddy Waters Sessions*. Muddy toured Australia and New Zealand, and then crossed the globe to jazz festivals in France and Montreux. In 1975 he cut the Grammy-winning *Woodstock Album*, as well as the *Mandingo* film soundtrack. He was then off to festivals in Poland, Germany, and Italy. The bluesman still made nightclub appearances stateside, but more and more gigs called for headline shows at stadiums and arenas.

Less frequently, Muddy was called to appear on blues bills with contemporaries such as B.B. King, Albert King, and Bobby Bland. "Ain't too many left that play the real *deep* blues," he explained to Robert Palmer in *Deep Blues*. "There's John Lee Hooker, Lightnin' Hopkins — he have the Texas sound, and Texas blues is very, very good blues — and, let's see, who else? Ain't too many more left. They got all these white kids now. Some of them can play *good* blues. They play so much, run a ring around you playin' guitar, but they cannot vocal like the black man. Now B.B. King plays blues, but his blues is not as deep as my blues. He play a type of blues that can work in a higher class place, like to a higher class of peoples — they call 'em urban blues. Bobby Blue Bland, the same thing. Albert King play a little deeper blues than they do. Otis Rush is deeper. I don't want to put down nothin' that'll make anybody mad, but it's the truth. There ain't too many left sings the type of blues that I sing."

1977 marked the beginning of Muddy's celebrated collaborations with Johnny Winter, a prominent Texas blues-rocker who — praise God — understood Muddy's music. With Winter producing and whooping it up in the background, they recorded *Hard Again* for CBS/Blue Sky in just two days; the album became one of Muddy's all-time favorites. With the mighty James Cotton on harmonica and Pinetop Perkins manning the 88s, this was arguably the tightest Waters lineup since the '50s. Muddy displayed spine-chilling authority as he roared through standards ("Mannish Boy," "I Can't Be Satisfied," "I Want To Be Loved"), premiered original material, and added excellent slide to "Bus Driver." The recording won him another Grammy and took the band across the U.S. and to Holland and France.

Muddy and Johnny next produced *I'm Ready*, covering "Hoochie Coochie Man," "Screamin' And Cryin'," and "Good Morning Little Schoolgirl." Their tour criss-crossed the U.S., and Muddy was invited to perform at the annual White House staff picnic in August. President Jimmy Carter introduced him to the 700 guests, saying, "As you know, Muddy Waters is one of the great performers of all time. He's won more awards than I could name. His music is well known around the world, comes from a good part of the country, and represents accurately the background and history of the American people." Muddy was featured singing "Mannish Boy" in 1978's *The Last Waltz*. Clips of him singing the same song and "Got My Mojo Working" during a German tour late in the year were presented in the film *Eric Clapton And His Rolling Hotel*.

While traveling with Clapton, the bluesman married 25-year-old Marva Jean King. Financially secure, he was able to buy a house in Chicago's suburbs. "Towards the end of his life," wrote Mary Katherine Aldin, "Muddy finally began to enjoy the recognition and honor that he had earned. He discarded the prowling, feral stage presence that had been his hallmark in favor of a more sedate and dignified stance, befitting the elder statesman of the blues that he had become. Younger musicians jostled for the chance to play with him, and he became, somewhat to his own puzzled surprise, the darling of the young white rock and roll crowd during the middle to late '70s."

Muddy and Johnny Winter sorted through tapes of their 1977 Detroit shows and 1978 Chicago appearances for their stunning *Muddy "Mississippi" Waters Live*. Waters bellowed past hits in fierce, declamatory Delta style and threw cross-sections of his whole stylistic spectrum into amazing slide choruses. His tone was other-worldly. The album left no doubt that Muddy Waters was still at the height of his powers. Johnny Winter produced Muddy's swan song, *King Bee*, in 1981. Among the songs were recuttings of "Feel Like Going Home," "Sad, Sad Day," and "Keep Me In Trouble (My Eyes)," as well as "Champagne & Reefer," a pro-marijuana song used to delight concert-goers.

Waters toured in support of the album — his slide playing was unspeakably brilliant during his northern California appearances — and was preparing to record another album. His plans were stilled on the night of April 30, 1983, when he peacefully passed away at home in his sleep.

Muddy Waters was survived by his wife, children, and many grandchildren and great-grandchildren. The death of the 68-year-old bluesman added only the postscript to one of the world's great musical legacies. His spirit and influence will live on as long as electric blues are played.

A SELECTED
MUDDY WATERS DISCOGRAPHY

Early recordings: *Down On Stovall's Plantation*, Testament (1941-'42 Library of Congress sides); *Chicago Blues: The Beginning* ('46), Testament; *OKeh Chicago Blues* ('46), Epic.

On Chess: *The Chess Box* (the essential anthology, covering 1947 through the early '70s); *Rare And Unissued* ('47-'60); *Trouble No More* (singles, '55-'59); *The Best Of Muddy Waters* ('58; reissued in '69 as *Sail On*); *The Real Folk Blues*; *More Real Folk Blues*; *McKinley Morganfield A/K/A Muddy Waters*; *They Call Me Muddy Waters* ('51-'67); *Muddy Waters At Newport* ('60); *Muddy Waters Sings Big Bill* ('60); *Baby Please Don't Go* ('62-'67); *Folk Singer* ('63); *Brass And The Blues* ('66); *Electric Mud* ('68, originally issued on Cadet); *After The Rain* ('69, originally Cadet); *Fathers And Sons* ('69); *Live At Mr. Kelly's* ('71); *The London Muddy Waters Sessions* ('72); *London Revisited*; *Can't Get No Grindin'* ('73); *"Unk" In Funk* ('74); *The Muddy Waters Woodstock Album* ('75); *Rolling Stone*; *In Memoriam*; *Profile*.

Chess reissues: *Back In The Early Days* ('47-'55), Syndicate Chapter; *Good News* ('55-'58), Syndicate Chapter; *Muddy Waters On Chess 1948-1951*, Vogue (France); *Muddy Waters On Chess 1951-1959*, Vogue; *Baby Please Don't Go*, Vogue; *Sweet Home Chicago* (late '40s-mid '50s), Aura; *The Original Hoochie Coochie Man* ('48-'63), Stack-O-Hits; *Mississippi Rolling Stone* ('48-'65), Stack-O-Hits.

On Columbia/Blue Sky: *Hard Again*; *I'm Ready*; *Muddy "Mississippi" Waters Live*; *King Bee*.

Other labels: *Muddy Waters, 1958* (live in England), Krazy Kat; *Mud In Your Ear* ('67), Muse; *Muddy Waters Live, 1965-'68*, CFPC; *Live In Paris, 1968*, French Concerts; *Live In Antibes, 1974*, French Concerts.

Anthologies: *Wizards From The South Side*, Chess; *The Super Super Blues Band* (with Howlin' Wolf and Bo Diddley), Checker; *Super Blues*, Checker; *Muddy And The Wolf* (portions of *Fathers And Sons*), Chess; *First Time I Met The Blues*, Chess; *Blues-Rock Cookbook — Montreux Festival*, Chess; *Blues From Big Bill's Copa Cabana*, Chess (also released as *Folk Festival Of The Blues*, Argo); *The Great Blues Men*, Vanguard; *Ann Arbor Blues & Jazz Festival 1972*, Atlantic; *Atlantic Blues: Guitar* ('72), Atlantic; *Blues Deluxe* ('80 Chicagofest), XRT.

With Otis Spann: *The Blues Never Die!*, Prestige; *Half Ain't Been Told* ('64), Black Cat; *The Blues Is Where It's At* ('66), Bluesway/MCA; *Take Me Back Home* ('66), Black Magic; *Heart Loaded With Trouble*, Bluesway; *Bottom Of The Blues*, Bluesway; *Nobody Knows Chicago Like I Do* (Bluesway reissue), Charly; *Rarest Recordings*, JSP.

With Little Walter: *The Best Of Little Walter*, Chess; *The Best Of Little Walter, Vol. 2*, Chess; *Boss Blues Harmonica*, Chess; *Little Walter*, Chess.

With Jimmy Rogers: *Chicago Bound*, Chess; *Jimmy Rogers*, Chess.

With Sonny Boy Williamson: *One Way Out*, Chess; *Down And Out Blues*, Chess.

With others: Baby Face Leroy, *Chicago Blues: The Early 1950s*, Blues Classics; Junior Wells, *Blues Hit Big Town*, Delmark; Luther Johnson, *Chicken Shack*, Muse; Johnny Winter, *Nothin' But The Blues*, Blue Sky; Willie Dixon, *The Chess Box*, Chess.

Soundtracks: *Mandingo*; *Dynamite Chicken*; *The Last Waltz*; *Street Girls* (also known as *Crackers*).

On film: *Jazz USA* ('60); *Blues And Gospel Train* (British TV, '64); *Chicago Blues* ('70); *Black, White And Blues* ('74); *The Last Waltz* ('78); *Eric Clapton And His Rolling Hotel* ('80).

Muddy Waters & Johnny Winter

August 1983

BY TOM WHEELER

MUDDY WATERS AND JOHNNY Winter were friends. As onstage performers and studio collaborators, the Mississippi blues bossman and the Texas rock star were also partners. But there were additional bonds perhaps even more profound than their deep, mutual respect as fellow professionals. Johnny's unbounded admiration for his mentor was matched by the appreciation that Muddy felt for his follower's efforts on behalf of the blues. This interview covers the Waters/Winter Grammy-winning album projects, as well as Muddy's techniques, tunings, equipment, and recordings. Throughout the conversation the interplay between the two guitarists reveals a glimpse of their unique relationship, and outlines the historical impact of Muddy Waters' blues odyssey from the Mississippi Delta to Chicago's South Side.

Johnny: Well, the first thing that you've got to understand is that I taught Muddy how to play guitar [*laughs*].

Muddy: Hey, that's right; don't laugh. You're still teaching me now. You play eight notes to my one!

When did you first get together?

Johnny: We met in Austin, Texas. We were on the same bill at a club called the Vulcan Gas Company, which later turned into the Armadillo. I can't tell you how excited I was to be on the bill with Muddy Waters. He's been my idol since I was 11 or 12, so I was there with my camera and my tape recorder. I was so honored just to meet Muddy, I wasn't about to ask to sit in.

Muddy: I asked to sit in with *him* [*laughs*]. I said, "That guy up there onstage — I got to see him up *close*." We didn't play together on the show, but we got together afterward and jammed a little and talked. Johnny had this old National, and I explained that I had played one kind of like that, so right off we had something in common.

Johnny: The first time we ever worked together was in 1974 or '75 on a TV show called

Soundstage, in Chicago. It was a tribute to Muddy, with a lot of people that Muddy had influenced — Junior Wells, Dr. John, Buddy Miles, me, Mike Bloomfield, Koko Taylor, and a few others. It was then that Muddy and I realized that we could definitely work together. When I finally got a chance to produce records with him, my whole thing was to make the record that Muddy wanted to make, with the musicians he wanted to work with. If Muddy gets pissed off, things change. He's the boss. My job as producer is to get things sounding right to him. And it's been very special and unusual, because we don't disagree.

Muddy: Our first album together was *Hard Again*. I was leaving the Chess label, and my manager went to CBS, and just like that they said, "Well, you should go to Johnny Winter's label, Blue Sky."

Johnny: Epic is part of CBS. They wanted Muddy, but they weren't sure exactly how to produce him. They distributed Blue Sky, so they asked me if I was interested. I said, "Hell yes! Let's do it!" It was that easy.

Muddy: And we didn't practice. We just got in there, and we'd run over a song and put it down. We caught it. The whole album took two days. We would've been done before, but Johnny would get tired and say, "Well, let's come back tomorrow" [*laughs*].

Johnny: I couldn't believe how he was running me ragged. The studio was downstairs and the control room was upstairs, and I was running back and forth saying to myself, "God *damn*, Muddy, you're gonna kill me." I figured we'd play about four hours, take a break, and work some more. But Muddy said, "No, I don't want to take no break, man!" [*laughs*]; it was one song after another, and they kept getting better and better. They'd run it down once just to go through it, but I'd go upstairs and listen to that first take and know that there was no reason to do it again. That's so rare, when everything's *right* the first time.

And *Hard Again* was a Grammy winner in 1977?

Muddy: *All* of our records were Grammy winners, all three of them. *I'm Ready* was in '78, and

then came *Muddy "Mississippi" Waters Live* in '79. *King Bee* is our fourth one together.

You've mentioned that your guitar style was influenced primarily by two people.

Muddy: Son House and Robert Johnson. I can tell you a little bit more about Son House than Robert Johnson. Robert's records were out in 1937, like "Terraplane Blues" and "Walkin' Blues." I was already doing my thing then, and I never followed him around to hear him or anything like that. But Son House I did follow around and listen to. And I do believe that the way Robert played, you could hear some of Son House in him. Robert was putting in more notes. It was about three notes to one. Robert was one of the greatest of the slide players.

Johnny: Muddy's told me that there were a lot of players to learn from in the Delta — not just the ones you've heard of, but many who never got recorded for whatever reason. Being even as great as Muddy is just isn't enough by itself. He's also very stable and very intelligent, and he held it together for many, many people, always working towards making it. Some good musicians were real itinerant, never worked at the same place twice, just didn't care, couldn't hold a band together ....

Muddy: Not with Krazy Glue [*laughs*].

Johnny: But Muddy knew he was damned good, even among all those others. When he was coming up, that music was everywhere.

Muddy: All over the place. Great people you never heard of who just didn't take it for a career. They'd just pick up the guitar and play it like heck and then put it down and forget it. I'd listen, and maybe I'd do some things a little different, maybe learn a few notes to add, and then other people would do it different ways and add more notes till you get up to this boy here — Johnny will stick about 18 notes in there instead of three [*laughs*].

Before you went up to Chicago, were you playing acoustic exclusively?

Muddy: Yes, starting with a Stella, and I had a Silvertone when I came North. First electric I got

> "*Muddy knew he was damned good, even among all those others.*"

was in 1944. That's when I hooked into it, and it was a very different sound, not just louder. I thought that I'd come to like it — if I could ever learn to play it. That loud sound would tell everything you were doing. On acoustic you could mess up a lot of stuff and no one would know that you'd ever missed. So electric was really rough.

Johnny: What made you get into electric?

Muddy: People were talking louder in the neighborhood taverns around Chicago, where I'd be sitting and picking my guitar. The people would be drinkin' a little booze and talkin' loud, and you couldn't get your sound over them.

Johnny: Hasn't changed much [*laughs*]. You just have to get bigger amps. Back in Chicago, were they amplifying harps before guitars?

Muddy: Where I was playing, they did it just about the same time. Rice Miller had a little microphone for his harmonica even before Little Walter was doing it.

Johnny: Rice Miller was one of the Sonny Boy Williamsons, the second one.

Muddy: And when I first got to Chicago, the first Sonny Boy [John Lee Williamson] would blow over the house mike sometimes. So the electric thing had started a little bit.

What was the Chicago club scene like when you arrived in 1943?

Muddy: It was going already, with people like Tampa Red, Memphis Slim, Big Maceo, Lonnie Johnson, and Big Bill Broonzy. Those people were heavy in Chicago.

Johnny: But boy, they didn't sound *nothing* like the blues Muddy started up there.

Muddy: No, it was different from what I do. I recorded for Columbia early on, and did a thing for Decca, even before I started recording with Chess. But I had a hard time trying to get it through.

Why was it difficult at first?

Muddy: Because I brought up the *deep-bottom Mississippi Delta blues*, and blues like Big Bill Broonzy's was entirely different. Mine was a rustier sound, a grittier sound. Big Bill and Memphis Slim and some of the others was singing very clear, and maybe they'd use a saxophone.

Johnny: It's funny that one little area of the Delta would have a sound all its own, but you could go just a few hundred miles one way or the other, and it wouldn't sound the same at all. You can't exaggerate how distinctive Muddy's playing is. In my band, if I stop playing, the main feeling keeps on going, but when Muddy stops, the whole feeling can change, because he's got that Mississippi thing and the Chicago sound all wrapped up together. It's pure style. Muddy Waters *is* Chicago blues, which is electric and has that group sound to it. But he's always kept the feeling of the Delta. And he's a very smart player. He'll do this one hot lead, sort of an Elmore James type of lick that you hear a lot, but Muddy will do it differently and put it in where you don't expect it, and it's just perfect and really grabs you in a new way. Many bluesmen overdo it, but Muddy never does.

What about his impact aside from influencing guitarists?

Johnny: One of the most important things Muddy did was to set up a particular instrumentation — piano, two guitars, bass, drums, and harp. And it became a model, with variations, for many who followed. So this was all part of the thing he did in Chicago. I read in a book once where down in the Delta Muddy asked his sister if she thought anyone would like his kind of music up in Chicago, and she said, "No, they don't want to hear that."

Muddy: When I got up there I had to keep feelin' around, testing out Aristocrat, which became Chess. Before, I had done some things for the Library of Congress. They weren't going to bring it out, but Pete Welding brought it out on his own label, Testament. It's called *Down On Stovall's Plantation*.

Johnny: That's a great record, just amazing.

Muddy: That was made when I was in Mississippi with Son Simms, Louis Ford, and Percy Thomas. We had mandolin, violin, and two guitars. Then I recorded for Aristocrat in '46. I made "I Can't Be Satisfied" and "Feel Like Going Home," and they came out in '47 and went over good and quick. And I was with Chess all the way until I got over with Johnny at Blue Sky just a few years back.

Johnny: We tried to capture the feeling of some of those old sounds on the records that we did together.

Of all your records, which ones stand out, partic-

ularly for the guitarist?

Johnny: The first one I ever bought was *Best of Muddy Waters*. That's good, and you can hear him in a small group setting.

Muddy: That record, and the first one I did with Johnny — *Hard Again* — are the two best albums I ever did.

Johnny: *Muddy Waters At Newport* is a real good live one from 1960. But there *aren't* any bad ones.

Muddy: I got some good stuff even on some bad ones [*laughs*].

Johnny: You can't go wrong with a Muddy Waters album. The only thing I didn't care for as well was when they added all that brass.

Muddy: When I did *Brass And The Blues*? Well, I liked that better than that *Electric Mud* record I did.

Wouldn't you consider *Electric Mud* a rock and roll album?

Muddy: I don't know what to consider it [*laughs*]. We ain't even going to get into it.

When it came out about 12 years ago, it made a lot of waves and people took notice, but your own opinion was, "Man, that's dogshit."

Muddy: That's what it was! But you're right — when it first came out it started selling like wild. It got up to around 80,000, and then they started sending them back. They said, "This *can't* be Muddy Waters with all this shit going on — all this wow-wow and fuzztone."

Johnny: It's worth buying just for the picture on the inside, though. See, the business people thought it'd work, because it had that hippie thing. Those people don't think the same way. They thought they'd take the blues and make it *modern*. You know: "Hey, if Muddy Waters is the big influence behind the Rolling Stones and all these people, all we gotta do is get the real man and put these hot modern players on there." They didn't understand the blues.

Muddy: I think Johnny knows more about my music than I do. When we went to do *Hard Again*,

> *"They said, 'This can't be Muddy Waters with all this shit going on — all this wow-wow and fuzztone.'"*

he was bringing up things I had forgot all about, and he was playing them just like they're supposed to be played, and I sat back and said, "*Well!*" He wanted to go back to the old sound, but I didn't know he went so far back. He knew about the tunings, phrasing, slide, picks, and everything.

Johnny: One thing I always wondered was how you got into thumbpicks.

Muddy: It was after I came to Chicago and was having that problem of getting myself heard. I was banging my hand all up, so I went to a thumbpick. That still wasn't loud enough, so I started playing electric. I used to play with a metal thumbpick, but the sound is too tinny to me, so I use a plastic one. No way could I use a regular flatpick.

When you switched to electric, did you change your style?

Muddy: No, no. But I did have to learn how to put that style into an electric guitar. Even today it hasn't changed that much. Only now I play with a band, and I give everybody a chance to play. I tell them, "I'm not going to hold you back. You go out there and make the people love you. *I* love you, but I can't make the people love you. *You* do that."

Johnny: Muddy's a lot different than many leaders. He's proud of his musicians, and he goes out of his way to help them. That's just one of the reasons why he's the father, one of the reasons I just glow when I talk about him. He gave Otis Spann his chance, plus James Cotton and Little Walter, Luther Johnson, and just so many others.

Muddy: Back in Mississippi it was usually just me, or maybe two of us.

Johnny: His style was already worked out by the time he got to Chicago. You did have somebody show you how to fret a little bit, didn't you?

Muddy: Yeah, Blue Smitty [Claude Smith]. See, I was mostly playing slide. When I started working with Blue Smitty and Jimmy Rogers, I learned a few note things. It didn't change my style, just improved it a little by putting some finger work on there. Smitty couldn't slide good, but he showed me how to go up there and do something else, and I put them together. I thank him today for it, because it was a very, very good improvement he did for me, because I didn't have to try to do everything with the slide by itself.

Johnny: A lot of the older guys never would use those other fingers, just the slide.

Did you try actual bottlenecks before you began using a metal slide?

Muddy: Yeah, I learned how to break my bottle. First I'd get me a bottle that I'd think was going to fit my finger. I had the slide in the wrong place at first, on my second finger, and later I put it on my little finger. So I had to get the right pop bottle to fit. Then I'd wrap some string around the neck and soak it in kerosene and light it and let it burn till it go out. Then you just rap it, and it breaks off just right.

Johnny: Every time *I* tried doing it like that I'd make the biggest mess [*laughs*]. There's a real trick to it.

Muddy: It's a short slide, because I don't play as many strings at once as Johnny. I play single strings mostly.

Johnny: I was so amazed to hear Muddy on record, because I couldn't see how in the world he could play slide and then be fretting it at the same time. I thought he was going back and forth between a regular guitar and a steel guitar on his lap or something. As much as I got off his records, I learned a lot more just sitting across from him and watching. It just knocked me out to see these things up close.

Can you tell us some of those things you picked up?

Johnny: Hell no! I don't want nobody else learning them [*laughs*]! No, really, there's a lot, but the main thing is hard to put into words, and that's feeling. And besides, there are some things that you can't learn.

Muddy: No matter what you do, some things come out all different, just your own. It's like singing. Your face, and what you're doing on your face, will change the tone of your voice. That's

> "**N**o matter what you do, some things come out all different, just your own. It's like singing."

where my tone is. It's like Johnny will go [*singing, with an ascending melody*], "Goin' down walkin', walkin' through the park." But I'll go way *down* at the end there, because my voice will go down there and Johnny won't go that deep down.

Johnny: Out of all the blues singers, I don't think anyone can do more with one note than Muddy. And every note is blues — whether voice or guitar. Every time I hear him, it's like the first time.

Do you consciously play vocal-style lines on guitar?

Muddy: Yes. I can't make the guitar say as much as my voice, but I try to get it as close as I can. I'm no hell of a guitar player, not the best guitar walkin' around the streets, but one thing I have tried is to make the guitar sound like my voice. See, I could never do like what Johnny does. But the *feeling* that I put into my guitar — a lot of players can't put it there.

Johnny: A typical guy now will play so many notes.

Muddy: That one note of mine will say something that the other guy can't say. The tone that I lay in there, the other guy can't get it out with 12 notes.

Johnny: Muddy will sing a line, and then he'll answer on guitar, almost like a second voice.

Muddy: That's from the Delta style, definitely. Me and my guitar, we have a conversation and talk together.

Is the guitar's tone as important as your vocal tone?

Muddy: Oh yes, it *has* to be there. I think on any guitar, if I could make a note on it, you could still know it's Muddy. But I really can't do nothing with other people's guitars. A lot of the sound is the amp. I'd rather always use my own amplifier. It's the Fender with the four 10" speakers, the Super. Even if I forgot my own guitar and had to borrow one, I could make the sound come out of that amplifier. I don't like the Twin — different sound. I like some of Johnny's amps. They're Music Mans, and them little guys is *tough*, man.

Do you ever pick up your acoustic anymore?

Muddy: I got two or three around the house, but I don't even hardly pick them up. You get lazy when you get up in age.

Do you remember your first electric?

Muddy: I really can't remember the name, because I bought it second-hand. It was one of those off brands. Jimmy Rogers and me were playing a club, and I left it there overnight. We got back and Jimmy's amp was gone and so was my guitar. So we couldn't work. When I actually started making records, I had a Gretsch with a DeArmond pickup on it.

Johnny: What was the arch-top you were playing on the cover of *Muddy Waters At Newport*?

Muddy: That was John Lee Hooker's, and I just grabbed it for the picture. My own guitar was up onstage, the same red Telecaster I got now. I got that one in 1957 or 1958.

Johnny: That's Muddy Waters' guitar, and it won't let anyone play it but him. You pick it up and it just says, "No!" You can't believe the action. My own action stays real high, but it's nothing compared to Muddy's.

Muddy: Yeah, I got a heavy hand. Everyone says, "Oh man, the strings are too high! What're you doing?" [*Laughs.*] A lot of guys want to squeeze and bend their strings up, like B.B., so they have the strings real low. My strings are *heavy*, like a .012 or a .013 for the first one. I don't need to worry about bending, because I can slide so high up there. But don't let Johnny talk about that slide — he's a dangerous man with a slide!

Johnny: My strings aren't so heavy, so I can't quite get that biting sound like Muddy. The heavier the strings, the better your chance of getting a good sound, definitely.

Are you playing mainly in standard tuning now?

Muddy: Mostly standard, 'cause it's tough if you're waiting in between songs to tune to G or A. And I'm too lazy to carry two or three guitars around like Johnny [*laughs*]. He's still a young boy — he can pull that stuff around. What would I look

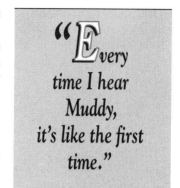

"*Every time I hear Muddy, it's like the first time.*"

like with two or three guitars like these kids? I don't need to be bothered with that. I got my one old guitar.

Johnny: I ain't heard no one complain.

Have you ever modified your Telecaster?

Muddy: Yes, in the '50s a guy in Chicago made me a neck for it, a big stout neck with the high nut to raise up the strings for slide. I needed to strengthen it up because of the big strings, and I think that the big neck has a lot to do with the big sound.

Johnny: You switch that thing on the front pickup and it's got so much bass it'll just about blow the amp up.

Sometimes during a verse—maybe just going into the turnaround — you'll switch the toggle from the bass or middle position to full treble and just let 'em have it.

Muddy: Yeah [*laughs*], I like to do that alright.

Johnny: I've never seen anyone do that so effectively, so dynamically. Sometimes he'll go the other way — like from a solo to backing up his voice, and he'll go from the brightest treble to the bass. He'll do it anywhere it works, going back and forth real quick, man, sometimes a couple times in one solo. One thing I always wondered, Muddy — there's a clicking sound you make, like the sound of the slide hitting the frets.

Muddy: I know what you mean. People don't know that I do a lot of this [*pats the strings against the pickup with his right hand*]. I do a lot of *pattin'*.

Johnny: And a lot of times I'll mix it up louder — because it just fits in there perfect. Those little things make a difference.

You've seen the blues go through many changes. Where do you see it going from here?

Muddy: I've seen it go up and down many times. Everything's improved over the years, and it's still changing. But if you're an old standard blues singer like me, my changed sound is still the same basic Muddy Waters style. If you change it too much, it's not blues no more. You can send it into rock and roll or even disco. You don't want to get too far away from it.

Johnny: I think people are moved by the blues because it's communication and emotional expression more than just music. Some people think it's about everybody sitting around and feeling bad together, but it's not at all. We have common problems, and you feel *better* by hearing that other people also have them, and hearing what they think about it and what they're doing about it: I don't have enough rent money, and neither does this guy here. Anybody can understand the blues if they halfway try. It might be braggin' blues about how cool you are, or down-and-out blues. No matter what kind, talking to people is more important than how many notes you play. John Lee Hooker is no Chet Atkins, but he gets up there and gets the point across.

Johnny, you've done a lot to help the blues continue.

Johnny: Well, a lot of people have been working their butts off all their lives, and the major record companies don't seem to care. So my commitment is to help make sure that people out there who want to play blues music will have a label and a way to be heard. I want to make sure that someone's not just playing great at home by himself because he can't get anyone to record him.

Muddy: And that's a heck of a move Johnny's making, because the big companies forget about the old blues singers, don't care. "What do we want with him? He can't sell enough records. We ain't got time." They look for somebody else.

Johnny: The younger guys can get out there and hustle, like Muddy and I did and everybody else. But you get *tired* of hustling when you're 60 or 70 years old, and people who might have started rock and roll or based their whole careers on what you did just don't even seem to remember. It pisses me off. You see someone who's still great, and during certain periods no one's interested in recording him. There's no excuse for it.

What kind of shape is the blues in right now?

Muddy: It's in good shape.

Johnny: It just keeps going. People say sometimes that they think the blues is dying. But it ain't going to die.

Muddy: It may change around a little bit, but it won't die. See, the groove was here [*long pause*] before time.

Johnny: During the '60s with all the hippie stuff, when the Rolling Stones and all the younger white musicians were acknowledging their gigantic debt to the older blues musicians, kids were listening to the blues. Their idols were telling them how great it is — guys like Eric Clapton and Mick Jagger. In a way it's more real now. They buy it because they really know who Muddy Waters is, not because Mick Jagger recorded a Muddy Waters song. I feel better about it now, but it did help in the '60s — anything to make people aware of where it came from, that's important. Muddy's the father. It's a debt that'll never be repaid in full. Lately I've felt great because he's finally starting to get the kind of recognition he's deserved for so long.

Muddy: Thanks to you.

Johnny: No, no, no. I ain't done anything. [*Johnny leaves the room to get his guitar.*]

Muddy [*whispering*]: That's my son.

77

Willie Dixon

December 1980

BY JAS OBRECHT

HE'S THE POET LAUREATE OF modern blues, the man who made Muddy the "Hoochie Coochie Man," taught Howlin' Wolf "Evil," and showed Sonny Boy Williamson how to "Bring It On Home." "Willie Dixon is the man who changed the style of the blues in Chicago," insists Johnny Shines. "As a songwriter and producer, that man is a genius. Yes, sir. You want a hit song, go to Willie Dixon. Play it like he say play it, and sing it like he say sing it, and you damn near got a hit."

For four decades, Willie Dixon has loomed at the forefront of Chicago blues, working as a bassist, arranger, band leader, producer, talent scout, agent, A&R man, and music publisher. Released in 1989, *The Chess Box* hints at the scope of his compositions: "Spoonful," "I Ain't Superstitious," and "Back Door Man" sung by Howlin' Wolf, "My Babe" by Little Walter, and Muddy Waters' "I'm Ready," "I Just Want To Make Love To You," and "You Shook Me," to single a few. Dixon himself is featured as a leader on several sides from the '50s and '60s. "Listening to these 36 compositions back-to-back tempts one to proclaim him *the* American songwriter," reviewed Joe Gore. "It's a high-water mark in American culture."

Willie Dixon was born in Vicksburg, Mississippi, on July 1, 1915. As a youngster, he learned to communicate in rhymes with his mother, a religious poet, and he remembers skipping school to follow around Little Brother Montgomery's band as it played atop a flatbed truck. A couple of stretches in Mississippi prison farms gave Willie a wider understanding of the blues. Learning harmony basics from a carpenter, Willie joined the Union Jubilee Singers gospel quartet as the bass vocalist. He left Mississippi in 1936 to box, winning the Illinois State Golden Gloves Heavyweight Championship. His subsequent professional career lasted four bouts (or five, if you count the fracas with his manager in the Boxing Commissioner's office). Guitarist Leonard "Baby Doo" Caston talked Willie into making music his career, and in 1939 they formed the Five Breezes.

The band broke up at the outset of World War

78

II, when Dixon was jailed for refusing induction into the armed forces. After a year of legal entanglements, Willie was free to gig around Chicago with the Four Jumps Of Jive. After cutting some sides for Mercury in '45, Dixon joined Caston in the Big Three Trio, whose harmony vocals hit a popular note with white audiences along the North Shore. After hours, Dixon headed to the South Side to jam with Muddy Waters and friends. Hearing Willie at the El Casino Club, the Chess brothers recruited him for their fledgling label. Dixon's initial contributions were as a studio musician, backing Robert Nighthawk's 1948 sessions. By 1951, he had full-scale involvement with the label. As the company's staff producer and chief talent scout, Dixon had a hand in the success of Muddy Waters, Howlin' Wolf, Little Walter, Jimmy Rogers, Sonny Boy Williamson, Magic Sam, and Buddy Guy. For a while in the late '50s, he plied his skills crosstown at Cobra, helping Otis Rush and Magic Sam get their starts.

Since the mid 1960s, Dixon's name has appeared on countless rock records — the Rolling Stones were early customers, followed by Cream, the Doors, the Jeff Beck Group, and Led Zeppelin. In more recent years, acts as unlikely as Hank Williams, Jr., Los Lobos, Oingo Boingo, and Megadeth have covered his songs. Willie's released several solo albums, including the 1970 Columbia classic *I Am The Blues* and 1988's *Hidden Charms*. Besides his love of music, Willie Dixon has another incentive for staying active in the business: Like his father before him, he has 14 children.

Who are the most impressive guitarists you've worked with?

I've played with just about all of them. The way-back guitarists were pretty good, like Big Bill Broonzy and Tampa Red, because they had unique styles of their own. Baby Doo used to play acoustic guitar, too. I like Matt Murphy. Elmore James had a unique style, too, although most of the time it was practically the same thing. Robert Jr. Lockwood had

> *"Hog Mason taught me a lot about bass, him and Baby Doo Caston. Sometimes I'd hop over the ring and we'd stand there and harmonize."*

a beautiful style when he played strictly blues; today he kind of mixes it up with a jazzy sound. He could play just about anybody's style, and then he had things of his own. Jody Williams had a very creative style, but he got out of music.

When you were starting out in the '30s, who were the bassists you listened to?

I liked this fellow who used to play with Duke Ellington a long time ago, Jimmy Blanton. I never met him; I just heard him, though I never actually tried to play like him. There was another guy we called Hog Mason who taught me a lot about bass, him and Baby Doo Caston. This was when I was boxing, working, and trying to learn how to play. I was fighting more than I was doing anything else, and I'd be at a gymnasium on 48th and King Drive and Baby Doo used to come up and sing and play the guitar there. Sometimes I'd hop over the ring and we'd stand there and harmonize. Then when I kind of got expelled from the fight game I just started singing with him.

Is this when you started playing bass for a living?

Yeah. In fact, Baby Doo made me a bass out of a tin can, and I used to play it all over Jew Town. We'd pass the hat around and get a little money. Then we'd go all through the different neighborhoods, singing like the Ink Spots and the Mills Brothers. I played the tin-can bass until I got a job on the West Side, a place called Martin's Corner. Since I wanted a bass fiddle, Jim Martin decided he'd buy me one. I paid him back $10 a week for twenty-some weeks. Baby Doo and Hog Mason used to always show up there and help me, and after three weeks, why heck, I could play about as good as I can now. I just wasn't quite as fast, I guess.

How did you get involved with recording?

I was on record sessions starting in '39; I did a thing for Decca with the Bumping Boys. Then I recorded with the Five Breezes and the Four Jumps Of Jive — in fact, I think this last one was the second session Mercury Records cut. With the Big Three Trio I got involved with Columbia. During that time I started recording spiritual groups, but the blues was always there, even in the beginning. I played with Memphis Slim, and did a lot of things for [record exec] Lester Melrose. Most of this was done with the tin-can bass. Then after the tin-can bass, I got involved with the first Sonny Boy Williamson — there was another harmonica player later who used the same name. Years ago they didn't have all the tracks that they have in studios now. I used to wrap cloth around the bass mike and stick it in the bottom of the tailpiece. It would come right through like an electrified bass.

Did you write songs with specific performers in mind?

There was always somebody asking me to write songs for them, but I would usually just write whenever I had a chance. If I felt certain people could do them, those are the ones I'd let have them. When I'd find out somebody was stuck for a song, I'd just say, "Look, I got something I think you can do with all ease, and it'll work." And most of the time, why, they worked. Like on the first song Muddy Waters made — I brought it to him when he was working along 14th Street. It was "Hoochie Coochie Man," and he liked it so well he went in the washroom, practiced a few minutes on his intonation, and he come right out and done it. And he's been doing it ever since. If I was writing for an individual, I would quiz him and get his feelings and expressions — the way he talked and sang. The first thing you have to do is try to get something he would like and that you feel the public would like, too. I would try to match his feelings about what he would be singing about with how he felt with other things I was going to add in. Most of the time they didn't know what chord changes they wanted, so I would tell them how to do them.

Were the royalties pretty good back then?

I'm afraid there were no royalties most of the time. They would always give you a contract saying they was going to give you some royalties, but you never got them anyway. They might give you $25 or $50 when you first recorded, but that would just about be the end of it. When rock and roll people started covering some of my songs, I started to get a little more out of it because they got so popular. It got to where I'd tell somebody I wrote the song, and they wouldn't believe it. Then when you'd go to the recording company, they would say, "Well, you're getting a royalty statement at such-and-such a time," and they'd give you a statement alright, but sometimes there wouldn't be any money with it, or very little. We didn't have a definite way of getting it, and the average lawyer you'd go to would be bought off by the recording company so they wouldn't have to pay you off.

What is your opinion of the cover versions of your songs done by popular rock bands?

Oh, I like them real well because a lot of the youngsters would use ideas I'd give them. There's no song that can't be changed in various directions. When Memphis Slim and I were working in Europe, they didn't have no rock and roll around except for a little bit that Chuck Berry done started. So the kids were all interested in blues and Chuck Berry's style. I would try to explain it to them, and sometimes I'd put it on tape. There was a group that called themselves the Rolling Stones; some of them say they met me at different halls I was playing over there. They were naked-face kids back then, and the next time I'd see them they were older — all stretched out, with hair all over their faces. I couldn't remember who they were.

What kind of bass are you using now?

I'm using an upright, an old Kay. I've had it about 18 years. A long time ago I had an electric bass when they first came out with them, but at that particular time they weren't doing much rock-style or jazz things, and I found out that old upright gave the blues and spiritual things I was doing a better background sound. Of course the electric does a beautiful job on the modern-type songs. I let Jack Myers have my first electric. I've only owned five different basses in my career, including a Fender I bought for my son once.

Do you use your bass when composing?

Sometimes I will. Most of the time I get the words that I would like to say and the expression I would like them said in first. To get the best results, I would like for these things to be a part of life because I've always felt like blues was the facts of life being expressed to people who didn't understand the other fellow's condition. Say, for instance, here's a guy you know who's in a very good condition. He's happy and there's something that made him happy, or he's in love and feels a certain way about a girl. You find out what he would like to say and get these words together in some kind of poetic form where they can be properly understood. Then you find the music to go with it. Or you might get a good tune in your mind and put the proper words in it. It all depends on what position you're in. Find words and tone qualities that make each other stick out. It's just like a picture on the wall: If you got a good picture, you want to have a good background. If you have a good background, you want a good picture. But you want them to contrast with each other to where one will stick out from the other and attract the attention of the public.

"I started creating middles to songs in order to give a complete story."

Which of your songs are you most proud of?

Frankly, I have several new songs that I think quite a bit of. It looks like most of the time I seem to be more proud of the latest song I'm involved in because it builds on the facts of life that exist today. There has been a lot of controversy lately between the majority of the public wanting to do one thing when what they consider is right is another thing. You have to decide what's what and bring out the truth. You can look at just about any blues song and see where the facts existed with certain people. It

makes you understand why they sung, do sing, and are very emotional about such things as the blues. It's not an imagination; it's a fact.

How has your style evolved over the years?

When I was a youngster they considered blues as just a 12-bar thing, done like Bessie Smith. But after I started working I found that it's earthly impossible for you to give a complete story with all the facts in 12 bars like they were doing it, so I started creating middles to songs in order to give a complete story. My style hasn't changed very much. Sometimes I found out that doing certain things in certain places can give you a better effect and attract attention to what you're doing. I can play just about any style, but I hang on to the blues because I feel this is my heritage. On top of that, it's my people's music through many generations. Most of the things that were created by black people have either been extinguished, forgotten, or placed out of proportion with everything that's happening today. It's necessary that the history of the blues be known — from where it came, how it is, and what it's for.

What do you look forward to in the future?

Bigger and better blues, and a bigger and better understanding among people themselves. I know if they listen to the blues, they gonna get the true facts of life without all the friction involved. It's got to create a better understanding among everybody.

A SELECTED
WILLIE DIXON DISCOGRAPHY

Solo albums: *The Chess Box*, Chess; *I Am The Blues*, Columbia; *Willie's Blues* ('59), Prestige; *Willie Dixon & Memphis Slim! Songs*, Folkways; *Willie Dixon & Memphis Slim: At The Village Gate*, Folkways; *Willie's Blues* (Bearsville reissue with Memphis Slim), OBC; *Willie Dixon & His Chicago Blues Band*, Spivey; *Catalyst*, Ovation; *What Happened To My Blues*, Ovation; *Live! Backstage Access* (Montreux, '83), Pausa; *Mighty Earthquake*, Pausa; *Hurricane* ('84), Pausa; *Hidden Charms*, Bug/Capitol.

Anthologies: *Blues Deluxe* ('80 Chicagofest), XRT/Alligator; *Blues From Big Bill's Copa Cabana*, Chess.

Soundtracks: *Blue Collar* ('78); *The Color Of Money* ('86).

Jimmy Rogers

August 1987

BY DAN FORTE

UDDY WATERS, HOWLIN' WOLF, Sonny Boy Williamson, Little Walter, Sunnyland Slim, Willie Dixon — all true pioneers of the raucous, impassioned music known as Chicago blues. But another essential component to any discussion of the genre is a guitarist who played with all of the giants listed above and more. Because he scored first as a sideman and later as a singer/songwriter on some of the most original blues recordings of the '50s, Jimmy Rogers' importance as a guitarist is criminally overlooked. But in the historic, unparalleled Muddy Waters band of the early '50s, Rogers' sinewy bass lines and chordal backups were as integral to the group's powerful, innovative sound as Muddy's soaring vocals, Little Walter's interweaving harmonica, or Otis Spann's meaty piano.

Listen to Waters' classic recordings of "Hoochie Coochie Man," "Standing Around Crying," "40 Days And 40 Nights," and "I Just Want To Make Love To You," not to mention Rogers' own "Ludella," "That's All Right," "Sloppy Drunk," and "Walking By Myself," and it's obvious that one can't play the blues Chicago-style without borrowing heavily from Jimmy. In the words of the Mighty Flyers' Junior Watson, who backed Rogers on his 1984 LP *Feelin' Good*, "His whole thing with Muddy was so precise—those intertwining guitars. I think it was all worked out, like, 'You play this, and I'll play this.' Their styles were so one-dimensional — this one thing is all they'd do — so they could count on the other guy playing a certain thing. That's why it worked — like Eddie Taylor with Jimmy Reed. The timing and rhythm of Jimmy Rogers' licks are what's amazing. And he hasn't lost any of that."

Although he gave up playing music for a living in 1960, not to return until 1971, Rogers is very active today, touring and recording in the U.S. and overseas, still based out of Chicago. His first-hand recollections give a rare insight into one of American music's most important turning points from one of its moving forces.

Born in Atlanta, Georgia, in 1924, Rogers (his real name was James A. Lane) moved to Memphis

84

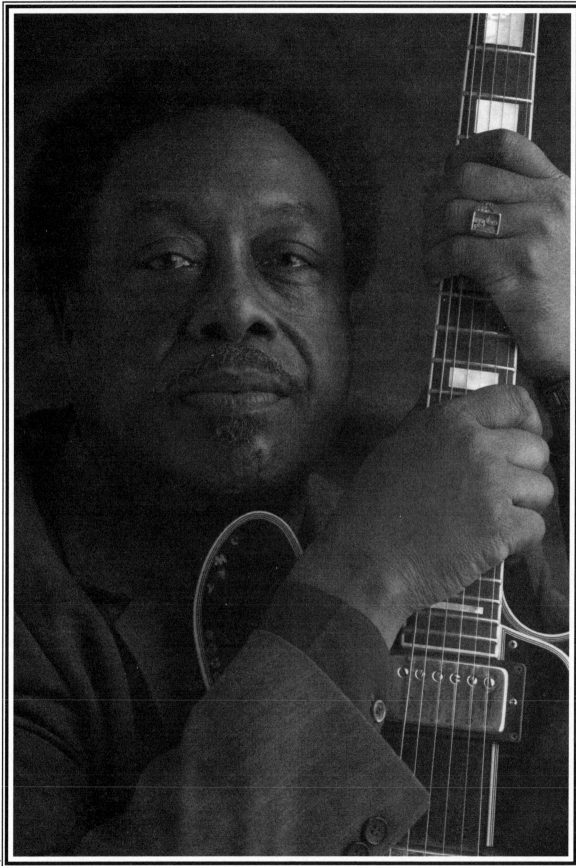

and later St. Louis while still in his teens. Raised by his grandmother, he would accompany her to Chicago visiting relatives in the late '30s. By the early '40s he had settled there for good. "I was learning to play before I came to Chicago, but I was real young. After I got to town, I played with Sunnyland Slim before Muddy came to Chicago, and with Tampa Red and Big Maceo. And I played harmonica with Memphis Slim some, and I played with Memphis Minnie on guitar. I had an acoustic. So I played with quite a few people before Muddy even came to Chicago. But Blue Smitty and myself were working together in Chicago the same year that Muddy Waters came to town, which was in 1946. I turned pro in 1946, but I had been playing before that."

He had also begun playing electric guitar. "Before Muddy came, I was playing electric guitar with Sunnyland. When Muddy came to Chicago, he wasn't playing electric. He had a guitar he brought to Chicago with him in 1946, but it was just a hollowbody with the 'S-curves' [f-holes] in it. It was an Epiphone, I think — an Epiphone or Gretsch. It's been so long, I forget. But anyway, he put a DeArmond pickup on it. That was his first electric. But we had DeArmond pickups and amplifiers and all that stuff before he came.

"My first guitar," he points out, "had the big hole in the center — the big soundhole. And I put a DeArmond pickup across that hole. A fellow there called John Henry [Barbee] had one, which give me the idea of getting it. And Blue Smitty had one made up like Muddy's — with the two 'S-cuts' on the sides — and he put a DeArmond pickup on his. I had a Gibson amplifier, the first amp that I owned, and then I went on through a chain of others until Fender came out, and I started buying Fenders."

Like most bluesmen, Jimmy played regularly in the open-air Maxwell Street market known as "Jew Town." "Yeah, me and my friends was playing out there," he smiles; "Buddy, Ed Newman, Porkchop, Stovepipe, Satch, John Henry — all those guys, a bunch of them. Most of those guys is dead now. We'd be out there from maybe 8:00 Saturday night

> "You'd hook up and play, and make you some money passing the kitty and stuff like that."

until maybe 3:00 or 4:00 Sunday evening. We played a few clubs, but mostly for parties. When we played in a club, at that time, you wasn't paid to play. You would come in, and the guy would furnish the electricity. You'd hook up and play, and make you some money passing the kitty and stuff like that. We'd play in maybe two or three joints a night that way and make pretty good money like that. In fact, we were making more money that way than I made when we started to call ourselves a band and started to be paid by the club owners. When we started playing, we were getting like $8 a night that way, apiece — three or four of us — but before that two guys, maybe three, would go from one place to the other, and you'd make $20 or $25 apiece. You'd make maybe 75 or 80 bucks a night on weekends. That was good money. Like Friday night and then Saturday night, and then we'd play in the street Sunday night until maybe midnight."

Jimmy also had a succession of day jobs, which is how he indirectly hooked up with Muddy Waters. "Off and on I was working days, but I was more interested in playing. The first job I worked on in Chicago was like a packing house — chicken packing in those big 60-gallon drums. Icing them and loading trucks, over at South Water Market in Chicago, right off Market Street. The next job that I had was at Midwest Shoe Manufacturing Company, on the West Side. Then I worked at some more packing houses — Liberty, Swift, Armour — and from there I went into construction. I was working at a radio cabinet company with Muddy Waters' cousin Jesse. Jesse would take up with us musicians, like me and Smitty; on weekends he would come around where we'd be playing, and he'd buy us whiskey and stuff. He just liked to be with us. So he got me this job at this radio cabinet place where he was working. He told me he had a cousin that was coming to Chicago. So then I did meet him when he came in, and we got to talking, and he said he was playing down south, down in Clarksdale, Mississippi, for house parties and what have you. And so we just started playing for parties. And from that, club owners hired us."

The guitarist details how what started as a modest, casual arrangement grew into the most important blues group in Chicago. "It was like myself and Muddy — at the time I was playing harmonica and some guitar — but Blue Smitty was our regular guitar player. I had been switching from harmonica to guitar with Blue Smitty, so when Muddy came in, he took one of the guitars, Smitty had the other one, and I was on harmonica. It was just three of us playing around like that. Then Blue Smitty wasn't too interested in playing, really, so he soon dropped out of it. And then Sunnyland Slim brought Little Walter to Chicago, and I met him. We'd be playing on the streets there on Maxwell Street, in Jew Town, where I was living at the time. That's where I met Little Walter at, down on Maxwell Street. He was about 17. So I took him down and introduced him to Muddy, and I told him he was a good harmonica player. In fact, Little Walter was about the best harmonica that was in Chicago — for the blues, at that time. I grabbed him right away, and we started practicing with him. We just formed a unit then: Muddy, Walter, and myself. I'd tune my guitar down like a bass, and Muddy was playing the slide. We did all right like that. We added a drummer in there later on, Baby Face Leroy [Foster]. He was a guitar player and could play drums pretty good, too. So we started touring around different places like down to Muddy's home, Clarksdale, Mississippi, and over to Arkansas and around different places, playing little nightclubs, in 1947."

Muddy Waters had recorded a few sides for the Library of Congress as early as 1941, while still in Mississippi. He recorded his first Chicago sides in '46, a year before Little Walter first recorded. (Baby Face Leroy, incidentally, also made a few stirring records under his own name, in 1949 and '50, backed by Muddy and Walter.) "Sunnyland got Muddy started on records," states Rogers. "We were making records, but they was on a small label, like underground. They wasn't getting off the ground too good. Sunnyland was working with Aristocrat, and that finally changed over and was the Chess label. Sunny knew Leonard Chess, and Leonard was like a talent scout for blues. Sunnyland said, 'I know a boy that plays hard Delta blues there on the West Side called Muddy Waters.' So they recorded him, just him and a bass player, Big Crawford. Sunny

played piano on some, but on others it was just a bass and the guitar."

Waters' earliest recordings for Aristocrat and Chess — songs such as "Gypsy Woman" (1947), "Little Geneva" (1949), and "Rollin' And Tumblin'" (1950) — featured spare backing, usually bassist Big Crawford and/or pianist Sunnyland Slim. "He wasn't getting the sound that he was getting when we were all of us playing together," Jimmy feels. "So he was down there sweating, man, and scuffling, trying to make the records. I told him, 'We have a good sound onstage, and the record don't sound as good.' And he talked to Chess, and they decided to start letting me record with him. We made 'Sad, Sad Day' and 'Just Make Love To Me' and all that stuff with the full band — Baby Face Leroy and myself, Otis Spann, and Big Crawford. But Big Crawford died shortly after he got into this, and then we started using Willie Dixon on the upright bass. All this stuff was happening like in a two-year period — from around 1948."

Although there was almost always upright bass on the recordings, the Muddy Waters band that played clubs consisted of drums, piano, harmonica, Muddy's slide, and Jimmy's rhythm guitar, playing bass lines. "At that time we didn't have a bass," Rogers points out. "I'd lower the guitar, tune it down and play the bass part. Dixon started playing bass on the records, but he wasn't playing the blues at clubs. He was playing like semi-blues or jazz-blues; they called themselves the Big Three Trio. And he was writing stuff already, but he started mostly helping arrange the blues stuff that Chess guys would do. And he got to the place that he could tell Chess what was going to sell and what wouldn't sell. He got enough good sellers out of it for Chess to start really paying attention to what he was saying."

Incidentally, on one or two sessions for Muddy, Rogers shared guitar chores with Little Walter. "That's how we made 'Still A Fool,'" Jimmy points out. "Muddy was just singing; me and Walter were playing the guitars. Walter wasn't considered a good guitar player; he clowned with it a little bit. But basically we had been playing, and he knew the sound, the way that I played, so 'Still A Fool' wasn't hard for him because he knew a little about the guitar. It was just up and down, the same thing, up and down. I was harmonizing, and he was just squeezing the string when it'd get to that point. So we made that particular side, but he didn't play guitar on any of Muddy's other records. [*Author's note: Some sources state that Walter also played guitar on "Honey Bee."*] But on a lot of songs Muddy would be standing over there in a booth, just singing, and we'd be over there playing. Most of the stuff Muddy played on is when you hear that *keen* — that slide. Sometimes after we would play, then he'd run a track [overdub] with the tape."

With the addition of Otis Spann, the band not only boasted of having arguably the greatest blues pianist of all time, but cut the die for most electric blues and rock bands that followed. "Otis Spann was playing with a fellow I knew over on the West Side, [singer/guitarist] Morris Pejoe. He made a record or two on Chess, but they didn't do too good. Otis was glad to work when I approached him about playing with me and Muddy. And he turned out to be a real good piano player. He was fantastic. He helped put weight behind the band. Then Leroy Foster dropped out of the picture, and we got another drummer called Elgin Evans. There was five of us; we held that five pieces there for a long time."

Whereas Waters' main influences on guitar were fellow Mississippians Son House and Robert Johnson, Rogers leaned more towards Big Bill Broonzy, one of the key figures in the blues' transition from rural to urban and already a big star in Chicago. "Big Bill was my favorite guitar man. Yeah, Bill used to call me his son; I knew him a long time. Tampa Red and Big Bill Broonzy and Big Maceo were really the leading hard blues artists that were in Chicago. And Memphis Minnie, but she was fading. Muddy talked about Robert Johnson, but he didn't know Robert too well. But he would talk about what he heard about Robert, see. Muddy knew Son House, and Son House was playing along this same style that Robert was playing. And so he picked up a lot of stuff from Son House, this Delta blues player. He had a lot of different stories about those guys back there. But, see, Muddy was, I'd say, about 10 years older than I am. So when he got to Chicago, he was like 30 years old."

> "Big Bill was my favorite guitar man. He used to call me his son."

Another big influence on Rogers' guitar style was Joe Willie Wilkins. "He never got too well known, but he was a good blues guitar player," Jimmy stresses. "He played with Sonny Boy Williamson on the *King Biscuit* show. But he was a home-type fellow. He would stay right around mama, hang around mama's dress tail. You could pull him away from Memphis for maybe a week, then he'd go back. Man, I didn't care *where* it was, I would go. I always was the going type. The further the better for me. I saw Joe Willie in Chicago once. He came to where we was playing at, and sat in with me and Muddy. And he was telling me, 'I'm getting the payback from when you played my guitar when I was with the King Biscuit boys.' He let me play his guitar one night, with Rice [Miller, a.k.a. Sonny Boy Williamson] and all of them. In fact that was the first electric guitar that I played — Joe Willie's."

Rogers never took up slide guitar because, in his words, "I never really liked it too much. You didn't have enough range with that slide; you're limited. You can't play chords. You've got to retune your guitar. If you've got it natural [tuning], when you play the slide, it's light and you're not executing too well. Muddy was doing enough sliding for me. And I really don't want slide on a record of mine. I'd take a harmonica, but I never wanted a slide in there."

His early influences combined with the necessity of covering the roles of rhythm guitarist and bassist accounted for Rogers' unique style, often consisting of bass lines and double-stops or single-note fills behind the vocal. "Yeah, with Muddy, I would do that," he says. "I was mostly a harmony player, see. It was actually mostly background, playing with Muddy. Also, I was used to harmonica because I played one myself. I know what it takes for a harmonica player to play, so I could play it on the guitar. That's the reason why the average harmonica player loved to play with me. I'd play heavy melody tones for the harmonica, to give the harmonica something to drive with. A lot of guitarists don't know how to play very well with a harmonica. You gotta know how to play harmony. You gotta know the changes and harmonize on the guitar to back up a harmonica. But most guys, they don't play that way. Most guys, they play that loud stuff like Albert King or B.B. King — single-stringing all the way through. And that don't leave no opening for a harmonica. That's why they don't like to play with a harmonica."

Rogers' relaxed but solid guitar work was the perfect foil for Muddy's intense vocals and whining slide. "I would pay attention to how he was singing," he stresses. "You got to be very alert. I would know how to phrase and how to change it. At the time that he was thinking of changing, I would watch him — pay close attention to him by ear, and watch what he was going to do. He'd pretty near do the same thing just about every time in the same order. So when I found out that that's the way he worked, well, I'd know then how to bring him. A lot of times he'd be lost — he wouldn't know when to make his change — but I'd change for him, see, and he was right there on the top of it. When he'd get through, he'd laugh, man — say, 'Man, that's good.' Because so many people didn't understand that. That's the good part about it."

Muddy's band wasn't the only electric blues band in Chicago, and not necessarily the first, but it was definitely the strongest. "There was lots of bands around," remembers Jimmy. "The Myerses, who were the Aces, they were playing. They had Junior Wells playing harmonica with them. They were called the Four Aces — Junior Wells, Dave and Louis Myers on guitars, and Fred Below on drums. And then when Walter left us, see, he had taken that band over, and Junior joined me and Muddy on the harmonica. They just changed places. We worked on like that for a couple of years, and then Junior went into the Army and we got another boy playing the harmonica, Henry Strong. Everybody called him Pot. He was learning to be a good harmonica player, but he got killed in Chicago. And then we got this boy who died a few years back in California called George Smith, and he played with us for about eight, nine months. After that, that's when we got James Cotton. Shakey Horton recorded some stuff with us, too, but

> **M**uddy's band wasn't the only electric blues band in Chicago, but it was definitely the strongest.

he didn't play with Muddy as a regular harmonica player, see — not too long. Cotton was working with him when I left the band." (The back cover of the Chess Vintage Series' *Chicago Bound* LP features a backstage photo of one edition of the Waters band, including Muddy, Otis Spann, Elgin Evans, Henry Strong, and Rogers, with an unidentified maracas player. Jimmy clears up the mystery: "That was Tommy Lee Armstrong. He wasn't really in the band, but we'd let him sit in on maracas. Actually, he was a sign painter; he's the one who painted 'Hoochie Coochie Man' on the bass drum.")

Nearly every player who worked in Muddy Waters' band during the '50s has since achieved legendary status. In town the group was intimidating, to say the least. "They called us the headcutters," Rogers laughs. "Anytime we'd go in a club, man, the other musicians had to back down because we had the floor. If some guy was playing over here, when we'd get off work we go to his club — just to have a nice time. But they wouldn't let us rest until they'd get us on the bandstand and tear the house up. Then we'd go to the next club."

The battles of the bands that had begun in the days of Big Bill, Memphis Minnie, and Memphis Slim were still commonplace. "On Sunday afternoons clubs like Sylvio's would have battles. You could win maybe $20 or a fifth of whiskey. We [the Muddy Waters Band] would lay down a lot," Jimmy reveals. "We could win them all, but we would lay down and let somebody else win. The public didn't like that at all — they'd know."

Sylvio's and most of the other South and West Side Chicago clubs were rough-and-tumble joints. "Sometimes the black clubs would be pretty rough," Rogers allows, "but it never harmed any of us. The Zanzibar was the roughest one — at 13th and Ashland, on the West Side. Just about every week somebody would get messed up. But what could you do? We was pumping the blues good and had a big crowd. Somebody'd look at somebody else's girl, and there you go."

By 1955 Rogers had already scored a succession of blues hits, so he left Waters to form his own band. "In Chicago the clubs that we were playing was too small," he explains. "We would pack the place, but the prices they was getting just wasn't enough to cover. Now, Muddy might've been getting a little more money, but he wasn't kicking it out to us. So then I said, 'Well, I could do this good or better with my own band.' Walter felt the same as me, so he left before I did. He tried to get me to leave when I made 'That's All Right,' because that was a big hit. Walter was going to pull off with me, but I said no, because we were trying to make an all-star unit."

Like Little Walter's early solo hits, Jimmy's recordings utilized Muddy's band and were usually done at the end of Waters sessions. "We made 'Juke' and let that go out under Walter's name. I could've taken it, or Muddy, either one, but we said no. We had made this up between the three of us. I told him to call it 'Juke.' Then we didn't have anything to back it up on the flip-side because Walter wasn't singing at the time too much. He would sing a couple of the late Sonny Boy, John Lee Williamson, tunes. One of them was 'Crazy About You, Black Gal.' And we just changed it; instead of saying black gal, he just sang 'crazy about you, baby.' I kept on pumping it to him: 'Don't say *black gal*, say *baby*.' So they had a song to go on each side of the 45."

The most amazing aspect of Rogers' solo recordings, especially considering that the first was done in 1950, was how sophisticated they were. They were much more melodic than the blues that was prevalent at the time, and many, while following three-chord, 12-bar changes, departed from the usual AAB lyrical structure. "I got ideas from big bands," he reveals. "I like a lot of jazz, man — big band stuff. A lot of my songs are just verses and choruses that go on and on, playing the 12-bar changes. But that's a different pattern [vocally]; the average blues player don't play that way. I guess that's why they say that it's different, because it *is* different. It sounds good to me, so we just go on with it like that. 'That's All Right' was already in the making before I started playing with Muddy, but I hadn't recorded it. I always felt that it would be a

> "*I* got ideas from big bands. I like a lot of jazz, man — big band stuff."

hit, but I wanted to wait and put it on a national label. It's been recorded a lot of times now. I like that version by Mose Allison."

By the time he was recording his own material, Jimmy had changed guitars. "I had a Silvertone," he recalls, "but when I made 'That's All Right,' I played a Gibson. The Silvertone was a nice little blonde, and that was the sweetest playing guitar, besides the Gibson, that I'd ever played. I've been using Gibsons ever since — a lot of years."

After Jimmy recorded with Muddy's band, most of his recordings featured his own group, occasionally with Chess session players brought in. "It would be my band," he explains, "but they had this dude Reggie Boyd who played on some stuff with me. He played the jazzy stuff on 'Rock This House' and 'My Last Meal' he was on, too."

Jimmy retired from music in 1960 and didn't return to active playing until 1971. "My kids were growing up, and expenses were going higher," he explains. "And I was a family man. Music wasn't doing too much for me at the time, so I had to do other things. I bought into a cab company with another fellow. Then I left that and had a clothing store. I would go around with some of the guys who was playing — Magic Sam or sometimes Muddy — after I closed the store at night. I'd go maybe on a Saturday night and play a number or two. But people would go, 'Where are you playing tonight?' and I'd go, 'Well, I'm not playing right now.'"

In 1971 Jimmy was forced out of retirement: "I started back a while after I got burned out. The store had burned down back when Martin Luther King got killed [in '68], and I lost a lot. They had a riot in Chicago, and they was burning up everything. So I got caught in it real bad. I had to do something. I already had an offer to go to Europe, but I'd refused it. I called back and within a month's time, I was in Europe. And that helped me to get myself started back again. I was getting good pay over there, and people was appreciating what I was doing. So I recorded a couple of records over there, and I was getting a pretty fair shake, I'd say."

Rogers played around Chicago with the Bob Riedy Blues Band, with whom he recorded, but he made his first full-fledged solo album, *Gold Tailed Bird*, in 1973, backed by the great Freddie King. During his years off Jimmy always kept a guitar in the house. "Yes, all the time I had a guitar. The ES-345 I play now I've only had for maybe four or five years. But I got another one at home. I love those 335, 345, and 355 Gibsons; I've got one that stays at Antone's [in Austin, Texas] all the time, and I've got about four guitars at home."

It wasn't too severe a culture shock to come back after a nine-year layoff because, in Jimmy's words, "I stayed in contact with the world. I would be practicing and learning more about what I was doing. So it wasn't bad. Me and Johnny Littlejohn started back together. Johnny was playing some guitar with Wolf, and we started playing gigs together. That was like in '71, '72, and then I went to Europe. I've always had good bands; I picked pretty good musicians all the time. I know what it takes. I had a guitarist named Jim Kahr in my group.

He lives in Germany now. He's a Chicago boy."

These days Jimmy's original Chess recordings are available on reissues, and he has several recent LPs out in the States and in Europe. He appeared on a live anthology from Antone's tenth anniversary, featuring Rogers as frontman (accompanied by Jimmie Vaughan), as well as backing Snooky Pryor, Eddie Taylor, James Cotton, and Pinetop Perkins. His latest release, 1990's *Ludella*, finds him in superb form working alongside harmonicist Kim Wilson, pianist Pinetop Perkins, and guitarists Hubert Sumlin, Derek O'Brien, and Bill Campbell.

Looking back over his illustrious career, Rogers is both proud and understated when he says, "We really did something for the blues — we all did. At the time when we were doing it, we didn't know; we were just playing to our satisfaction, mostly. We didn't really know how strong the blues was going to become."

A SELECTED JIMMY ROGERS DISCOGRAPHY

Solo albums: *Chicago Bound* ('50-'56), Chess; *Jimmy Rogers*, Chess Masters; *The Classic Chicago Blues*, Chess Japan; *Left Me With A Broken Heart*, Chess France; *Jimmy Rogers & Left Hand Frank*, JSP; *The Dirty Dozens*, JSP; *Chicago Blues*, JSP; *Gold Tailed Bird*, Shelter; *Feelin' Good*, Murray Brothers; *That's All Right*, Black And Blue; *Sloppy Drunk*, Black And Blue; *Stickshift* (one side by Rogers), Teardrop; *Ludella*, Antone's.

With Muddy Waters (on Chess, except as indicated): *The Chess Box*; *Rare And Unissued*; *Rolling Stone*; *Sail On*; *The Real Folk Blues*; *More Real Folk Blues*; *Trouble No More*; *Back In The Early Days*, Syndicate Chapter.

With others: Sonny Boy Williamson, *Down And Out Blues*, Chess; Bob Riedy Chicago Blues Band, *Lake Michigan Ain't No River*, Rounder.

Anthologies: *Wizards From The Southside*, Chess; *The Second Time I Met The Blues*, Chess U.K.; *Tenth Anniversary Anthology, Vol. 1 — Live From Antone's*, Antone's.

John Lee Hooker

BY JAS OBRECHT

FORTY-ONE YEARS AGO, JOHN LEE Hooker sat alone in a Detroit studio and recorded his first songs. One of them — "Boogie Chillun" — was destined to become a million-seller and get the world jumping to a boogie beat that's reverberated through popular music ever since. Over the years, Hook's cut more than a hundred albums and worked with some of the finest musicians in blues, and yet the very heartbeat of his music remains his powerful voice, propulsive guitar, and unique songwriting. Like Lightnin' Hopkins, Muddy Waters, and very few others, he's a musical law unto himself and a direct link to first-generation blues.

His latest album, *The Healer*, is no exception. While Carlos Santana, Bonnie Raitt, Robert Cray, Canned Heat, Los Lobos, George Thorogood, Roy Rogers, and Charlie Musselwhite all appear as guests, the deepest track of all is "Rockin' Chair," a spine-chilling four minutes of ferocious solo guitar and that haunting, unmistakable voice. "Yeah," insists the man, "that *is* the closest to my heart."

Born to sharecroppers in the Delta town of Clarksdale, Mississippi, on August 22, 1917, John Lee Hooker learned guitar from his stepfather, Will Moore. He sang gospel and played blues in Memphis with Robert Nighthawk before moving to Detroit in the '40s, where he worked in a factory by day and played clubs by night. After his first Modern Records session, Hooker recorded for other labels, using pseudonyms such as Texas Slim, Delta John, Birmingham Sam & His Magic Guitar, Johnny Williams, and Johnny Lee to avoid contractual problems. (It's estimated that between 1949 and '53, he issued some 70 singles on 24 different labels, using a dozen different names.) He proved to be as prolific as Lightnin' Hopkins, following "Boogie Chillun" with other big R&B hits such as "Crawlin' King Snake" in '49 and "I'm In The Mood" in '51. In the '50s Hooker began recording with experienced R&B sidemen such as guitarist Eddie Kirkland, who helped him mold a more disciplined, commercial sound.

Signing with Chicago's Vee Jay Records in 1955, Hooker seldom recorded without guitarist

Eddie Taylor and other sidemen at his side. "Dimples," cut in March '56, became his first British hit a few years later. Hooker returned to his old style for his 1960 and '63 performances at the Newport Folk Festival, recording solo or with a bassist for the tracks released by Vanguard. He made his first foray into Europe with the American Blues Folk Festival of 1962, and returned home to find that "Boom Boom" had become his first crossover hit, reaching #60 in the charts. The Animals' 1964 cover of the same tune became a huge British Invasion hit and introduced Hooker to white audiences at home. He next signed with ABC, releasing albums on its Impulse and Bluesway subsidiaries. His *House Of The Blues*, a collection of early-'50s Chess sides, reached #34 in the British charts in '67, while 1971's *Hooker 'N' Heat* charted in the U.S. Later in the '70s Hooker cut for Atlantic, Tomato, and European labels, and in 1980 he played the role of a street musician in *The Blues Brothers*. Six years later Steven Spielberg featured his music in *The Color Purple*, and Hook's latest guest appearance on vinyl is in Pete Townshend's musical, *The Iron Man*.

Today John Lee Hooker enjoys more trappings of success than perhaps any other bluesman. The walls of his palatial house in the hills above Vallejo, California, are decorated with gold records, music awards, concert posters, letters from governors, and snapshots posed with George Thorogood, Jerry Garcia, Carlos Santana, and promoter Bill Graham. His modest collection of about 50 albums includes titles by Clifton Chenier, Wayne Cochran, Albert King, James Brown, Junior Parker, Champion Jack Dupree, Muddy Waters, Charles Mingus, and a few of his own old albums. The license plate of his white Cadillac reads "Doc Hook," while his sporty red Toyota is registered as "Les Bogy." Our conversation took place in the shade near his hot tub. We left the interview in Hook's exact words.

While *The Healer* features many well-known musicians, the strongest tracks are the ones where you're by yourself, especially "Rockin' Chair."

> "*It chills you, it's so deep. Sometime when I play stuff like that, tears come out my eyes.*"

That's my favorite tune! The others is good for dancing, some of them, but getting right down to the nitty gritty and the real funk, this is it. Just playing the guitar, sittin' there in my old-time rockin' chair. A lot of people like that, too. It is *the* closest to my heart. It, and another one on there — I can't think of the name of it, but it's with Musselwhite. Oooh!

"Rockin' Chair" seems to be in the oldest style you play in.

Oh, boy! Whew! That's *direct* to my heart. That's a funky blues. People can just sit there and just *meditate* and think about how it feels sometimes. It'll send a cold chill up and down your spine. It chills you, it's so deep. Sometime when I play stuff like that, tears come out my eyes.

When you were working in Detroit in the early days, you often played like that, with just your guitar, a small amp, and your right foot keeping the beat.

That's the way I used to play. No band, no nothing. Just John Lee Hooker and his feet.

Did that style develop from playing by yourself a lot when you were young?

No, it come from my stepfather, Will Moore, from whom I learnt to play. He taught me how. I used to listen to him. My real father, he didn't care for that kind of music in the house, because he was a minister. My real father and my mother, they wasn't together. They separated or divorced or whatever. My mother, she got remarried.

How much of your style today is similar to Will Moore's?

As the years went by, just a little bit changed with new, young musicians around. Well, maybe my basic style have changed a lot. I listen to my old records, way back, and look at my new stuff, and it's a difference. What I'm doing now is still funky, but my old style was just nothing but me by myself just playing the hard, hard blues. Now with a band, it changes quite a bit.

If someone wanted to hear John Lee Hooker's

best guitar work, where should he begin looking?

I would tell him to start lookin' at the years gone by. Back when I was younger coming up, I was playing more hard blues by myself. I could play more guitar and do more by myself. I could do the same thing now if I went on and started playing by myself. But to get the best hard stuff I did, you want to go back to Detroit days when I was playing by myself in coffeehouses. I played more guitar. I had no band to interfere. I didn't need to give no band no breaks and solos. I could do what I wanted to do when I wanted to do. With the band, it gets in the way a lot.

A band restricts you to playing in a certain format.

Yeah! Now you said it. When you got a band, you got to concentrate on what to do. When I'm by myself, I just do it when I want, change when I want, not change when I don't want. I can sit there and play a whole lot of guitar and just go to it.

Do you see a similarity in your approach and Lightnin' Hopkins'?

Oh, yeah. Lightnin' did it all the time. That's where he was comin'. He didn't believe in all them bands and things.

Are there certain blues albums that you like to listen to a lot?

Oh, yeah. I would start with Albert King and Jimmie Ray Vaughan — well, Stevie Ray Vaughan. Jimmie, too, is nice. Layin' these blues on you. And Muddy Waters and on and on. The great ones have stood here and then have gone, but they still live on in my memory, whom I love so much. Just a great memory.

Right now, it seems like there are tens of thousands of blues guitar players.

Whoo! Well, I hate to say it, but it seems like there's *too* many. And a lot of them is really good! They are good ones, but if you look around, a lot of 'em sound alike. You hear one, you just about done heard them all. So in your mind, they all are good,

> **"Some of them play a tremendous lot of guitar, but what I play is with a solid drive, a funky beat, and nobody got it but me!"**

but if you go in to record with them, you just say, "Hey, this guy sounds like so-and-so. He sound like B.B. He sound like Stevie Ray." They don't have a unique style all to themself, like I got. Some of them play a tremendous lot of guitar — they play much more guitar than I do — but what I play is with a solid drive, a funky beat, and nobody got it but me! That's what make me stand out. In fact, all of them sound almost alike — *do do do do do* [*mimics stratospheric wailing high on the fingerboard*]. It's good, but...

You know how some guys try to copy another player exactly?

Yeah!

What would you have someone learn from you?

That's a good question. What would I have them learn from me? Just learn to stop trying to make all the fancy chords and a whole lot of guitar all the way down the neck real fast. Forget about the fancy chords and concentrate on just a funky beat and something with a lot of soul and just a feeling to it.

You've played with dozens of great guitarists, from Eddie Kirkland on down to the musicians on your new album. Which of them could send chills up and down your spine?

Albert King [*laughs*]. I don't know why, but there's just something about his guitar. He got a outstanding style of his own, and a lot of people try to copy him, too, but they don't get it. I don't know, there's something about Albert — I hear his voice and his guitar, and it just chills me.

He's one of the last guys you'd want mad at you.

[*Laughs*.] He sure as big as this house! He's the *last guy* I want mad at me! Yeah. Well, you know, me and him good buddies. I respect him; he respect me. We're always glad to see each other. B.B.'s the same way. Me and him are really good friends. He's a tremendous guitar player. A lot of 'em try and sound like him. I think he changed over the years, too. He's gone to the big-band style, the Las Vegas style. But he can play some hard blues when he just want to. But he don't do too much of that now. He's on the Vegas trip and circles. That's where you make a lot of money, but with me, I just like to please myself.

Throughout your career, you've seemed to remain true to your own vision of music.

Yeah. We all like money, you know, but the main thing is, I want to please myself. I'm doin' alright money-wise, but I want to play what pleases me. I don't want to play Vegas circles. I want to please the other people, but I want to please myself, too. And so I just stays in what pleases me. When I was making this record, I had all these good people on it, but it was an entirely different style, like "The Healer" and Los Lobos. But I said, "Hey, I got to play some funky blues on here. I want to play some funk." Now, this other stuff will sell real fast, like Los Lobos and Carlos Santana — I'm sure they're going to go AM — but I wanted to please myself. I wanted to play some deep funk!

When you were growing up in Mississippi or working in Memphis, did you ever dream about someday being one of the greatest bluesmen in the world?

No, it didn't never occur. I know I had the know-how. I know I had the stuff to do it with. I know I had the voice. I know I had the unique style. But I never would have thought that I would have come to get my foot in the door where I had a chance to prove what I could do. I never knowed that I would come to be this great, this popular on this planet, enjoying these things as one of the greatest bluesmen in my field that is. But I always thought I could be if I had the chance.

Didn't you work in the Ford Rouge plant after you moved to Detroit in the '40s?

Yeah, I was a janitor. I pushed a broom. I was so into my music, but I had to work to survive. I always did like to be independent. I wanted to be on my own. I didn't want hand-outs, and I had to work to support myself. And I didn't want to be doing it in

the factory. I would play my guitar at night, be up late, and they would catch me asleep, wake me up. They wouldn't fire me, because at that time it was so union, and then they wanted help so bad, they did give me all kind of chances. They'd wake me up if they found me asleep [*laughs*]: "Little John" — they used to call me Little John — "Little John, get up! Wake up."

Back then, you recorded under a lot of different names — Texas Slim, Delta John, John Lee Cooker, John Lee Booker. Did the record companies give you those names, or were they your idea?

That was me. I want to say this very slowly [*looks carefully around the yard and tips his hat back on his forehead*].

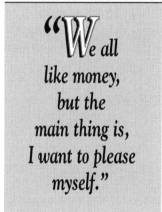

"We all like money, but the main thing is, I want to please myself."

I was the hottest blues singer when I got my foot in the door with, like, "Boogie Chillun," "In The Mood," "Hobo Blues," "Crawlin' King Snake." Everything I did [*snaps fingers*] just turned to gold. I had this manager, Elmer Barbara, and all these record companies would come to him. They said, "This kid got something so different." And I was under contract with Modern Records in L.A., and they was crooked — some of the biggest crooks ever lived. So Barbara would come to me late at night and say, "Man, I got a deal! This record company want to do something with you. I know you under contract, but we can change your name." I said, "I don't care," and this kept going on. Every different little record company would come to me, and I'd say, "Call me what you want to — as long as you got the money." They did give me a name, and I went in the studio late at night.

Would you change your style?

Sometime, but the company knew. There wasn't nothin' they could do about it.

How would you record guitar back then?

I had an old Stella with a pickup in it. I thought at that time it was a great, great sound. Tremendous sound that was really good until the electric come along. T-Bone [Walker] give me my first electric guitar. Then I thought that was the best I ever seen. It was a Fender — no, no, it was Epiphone [arch-top].

Given your choice of any amp, what would you choose?

Fender. I love Fenders and Gibson guitars. I thought two or three times about endorsing Fender amplifiers — get 'em free, 'cause that's all I use. I love the sound of the Twin.

What's your favorite guitar?

A Gibson. I got two Gibsons and two Epiphones. [*Ed. Note: Rich Kirch, backup guitarist in Hooker's band, details: "The Gibson ES-335 that John uses now — serial number 26201 — was given to him by Carlos Santana on his birthday a few years ago. He plays that one all the time. His blonde Epiphone is his favorite one; it's on a lot of the old records. I'm not sure what year it is, but it's a semi-hollowbody with a single cutaway. He also has a Lucille guitar — the Gibson B.B. King model — and another 335. He gave one of the 335s to Junior, his son."*]

You're holding a Les Paul on one of your early albums.

Yeah, that's when I first started out.

Do you ever use picks?

No.

How do you tune your guitar?

Regular tuning and open tuning. Open A [E A E A C# E] and open G [D G D G B D]. [*Kirch adds, "John plays most everything in E, except to boogie, when he usually tunes three strings up so he's in open A."*]

Have you ever been interested in playing slide?

No.

Why?

No reason. I just never did care for it myself. I love to hear it, but for myself, I wasn't into it. I didn't want to do it. It wasn't the sound that I wanted, which is good. Oh, I love Bonnie Raitt's slide; she's one of the best slide players I ever heard in a long time. She's one of the unique ladies I ever seen. I love her voice, I love the style of guitar. She can do that slide.

Your cousin Earl Hooker was great, too.

Oh, yeah. Well, he was number one. Bonnie Raitt got her style from Fred McDowell. She used to go out there [to Como, Mississippi]. I knew him real well.

If you could put together an all-star blues band, who'd be in it?

That's a good, big, big question. The famous people, like? Well, you can only get so many guitars in one band, so I would say Albert King — the Big Man, I call him. The others, right now I really can't put my hand on it, but number one, I really would pick Albert King to be one of them. There are many, many more that's good — tremendous good. Of course, I don't copy him; I don't do none of his stuff. But I don't do none of nobody's stuff but mine. So I'd get him first, and all the rest of it I'd fill in. If I could pick one who's gone, I'd pick Otis Spann. He was one of the greatest piano men that ever lived. Drummer, I don't know. There's some funky bass players. The guys that I'm used to playing with — and I heard a lot of 'em — one of them's gone, Geno Skaggs. The young kid I got now, Jim Gayette, I never thought he was that good until I really take a good listen to him. He's a funky little bass player—he play funk, play rock, play it all.

Did you know any of the early bluesmen, or were you familiar with the work of, say, Robert Johnson or Blind Lemon Jefferson?

I didn't never know any of those gentlemens; I only know them through my stepfather, so I don't have too much to say. I don't know their background, but all the blues today — they was the root of all that music. It come from them. It come up progressive from those guys, and it could rise and rise and rise, but it was still from them. They was the one who created all of that.

When you began performing, did it seem almost impossible that a blues performer could play to a white audience?

Right. No, you couldn't imagine it. But I had a feeling that it was comin', but when? I know it would come sooner or later. Now it's here in the full. I know back then that the blues was just only for the older black people in just a certain area. You get a hit record then, it wouldn't be half of the hit it is now. Just a half a big hit now is *big*, but back then the #1 record didn't make a lot of money 'cause it only went to a certain people, the older black people. But down through the years it all changed.

Is right now a good time for the blues?

Oh, yeah. All over the world. To the non-English-speaking people, Japanese, France, Russia, the Communist countries, the blues have just cut their way into every country in the world, all over the world. Young, old — they found out the true identity of music that is the blues. It is the first music was here. It is the one tells the story. It is the one to tell the life story of a human being or a man and a woman. Who started this? Eve and Adam in the Garden. When the blues was born, it was born with Eve and Adam. Over years and years and years, they beginning to find out the roots of this stuff and what it means to people. The rich, the poor—they all have the blues. No matter how much money you got, when your woman or the one you love have left you or you can't get along with her, all the money in the world cannot fill the place of happiness in your home. Because money can't talk to you. So that's the reason the rich people, they get the blues. They get worried and upset, and then they can't talk to that money at night. They can only spend so much, but they cannot buy happiness. So everybody realizes that now. The young, they study the blues. It's in the library. They read about it.

See, what they call rock and roll haven't been around over 35 or 40 years. What is rock and roll? That was all taken from the blues. Everything that we are saying, they are saying: "My woman done left me [*scat-sings a solo*]." The blues was saying all along, "My woman done left me heartaches," or, "My baby gone, she won't be back no more." Well, rock and roll say the same thing, but they got the really up-to-date form and they call it rock and roll. It's the blues.

Johnny Shines tells of how a guy could walk up to a bus stop and tell people how his house just burned down and his kids died, and most people

> *"The blues is here to stay. That's all I can tell you. And they stronger than ever."*

would probably just walk away.

Right.

And yet that night those same people might spend $15 to hear him sing about it in a club.

Right. Oh yeah! Yeah, you know, that's the blues. The blues is here to stay. That's all I can tell you. And they stronger than ever. I have to admit that when I first started playing the blues and first started making a record, I wasn't making that much money. Just a little bit, but at that time I thought it was big money. You know, you make $1,000 for a week or $500 a night — that was *big* money to me. But now I consider $500 — I go out for dinner a couple of times, it's nothing. But back then that was a lot, a lot of money. Now all the kids, especially the young white kids, oh, they eat the blues up. They love 'em. And they playing them, too. The young kids, they can play them. It first got big in England. The blues got *real big* in England before it got big here in the '60s. The Stones and Animals and things like that — ooh, boy!

The Animals' cover of "Boom Boom" is probably where most white kids in the '60s heard of you for the first time.

It was! It was! And when I went overseas, it was just like God just let Jesus go over there. That's all you could hear: "John Lee Hooker!" But they had never saw me. But everybody over there was playing my stuff.

Was the audience very different from what you were used to?

Ooh wee! You know, this is the truth: Before I got to the concert hall — even if it was rainin' — the place be full with a line around the block. They had to start puttin' on two shows a night to accommodate those people. Before I got there, the guys was playing all my music — Eric, Jimi, Georgie Fame, Spencer Davis, they all was doing it. John Lee Hooker. And then on the radio it was big over there. When I went over there, oh boy, it was just like the President coming. It made me feel good, you know. That's where it started from, and then I come back over here, and it started catching over here real big. Then everybody in the world got it — the white kids, the black kids.

When the white kids became interested in your music, did you lose some of the black audience?

No. With dedicated fans, no matter who come in, they still are gonna like who they like. Just like a baseball team. I live here [near Oakland] and I like the Giants, but I'm a strictly Dodger fan. Although they ain't doin' nothing, but I still like 'em and I'm still with 'em. Oh, I love baseball.

What else do you like outside of music?

I love being home. I'm a regular home person. I like just to lay back.

Do you play guitar much when you're home?

Oh, yeah.

During concerts, it often seems that you compose songs on the spot.

Sometimes, yeah. Sometimes, no.

Do you have a good memory for songs?

I've got a hell of a memory. I don't forget nothing. Once I get it in there [taps forehead], I just [snaps fingers three times]. I can lay down at night and think of a song, get up, and sing it word by word and don't forget nary a word.

Do you sing songs that aren't blues?

Yeah. Like *The Iron Man* with Pete Townshend. And I was surprised I did that. He kept telling me I could do it, and I cut it in New York. That was completely out of my style, but it don't sound bad.

You also contributed a version of "Red House" to a Jimi Hendrix project, *Variations On A Theme — Red House*.

Oh, yeah. I did it real bluesy and funky. That's really nice. Mr. Jimi Hendrix, one of my favorites.

He was one of my idols, and I was glad to do it. The guy that used to manage him [Alan Douglas] said Jimi would talk about me a lot, and he was the one who had me do this. It's going to be in music stores for people who like Jimi Hendrix and stuff like that.

Did you know Hendrix at all?

No, I wished I had, because I was a great fan of his.

You seem to have a very smart business sense.

Oh, yeah. I'm very deceptive. Money ain't anything, but I just don't run through it. I know I'm not going to be doing this all my life, and I know that if I live on, I'm going to retire and just have a good life, a good home, and have money to kick back and do what I want to do, go where I want to go. Some of them live so fast when they're making big money, they run right through it. And when they can't do this....

> *"I've got a hell of a memory. I don't forget nothing. I can lay down at night and think of a song, get up, and sing it word by word and don't forget nary a word."*

Did you learn that lesson the hard way?

Yeah [*laughs heartily*]. Yeah, yeah, I did. I learned it the hard way. But now I'm very well set. I got a pretty nice home. I'm into real estate. I got three more homes in Oakland that I leased out. But like I said, I learned it the hard way. I could have run through partying, women, whiskey, living the fast life, and I wouldn't have had nothing. You get through, and it's just a dream. It's a dream you went through, and you got nothing — all that stuff's behind you. And then when you're old, that's gone. When all your money and success is gone, all your so-called friends are gone. They ain't friends; they leeches that hangin' on as long as you got something. I learned it the hard way. I *love* people — don't get me wrong. Oh, I love people. Friendship is the best thing in life. I go out of my way to help people. I'm a kindhearted person. I have a lot of people; I know some of them appreciate it, some of them don't. I hate to say it: Some of them are leeches. *I* know they are, but I don't tell them. I know what they're thinking before they do it. I *know.* I can look right through people, but I still love 'em.

And you've always got your guitar.
Yeah, always got that! When the women gone, I always got my guitar. My woman can leave me, but my guitar ain't gonna leave me. Always got that. Remember that song "Red House" that Jimi did — "way back yonder 'cross the hill"? He say, "I still got my guitar!" [*Laughs.*] Yeah, I still got my guitar.

A SELECTED
JOHN LEE HOOKER DISCOGRAPHY

Earliest material (primarily solo sides): On Red Lightnin': *No Friend Around* (late 1940s-early '50s). On Specialty: *John Lee Hooker...Alone* ('49-'51); *Goin' Down Highway 51* ('48-'51). On United: *Drifting Through The Blues*; *The Blues*; *Folk Blues*; *The Great Blues Sounds Of John Lee Hooker*; *Original Folk Blues*; *The Greatest Hits Of John Lee Hooker*. On Ace: *John Lee Hooker Vol. 1* (Modern reissues). On King: *Moanin' And Stompin' The Blues*. On Krazy Kat: *Detroit Blues, 1950-'51*. On Sensation: *40th Anniversary Album* ('48-'52). On Blues Classics: *Detroit Blues — The Early 1950s*. On Chess: *John Lee Hooker Plays & Sings The Blues* ('51-'52); *House Of The Blues* ('51-'52); *Mad Man Blues* (early '50s); *John Lee Hooker* ('51 to '54, Japanese import). On Atlantic: *Atlantic Blues: Guitar* ('53).

Mid 1950s through '60s (usually with small group): On Vee Jay: *I'm John Lee Hooker* (superb debut album, recorded between '55 and '59); *Travelin'*; *The Big Soul Of John Lee Hooker*; *Concert At Newport*; *In Person*; *On Campus*; *Soul Meeting Saturday Night*; *Hall Of Fame*; *Is He The World's Greatest Blues Singer?*; *John Lee Hooker Gold*; *The Best Of John Lee Hooker*. On Archive Of Folk (Vee Jay reissues): *John Lee Hooker*; *Hooked On The Blues*; *John Lee Hooker Sings*. On Charly (Vee Jay reissues, '55 through '64, except where noted): *This Is Hip*; *Everybody's Rockin'*; *Moanin' The Blues*; *Boogie Chillun*; *Solid Sender*; *Original Bluesway Sessions* (reissue of Bluesway's *Urban Blues*, '67, with Wayne Bennett and Eddie Taylor, and *Simply The Truth*, '68); *House Rent Boogie*. On Dynasty: *In Person* (Vee Jay reissues, late '50s-early '60s). On GNP: *Best Of John Lee Hooker* (Vee Jay reissues). On Tradition: *The Real Blues*. On Atlantic: *Don't Turn Me From Your Door* ('53 and '61). On Muse: *Sittin' Here Thinkin'* (mid-'50s). On Vanguard: *The Great Blues Men* (one Newport cut); *Great Bluesmen/Newport*. On Ace: *The Folk-Blues Of John Lee Hooker* (on acoustic; originally issued by Riverside, '59); *That's My Story* (Riverside trio cuts, '60). On Fantasy: *Boogie Chillun* (solo, '60s); *Black Snake* (reissue of Riverside's *The Folk-Blues Of John Lee Hooker*, '59, and *John Lee Hooker Sings The Blues*, '60). On Jasmine: *It Serves You Right To Suffer* ('65 Impulse sides with jazz trio). On ABC/Bluesway: *Live At Cafe Au-Go-Go* (with Muddy Waters Band, '66). On Chess: *The Real Folk Blues* ('66). On MCA: *Urban Blues*; *Tantalizing With The Blues* (Bluesway/ABC reissues, '65 through '71); *Lonesome Mood* (Bluesway sides with Earl Hooker, '69). On Black And Blue: *Get Back Home* (solo in '69). On BGO: *Live At Cafe Au Go Go* (late '60s, originally issued by Bluesway).

1970s and '80s: On Rhino: *Hooker 'N' Heat* (solo and with Canned Heat, '70); *Infinite Boogie*. On See For Miles: *Never Get Out Of These Blues Alive* (reissue of '71 album, plus tracks from 1970's *Endless Boogie* and *John Lee Hooker Featuring Earl Hooker*). On Labor: *Alone, Vol. 1* (powerful '76 solo sides). On Ornament: *Live & Well* (live in Germany, '76). On Festival: *Black Rhythm & Blues* (live in Europe, '70s). On Tomato: *I'll Play The Blues For You* ('77; half of the cuts are by Albert King). On Charly: *The Cream* ('78; reissue of Tomato's live LP). On JSP: *Hookered On The Blues* (live in '80s, solo and with band). On Pausa: *Jealous* ('86). On Chameleon: *The Healer*; *The Hook* (a retrospective). On Atlantic: Pete Townshend's *The Iron Man* (Hooker sings two cuts).

Soundtracks: *Mr. Brown* ('72); *The Outsider* ('79).

On film: *Jazz USA* ('60); *American Folk Blues Festival* (BBC, '68); *L'Adventure Du Jazz* (France, '69/'70); *Roots Of American Music* ('71); *Gettin' Back* (Ozark Mountain Folk Fair, '74); *The Blues Brothers* ('80).

Albert King

September 1977

BY DAN FORTE

LBERT KING HAS INFLUENCED SO
many blues-rock guitar players, it would be
futile to try to name them all. As Elvin Bishop
puts it, "Everybody in the world that I know
of who plays any kind of blues guitar was
affected by him to a small degree at least. A
couple of his little pet licks are just part of the
language."

The hefty 6'4" ex-bulldozer-driver-turned-
bluesman first stepped onto the stage of the
Fillmore Auditorium in San Francisco on February
1, 1968, as opening act for English blues singer John
Mayall and Jimi Hendrix, the space-age black
Albert had known years earlier as Jimmy James, Jr.
For Albert King, the show became the launching
pad for an overnight success story which, like so
many others, came after 15 years of playing the
blues on the chitlin circuit. For the predominantly
young white audience in attendance during the four
days Hendrix, Mayall, and King played the
Fillmore, the event is remembered as one of the
most musically satisfying in the auditorium's history
of rock concerts.

As Jerrold Greenberg of *Rolling Stone* documented the concert, "The least contrived, certainly
the most 'old-fashioned' of the three, Albert King
was nonetheless the only consummate artist among
them, the only one who could play on the full
emotional range of his audience with as much facility as he used to sustain a note on his guitar."

Albert's facility on the instrument didn't come
from chord books or guitar lessons at the local music
store. Even picking up licks by watching other players was rendered difficult because of the fact that
Albert is left-handed and plays a right-handed
guitar. Unlike Jimi Hendrix, who restrung his guitar
so that he was playing normally for a southpaw,
Albert actually plays upside-down and backwards.

Born in Indianola, Mississippi, on April 25,
1924, King was first attracted to the guitar at an
early age through his stepfather, Will Nelson. "He
had a guitar," Albert recalls, "but I couldn't play it. I
used to climb up on a chair and hit the box hanging
upside the wall; sounded good to me."

When he was about six, King started playing a

102

homemade one-string "diddley bow," sort of on the principal of a washtub bass. "I used to put me a strand of wire upside the wall," he explains, "and put a brick at the bottom and a bottle at the top to tighten it. I'd play it and take another bottle to slide up and down the wire."

Also during this time, Albert was exposed to his first blues music. "The first one was Blind Lemon Jefferson," he states. "Later I heard him on records, but I used to see him in these parks, like on Saturday afternoons in these little country towns around Forest City, Arkansas. We'd work till noon on Saturdays, and then my stepdad would hook up the wagon, and sometimes my sister and I and the other kids could go to town. This one particular day he was there playing acoustic guitar, and he had his cup. He sounded something like that folk singer, Richie Havens; something on that order. He had a crowd of people around him, and we'd put nickels in his cup, and he'd play a song. It was amazing to me to see him count his money. He could feel the face of the coin and tell you what it was. Then he'd put it in his pocket and play some more. I also heard this lady Memphis Minnie. She used to come to town and sing to the electric piano — they called it the 'self-playing' piano. Not the kind you pump with your feet; the kind you just turn on and it goes to playing the sheet music on a spool. She brought her music with her that would fit right in that. I was a little boy, and I used to sneak and peep in the door before they'd run me away."

In the tradition of countless country and blues musicians, Albert's first guitar was one he made himself out of a cigar box. "It was a wooden cigar box for the body and a little tree that I cut off and shaved up to make the neck. And I used wooden pegs for the keys, with holes in them to wrap the wires around. Years ago they used to make whisk brooms that had real thin stainless steel on them. Sounded good. I had all of the strings tuned different, but I had to use the same grade wire on all six. I kept that guitar for a long time, but it got burned up in a fire."

His first legitimate guitar, a Guild hollowbody

> *In the tradition of countless country and blues musicians, Albert made his first guitar out of a cigar box.*

acoustic, didn't come until Albert was 18. "See, this guy had a guitar," he remembers. "He'd paid $2.00 for it. Well, he had a girl, and they wanted to go to the afternoon movie show, but he didn't have the money. I didn't have a little girl, but I had my allowance that my mother gave me. So it was getting close to show time, and this girl was getting really upset to get in to see the movie. I offered him my $1.25 for it. 'No, I ain't gonna sell my guitar. Give me $1.50.' I said, 'You just wait around; that girl's gonna be ready to go to the movies soon.' It was really funny. All the guys who didn't have nobody were gathered around waiting to take her. Well, I had my mind on that blasted guitar. She was getting ready to go in with another guy, and he couldn't stand that, so he came over and said, 'Give me the $1.25, man; you can have the guitar.' So that's how I got my first guitar, and I just started rapping on it from the left side."

Obviously, playing upside-down and backwards presented its share of problems, but because of the unorthodox approach it necessitated, one of the unique blues guitar sounds was created. "I knew I was going to have to create my own style," declares King, "because I couldn't make the changes and the chords the same as a right-handed man could. I play a few chords, but not many. I always concentrated on my singing guitar sound — more of a sustained note."

After working on construction crews around Little Rock and Osceola, Arkansas, and singing occasionally in a family gospel quartet called the Harmony Kings, Albert bought his first electric guitar and amplifier, an Epiphone, for $125.00. After traveling north to Benton Harbor, Michigan, where he picked cherries during harvest time, King moved on to Gary, Indiana, in 1953. "I stopped playing guitar there," he recounts, "and got a job playing drums with Jimmy Reed, playing them little small joints. Well, Jimmy got to where he wouldn't stay sober and wouldn't work one half of the time, so I said, 'Hell, I'm going to make a record myself.' Al Benson in Chicago had a label called Parrot, so I went over and auditioned for him. He was a big shot; I had to make an appointment to see him. I played and sang, and he said, 'Okay, be in the studio tomorrow night.' So we recorded 'Bad Luck Blues' and 'Be On Your Merry Way' [reissued on *Door To Door*]. He said, 'I've got to see if it's going to sell, then I'll give you a contract later' [*laughs*]. I didn't get no contract, I didn't get no statement — the record sold about 350,000 copies. I didn't get no money out of it, but it kind of helped make a name for me, you know."

Several singles for the Bobbin and King labels were recorded a few years later, and it was these recordings that the more conscientious blues fanatics began cutting their teeth on. Johnny Winter relates, "When I first heard him, I think it was one of those Bobbin records, 'I'm A Lonely Man' — my favorite Albert King song. I learned that and played it for about five years every night, note for note, man. I love his guitar playing. I got every single record he made."

Michael Bloomfield's first exposure to Albert came from the King recordings, made in 1959. "Sam Lay, who played drums in the Butterfield band, used to be Albert's drummer," says Bloomfield. "He gave me this record on King called *The Big Blues* by Albert King; I'd never heard of him before. I was knocked out; the guy was just a fabulous lead guitar player. His style was superb, comparable to Otis Rush or Buddy Guy or any modern blues guitarist, but it wasn't as well-formed as when his first Stax record, *Born Under A Bad Sign*, came out about six years later. I could hear that the way he played guitar was different than the other guitarists, but I couldn't figure it out until I saw him in person. Then I realized that he played backwards. He was a huge, immense man, and his hands would just dwarf his Flying-V guitar. He played with his thumb, and he played horizontally — across the fingerboard, as opposed to vertically. If he had to go seven frets, he'd bend the guitar seven frets!"

King began playing without a pick, because, as he puts it, "I never could hold a pick in my hand. I started out playing with one, but I'd be really gettin' into it, and after a while the pick would sail across the house. I said to hell with this. So I just play with the meat of the thumb."

As Bloomfield pointed out, Albert probably bends more notes (with more accurate intonation) than any other bluesman. On some tunes — for instance, "Blues At Sunrise" on *Albert Live* or "Angel Of Mercy" on *I'll Play The Blues For You* — he'll *begin* with a bend. "It just came to me when I started," he shrugs. "I couldn't make the runs. This is what really got me into the bending note sound. I listened to the blues by Howlin' Wolf, Lonnie Johnson, and all those guys — but when T-Bone Walker came, I was into that. That really gave me an idea of what I wanted to do; that opened it up. That was the sound I was looking for, because he had an incredible blues sound. But all those licks and things he was making, I couldn't do. I said, 'I'm gonna have to try to do something with these strings' [*laughs*]. So I developed that string-squeezing sound."

Yet another unorthodox method King employs is his tuning. Steve Cropper, who played rhythm guitar on many of Albert's Stax sessions and appears on *Jammed Together* with Albert and Pop Staples, explains: "He tuned to an E minor chord, with a low C on the bottom. That's a low son-of-a-bitch, like a tuba, but he doesn't play it that much; that string gets overlooked a whole lot. He mainly concentrates on the top three strings, the highest ones. We were in the studio once, and I said, 'Boy, that sure would sound good if it had Albert King playing on it.' He was out of town, so I took one of my old guitars and strung it backwards and tuned it to his chord and tried it. And it worked, because I'd been around Albert, and I knew how he played — I'd picked up his guitar and goofed with it a couple of times. So I set one up with that action, and it sort of got the Albert King sound."

Cropper, the rest of Booker T. & The MGs, and the other Stax sidemen were largely responsible for presenting King in a way that was identifiable to both black and white listeners. As Mike Bloomfield states, "Between [MG's drummer] Al Jackson's production, Booker T. & The MG's rhythm section, the choice of material, the Memphis Horns, and Albert's playing, he was the only bluesman I know of who had a completely comfortable synthesis with modern black music — R&B, so to speak — and sold copiously to a black audience as well as the white audience. He was the only singer who had clever, modern arrangements that would fit in with the black radio market *and* with the white market and in no way compromised his style. That's sort of amazing, in that B.B. King never did it, except once with 'The Thrill Is Gone,' but Albert did it time after time. Also, if you listen to those Stax records, his guitar was always very loud, right out front. Like on 'Cold Feet' [*King Of The Blues Guitar*], he's really got that guitar turned up, screaming."

MGs' bassist Donald "Duck" Dunn, who played on several King sessions, points to the late Al Jackson as being instrumental in developing this synthesis Bloomfield spoke of. "We took a blues artist and put a few different rhythms behind him — it wasn't just that shuffle type of stuff — and you've got to attribute a lot of that to Al Jackson and his drum patterns."

Steve Cropper, who doesn't especially consider himself a blues fan or player, elaborates: "Al gave it a little bit different flavor. Like, 'Crosscut Saw' [*Born Under A Bad Sign*] has a sort of bloopy, crazy kind of lick, and that was Al's innovation — which consequently made everybody else play a little different. The only one who didn't play different would be Albert King — who played like Albert King."

Though his influences cover the entire spectrum of blues — from Howlin' Wolf and Sonny Boy Williamson (who he heard as a boy in Arkansas) to Kansas City blues shouters such as Big Joe Turner, to the slide guitar of Elmore James, to Chicago blues in the mold of Little Walter, to Delta blues a la Son House — the combination of Albert King and a Memphis studio with Stax musicians made for a distinctively "Memphis" sound, one which wasn't too far removed from the R&B hits of the day. "We were, basically, on top of the music scene as far as what we thought the R&B public wanted to hear," says Cropper, "so it was a little more polished, a little slicker than some of the other blues coming out. He had his own unique style, and it still got in the blues rack. But the songs that we picked for him and some of the arrangements we did wound up in the pop and R&B racks, too."

As music critic Robert Palmer declares in the liner notes to *Albert Live*, the impact this sound had when *Born Under A Bad Sign* came out "was as inescapable among blues players as John Coltrane's

> *The most distinctive element of the Albert King style was his uniquely female-like guitar tone.*

influence was in jazz."

Probably the most distinctive element of the Albert King style was his uniquely female-like guitar tone. In Mike Bloomfield's words, "He approaches lead playing more vocally than any guitar player I've ever heard in my life; he plays exactly like a singer. As a matter of fact, his guitar playing has almost more of a vocal range than his voice does — which is unusual, because if you look at B.B. or Buddy Guy or Freddie King, their singing is almost equal to their guitar playing. They sing real high falsetto notes then drop down into the mid-register. Albert just sings in one sort of very mellifluous but monotonous register, with a crooner's vibrato, almost like a lounge singer, but his guitar playing is just as vocal as possible. 'I Love Lucy' [*King Of The Blues Guitar*] is a good example of that; he makes the guitar talk."

Bloomfield and other blues guitarists of the 1960s were instrumental in persuading Fillmore impresario Bill Graham to book bluesmen like Albert King into the Fillmore Auditorium. Graham details: "In the mid '60s, once the Fillmore got started, I began to speak to a lot of the musicians I respected and ask them where they got whatever they did. They mentioned Howlin' Wolf, Muddy Waters, Chuck Berry, Freddie, B.B., and Albert King, Mose Allison, Fats Domino, and artists who were relatively unknown to the mass Caucasian market that sprung up in the '60s. So I decided to track down some of these artists and listen to their records to see if I could expose their talents to these people who didn't know they existed. It may sound corny, but it's almost like dealing with your child. If your child says, 'I want the ice cream,' you say, 'Well, you've got to finish your meat first.' And the beauty of that era was that I did not have to worry about draw, getting people in, because the headliner would take care of that. Then I'd say, 'Who would I like to expose this particular audience to?' If you had a Grand Funk Railroad or a Black Sabbath, a loud group of that era, you couldn't bring in a tasty blues artist. Not that I have anything against those fans, but they're looking just for energy. But when you had a Jimi Hendrix, the

Hendrix fan, who was into guitar, would listen to a John Mayall or an Albert King. So Albert was the meat, even though they got to enjoy it."

And so King came to the Fillmore to share billing with one of his many guitar disciples, Jimi Hendrix. "I knew Hendrix," he states. "I knew him personally from when he was a boy, in Nashville, Tennessee; he was Jimmy James, Jr. He came to St. Louis during the time that Ike Turner was real hot. He sat in with Ike, and they made fun of him. I talked to him; he said he was leaving for California. I didn't see him till years later when I was hired to play the Fillmore, and he had that big hit, 'Foxy Lady.' Bill Graham brought me into that circuit; he's a hell of a promoter."

King was soon a headliner and a regular member of the Fillmore family. "Albert was one of the artists I used many times for various reasons," says Graham. "He wasn't just a good guitar player. He had a wonderful stage presence, he was very congenial and warm, he was relaxed onstage, and related to the public. Also, he never became a shuck-and-jiver. One of the sad things that happened in the '60s — it's not a nice thing to say, but it happens to be true — was that the blues artists began to realize that anything they did onstage, white America would accept. And a lot of them became jive. But Albert remained a guy who just went onstage and said, 'Let's play.'"

Bloomfield reiterates, "I've never seen him once when he wasn't vital, exciting, and not shucking. I've seen every blues singer there is shuck at one time or another, but I've never seen Albert do it once. He's always giving 100% of himself—much more than I ever would."

The second Stax LP, *Live Wire/Blues Power*, was recorded live at the Fillmore, where Albert told the crowd in his famous blues monologue, "Blues Power": "When you're playing the blues, they're so strong, that's the reason they call it blues power. And would you believe I invented blues power?" Judging by the audience's reaction, most were believers.

King became a favorite at blues festivals such as the one at Ann Arbor, Michigan, and would often

> "A lot of guys became jive, but Albert remained a guy who just went onstage and said, 'Let's play.'"

take part in fierce jam sessions, taking on all comers. "I jammed with him many times," says Michael Bloomfield. "He was incredibly powerful. I remember seeing him and B.B. King jam at the Fillmore, and Albert cut B.B. to death, man. He had that big Acoustic amp, and it sounded like bombs exploding. He mastered that sound [*slurs up then drops down*] — very extroverted style. He's one of the few blues guys who can play with changes, too. You can put him with some chord changes, and he sits very comfortably with any sort of mode. He understands where his music will fit in, whereas other blues guitarists get a mental block if it's not 12-bar or 8- or 16-bar blues. Plus, he's into feedback and into sustain. He watched the modern rock and roll players and said, 'Okay, I like sustain, I like feedback.' Then he just shot for it and used it consistently."

Indeed, Albert's playing is possibly the most contemporary (or at least the most adaptable to contemporary sounds) of all bluesmen playing today. On his recent LPs many of the tunes are not based on standard blues progressions or rhythms. "That's why I do those numbers—so I can change my style," he stresses. "I can't play 'Don't Throw Your Love On Me So Strong' forever; I can't play 'Blues Power' and 'Born Under A Bad Sign' forever, you know. I've got to have something else in there, so a lot of the new tunes aren't I-IV-V blues. I decided I had to learn to play more than one style, more than one song. So by my learning from the other records and the ballads and the rock and roll, and putting my own ideas into them, that's what keeps me right on top of what's happening now."

Always willing to listen and learn, King even took night classes in music theory a few years back. "I went to school to learn how to voice horns," he recalls. "See, I had a band that was giving me problems, hitting the wrong notes. And when I'd tell them they played something wrong, they'd say, 'Well, you tell us what to play, and we'll play it.' They knew that I didn't know what notes to tell them to hit. So I sneaked off and started school on my off nights in St. Louis, and I learned how to

107

voice horns. On my records now I have an arranger, but I help him. I decided that my horns were going to be different. I went around, I listened to B.B. King's horns, to Bobby Blue Bland's horns. They got all those horns up there, and they ain't doing nothing. And out of ten players, wouldn't be but one or two who know how to take a decent solo. But every man in my band can take a solo."

In recent years, Albert has probably placed his blues lines in a wider range of contexts than any other guitarist. Besides the several Memphis sessions for Stax, he has gone to Muscle Shoals, Alabama, to record with Southern rockers on *Lovejoy*. In 1969 he became the first blues guitarist to perform with a symphony orchestra, when he was a guest artist with the St. Louis Symphony. He even made a cameo appearance on a comedy album, *A Star Is Bought*, trading blues licks and verses with ethnic shtick by Albert Brooks.

King is still trying to stay on top of things, always looking for new ideas while relying on his tried-and-true licks. One of the new additions to his sound is the occasional use of an MXR Phase 90 phase-shifter. His amps are and have been for several years Acoustics. His main guitar is a custom-made copy [by Dan Erlewine] of his '58 Gibson Flying V, Lucy, which he still owns but keeps at home. The newer model has "Albert King" inlaid on the fretboard and "Lucy" on the headstock. As for details such as string brands, King shrugs, "I used to use Black Diamond, but now any kind I can get my hands on will do. I use a light-gauge first, second, and third — with a wrapped G — and then heavy gauge on the bass strings. And I usually play with both pickups on the guitar, with the treble turned up."

Whatever the ingredients, the result comes out sounding uniquely like Albert King. In the words of Bill Graham, "I'm not a musician, so I can't speak in technical terms, but for me his tone is as clean as anybody's. I think a very good guitarist could get himself to sound like a Clapton or even a Hendrix,

> *In recent years, Albert has probably placed his blues lines in a wider range of contexts than any other guitarist.*

and you can hear people do Chuck Berry imitations, but there's a certain thing about Albert's tone. I'm not saying it's better than anybody else's, but it's very distinctive. There are only two guitarists who I could pick out if you played a thousand different guitarists — Carlos Santana and Albert King."

Of course, the other half of the equation which adds up to the Albert King style is *what* he plays, the actual notes. Here King relies mainly on simplicity and good taste, rather than speed and flash. "His attack, the timbre, the tone — it's always right," says Mike Bloomfield. "I can listen to ten minutes of him playing the same licks over and over and never get bored. He can take four notes and write a volume. He can say more with fewer notes than anybody I've ever known. With the rapid demise of so many blues singers in the past few years, I sure hope Albert can stay healthy and play for a long time."

Today King continues to tour in his own Greyhound bus with "I'll Play The Blues For You" painted on the side. And if his recent *Albert Live*, recorded when he headlined the Montreux Jazz Festival's blues show, is any indication, the man is not about to slow down. In a jam that appears on that LP, Albert's style was easily identified alongside Irish rocker Rory Gallagher and slide guitarist Louisiana Red. "I'm gonna hang these young boys by their toes up here tonight," he told the audience. "They done sicked this one young fellow [Gallagher] on me, and now they sicked this bad Red fellow on me. Who else is coming up here? I want to be ready. They're gonna fool around and make me turn loose on Lucy here in a minute."

And with that, Albert played those famous pet licks, cut through with that one-of-a-kind tone, and showed everyone why he was the man closing the show that night. As he ended the set with his signature song, King sang, "Ain't got no big name/Lord, and I ain't no big star/I'll play the blues for you/On my guitar."

And, without shuck or jive, simply taking care of business, Albert played the blues.

A SELECTED
ALBERT KING DISCOGRAPHY

Solo albums (on Stax): *Born Under A Bad Sign* ('67); *I'll Play The Blues For You; Lovejoy* ('70); *The Lost Session* (produced by John Mayall, '71); *The Pinch; Years Gone By; Blues For Elvis* (originally issued as *King Does The King's Thing*); *I Wanna Get Funky; Live Wire/Blues Power; Blues At Sunrise* (Montreux, '73); *Chronicle* (one side each by King and Little Milton); *The Best Of Albert King* ('68-'73); *Montreux Festival; Jammed Together* (with Steve Cropper and Pop Staples). Other labels: *Travelin' To California* (King and Bobbin sides, '59-'63), Bellaphon; *Let's Have A Natural Ball* (King and Bobbin, '59-'63, including material from *Travelin' To California* and *The Big Blues*), Modern Blues; *Laundromat Blues* (Stax, '66-'68), Edsel; *Door To Door*, Chess; *Masterworks* (includes Stax sides), Atlantic; *King Of The Blues Guitar* (Stax reissues), Atlantic France; *Albert Live* ('77), Utopia; *New Orleans Heat* ('77), Charly; *Truckload Of Lovin'* ('78), Charly; *I'll Play The Blues For You* ('77; half of the cuts are by John Lee Hooker); *Albert* ('78), Tomato; *King Albert*, Tomato; *San Francisco '83*, Fantasy; *I'm In A Phone Booth, Baby* ('84), Fantasy.

Anthologies: *Door To Door* ('53-'61), Chess France; *Atlantic Blues: Guitar* ('66-'67), Atlantic; *Blue Monday*, Stax; *Best Of Wattstax*, Stax; *It's Christmas Time Again*, Stax.

With others: Toru Oki, *Toru Oki Blues Band*, CBS Japan; Albert Brooks, *A Star Is Bought*, Asylum.

On film: *Wattstax* ('72 concert), Columbia; *The Blues Alive* (with John Mayall's 1982 Bluesbreakers reunion tour), RCA/Columbia Home Video.

B.B. King

September 1980

BY TOM WHEELER

RILEY B. KING IS THE WORLD'S preeminent blues guitarist. There is hardly a rock, pop, or blues player anywhere who doesn't owe him something, although because much of his influence has been indirectly transmitted through rock stars, more than a few may be unaware of that debt. His dedication is as inspiring as his talent, and it's hard to imagine someone working harder at music, or anything else. For decades Riley, better known as B.B., has worked a staggering 300 nights a year or more, in part because he feels that he must live up to a long-held title. They call him King Of The Blues.

"There are days when I don't feel like going onstage," he admits, "but whether I want to go on or not, I *must* go on. Usually when I'm up there, I try and do like an electric eel and throw my little shock through the whole audience, and usually the reaction comes back double-force and pulls me out of it, because the people can *help* you entertain; they become a part of it. It's something like radar: You send out a beam, and it hits and comes back with even more energy."

Sweating in the spotlight, working on the fretboard, B.B. seems like a string-bending surgeon with his deft and confident left-hand technique. Unlike many self-taught guitarists, he plays very efficiently, without the wasted effort that comes from using the wrong fingers. He takes a breath. From his expression you know that in a split-second Riley B. King will lay himself bare. He extends an irresistible invitation to share in the simple transfer of joy and pain which he has perfected: He stings Lucille; Lucille stings you. David Bromberg recently put it this way: "Usually in a good concert you'll hear people say 'ooh' or 'aah' at various times, but when B.B. plays they all go 'ooh' at the same time and 'aah' at the same time. He doesn't just play his guitar; he plays his audience."

Many of the post-Beatles guitar stars were of course technically accomplished and innovative, but in most cases, beneath the arrangements and the special effects were guitar licks unmistakably attributable to B.B. King and other American blues-

men who, in the U.S. at least, were then known only to limited numbers of blues buffs. Aside from phrases and blues scales, the dynamics of rock guitar as a communicative vehicle also owe much to the originality of B.B. King. He can make Lucille talk in an almost literal sense, with screams, sassy put-downs, cute little tickles, or an unabashed plea for love. He can articulate the hopelessness of poverty or a love gone wrong with a poetic subtlety rarely matched by mere words.

When he was developing what has become one of the world's most readily identifiable guitar styles, B.B. borrowed from Lonnie Johnson, T-Bone Walker, and others, integrating his precise, vocal-like string bends and his patented left-hand vibrato, both of which have become indispensable components of rock guitar's vocabulary. His economy, his every-note-counts phrasing, has been a model of taste and style for thousands of players. Mike Bloomfield was awestruck upon hearing Eric Clapton in the mid-'60s. Later describing his impression, he groped for superlatives: "He was as good as... *B.B. King.*" For Bloomfield, an ardent musicologist, it was the ultimate tribute.

According to one prevalent view, there is some quantum of suffering which must be endured before an entertainer "qualifies" as a blues artist. Under anybody's standard, B.B. King has qualified many times over. He was born on a Mississippi plantation and earned 35¢ for each 100 pounds of cotton he picked; he once calculated that he had walked thousands of miles behind a plow during his years as a farmhand. It was only during the rainy season that he was allowed to leave the farm to attend school, and he walked 10 miles to join his 85 classmates in their one-room schoolhouse. For two decades he took his music to scores of obscure and often sleazy bars throughout the South, where isolation crushed the dreams of many a performer.

At age 24 King was performing in a bar in Twist, Arkansas, when two men started a fight, kicking over a barrel-sized kerosene lamp. The building erupted in flames, and the panic-stricken crowd scrambled into the street. Not having enough money to replace his $30 guitar, B.B. raced back in to save it. The man who was later to acquaint much of the world with the blues was almost burned to death, and just after his escape the building collapsed, killing two other men. When he learned that the fight had been over a woman named Lucille, he gave that name to his beloved instrument and its many successors "to remind me never to do a fool thing like that again." The story is the stuff of legends, but legends sometimes spawn stereotypes, and B.B. King is a complex man, one who in the interview below disavows several popular images of blues entertainers.

The young B.B. King spent countless hours in the small recording facilities used by Kent (later Kent/Modern), Crown, and Blue Horizon, turning out regional hits in the early '50s. He estimates that he's recorded over 300 sides in all, although because of poor distribution and low retail prices he never reaped much profit on many of them.

He cut more LPs after signing with ABC-Paramount in 1961, one of the best of which is *Live At The Regal.* He was transferred to ABC's now defunct Bluesway label in 1967, and he made the R&B charts a year later with "Paying The Cost To Be The Boss." Producer Bill Szymczyk contributed much energy to *Live And Well* in 1969, and it was hailed in *Downbeat* as "the most important blues recording in many years."

Finally in 1970, over 20 years after cutting his first record, B.B. scored a nationwide hit with "The Thrill Is Gone." Though it employed a string section and thoroughly modern production, he is suspicious of the emphasis so often placed on elaborate recording techniques, noting that many early blues classics were cut in garages or mobile facilities. In fact, his first major R&B hit, RPM's "Three O'Clock Blues," was recorded in 1950 in the Memphis YMCA. It stayed on top of the regional charts for four months, and as he discusses below, it changed his life.

B.B. has been acclaimed in virtually every

> *King can make Lucille talk in an almost literal sense, with screams, sassy put-downs, cute little tickles, or an unabashed plea for love.*

112

music poll, and his affection for music of almost all types continues offstage. In his hotel room, a bed or table is usually covered with mounds of cassette tapes, perhaps 50 of them, "just for my own listening enjoyment." He often practices long into the morning hours, even during periods of grueling roadwork, and spends much of his free time listening to the records in his mammoth collection at home.

B.B.'s approach to his art is not only the cornerstone of a distinguished career but also a metaphor for a remarkable philosophy of self-improvement and universal brotherhood. In 1973 he and Fayette, Mississippi, mayor Charles Evers cosponsored a memorial festival commemorating slain civil rights leader Medgar Evers. B.B. was a founding member of the JFK Performing Arts Center and has received public service awards from B'nai B'rith and many other organizations. He cofounded the Foundation for the Advancement of Inmate Rehabilitation and Recreation. He has played many prison benefits and been cited for his service by the Federal Bureau of Prisons. He is a licensed pilot and an accomplished player of several instruments other than guitar. He received an honorary doctorate from Mississippi's Tougaloo College, and his hometown renamed a park after him and painted a guitar on the street near the corner where The King Of The Blues used to play for dimes. The town turned out to see him put his large hands in the wet cement, and the tribute was a highlight of B.B. King's life.

In the following interview B.B. reflects upon his professional standards, guitar techniques, and his more than 30 years as a bluesman. He rejects certain public perceptions of blues performers and explains the evolution of his relationship to his art. B.B. King is witty, gracious, independent, and significantly more eclectic than his contemporaries. At the core of his career is a dedication to his ideals, to his fans, and to his belief that music is a social tool, a vehicle for bringing people together.

When were you born, and where did you grow up?

I was born in 1925 in the country outside of Itta Bena, Mississippi, which is not too awful far from Indianola. My parents separated when I was around four, and I spent some time in the hills of Mississippi, up around Kilmichael. That's where I lost my mother, when I was nine. I was a farmhand all of my life, until I was inducted into the Army and sent to Camp Shelby near Hattiesburg, Mississippi, in 1943. I was plowing, driving tractors and trucks, chopping cotton — everything that one does on a farm, I did some of it.

When did you first encounter music?

The first music was in church. From that time until now, that . . . certain something was instilled into me. I had been baptized as a Baptist, then I was in the Holiness — the Church Of God In Christ — and the singing and the music in the churches was something that a small boy, even in his fifties today, will never forget.

What did your family think of you playing the blues when you started?

I couldn't play them at home. I was formerly a spiritual singer, and they wouldn't go for the blues, not around the house [laughs, shakes his head], not then. That's one thing about the early days of the blues. A few of the spiritual people liked blues, but they would play their blues after 12:00, when they were in their room and nobody could hear them. But you always had a few devils like myself and a few others that would listen to anything. You played it and it sounded good, we would listen to it. I was singing spirituals in my first group, the Elkhorn Singers, but I'd love to go to juke joints at that time.

What made you choose the guitar?

I think that a lot of that has to do with the Sanctified Church, because this preacher played guitar in the church, and that was one thing. But also, guitars were kind of available. The average home had a guitar and a harmonica, usually; you could always find them around. But saxophones, trumpets, pianos, and things like that were rare. Only the middle class families would have a piano. Sometimes a lot of us would like to sneak in the church to play with the piano, and many of us got jobs as janitors, because this enabled us to be near it. We'd be cleaning up the church or something like that, and get a chance to fool with a piano a little bit.

Do you remember your first guitar?

My first one was a Stella, about two-and-a-half feet long, with the big round hole in it, and it was red, one of their little red guitars. I was making $15 a month, so I paid seven-and-a-half the first month and seven-and-a-half the next one. I kept it for a long, long time. It was stolen, but I don't remember when. The next one was a Gibson I bought in Memphis with the help of my cousin, Bukka White. It was an acoustic, but we had just learned about DeArmond pickups. I didn't have enough money to buy the regular electric, so we bought that and put a pickup on it that cost $27. The very first Fenders — I had one. I used it when I first went out on the road, '49 or early '50. I also had a little Gibson amplifier that was about a foot wide, and about half a foot thick [*chuckles at the recollection*], with a speaker in it of about eight inches, I suppose, and that was my amplifier, and I kept it for a long time.

> "*I never passed the hat, but the people knew that I'd appreciate a dime if I played a tune they'd requested.*"

When did you begin playing professionally?

In the middle 1940s, in Indianola, on the corner of Church and Second Street. Second Street is like the main part of town, and Church Street crossed it and went into the black area, what we called "across the tracks." I never passed the hat, but the people knew that I'd appreciate a dime if I played a tune they'd requested.

Why had you picked that particular corner?

I was afraid to sit in the square near city hall, because I probably would have been run out of there. I forget the name of the sheriff that we had then [*laughs*], and on my corner both the blacks and the whites would see me. It wasn't something I planned; it was just like a good fishing place — it seemed like a nice spot to be. You'd find me on that corner on Saturdays, and sometimes after I got off work I'd take my bath, get my guitar, and hitchhike to other little towns like Itta Bena or Moorhead or Greenville. Most times I was lucky. I'd make more money that evening than I'd make all week driving tractors. I'd probably have enough money for a movie. Next day, go to church, then back to work.

At the time I was making $22.50 a week with the tractors.

Do you remember your first paying job as a musician?

I don't remember my first paid gig, but I remember the first gig where I started working for like a week at a time — 1949 that was, in West Memphis, at a place called the 16th Street Grill. That lady was paying me $12 a night, room and board. I was 24 years old, and that was more money — I didn't know there was that much money in the world. So that's how that started. That was me alone up there — sing, and then play, as I normally do. Sing and play. Working there made me think about going on the radio as a disc jockey, because the lady at the grill told me that if I could get my own show like Sonny Boy Williamson and Bobby Nighthawk and quite a few of the guys, she would give me a steady weekly job, and I *loved* that idea.

How did you acquire the name "B.B."?

The idea came from the local radio station where I was working, WDIA. I was singing some advertisements for Pepticon, one of these cure-all patent medicines. Later, when I became a disc jockey with my own one-hour show, they would call me "the blues boy," or "the boy from Beale Street." A lot of times they'd shorten it to B.B., and I liked that, and it stuck with me all this time.

Before you were nationally recognized, was there much contact between you and your contemporaries such as Muddy Waters? Were you aware of each other; did you have each other's records and so forth?

No. I had *their* records, but see, Muddy Waters and John Lee Hooker and all of those guys were playing *before* me, and they didn't know me from Adam. I was *plowin'* when they was *playin'* [*laughs*]! I liked them, and I imagine that they were aware of each other. But they didn't know anything about me, no. Like Ike Turner was about 14 years old when I first met him, in Clarksdale, Mississippi. I had this great big band at that time, which consisted of my guitar, a set of drums, and a saxophone. That was a *big band*, wasn't it? When Ike saw me [*laughs*], he said, "Oh, *man*, you need *help!*"

What was it like gigging for years in small, segregated clubs all over the South?

Well, you hear this term "chitlin circuit." That's not one of my terms, but they're talking about the joints where we used to play before we started to play the white establishments. These clubs were small, most of them, and always across the tracks, in the black area. A lot of the promoters couldn't afford to pay you very much money, and if they didn't have a pretty good crowd, sometimes you didn't get paid at all. I only have about $180,000 owed up to me from my playing during my career. I'd say 90% of the promoters were for real, just like they are today. But then you had the other 10% — the young promoter, probably his first time to give a dance or concert. If he didn't make it, that was it, because he had thrown in everything he had to do this one concert, which he felt would be a gold mine. He'd say to himself, "Well, if I can get B.B. King or Junior Parker or whoever, *this* night they're going to pull me through," and a lot of times that didn't happen, and when it didn't happen for that promoter, you didn't find him. He wasn't around afterwards.

When you started entertaining, did you think of yourself mainly as a singer, as opposed to a guitar player?

When I first started, couldn't nobody tell me I couldn't sing. See, if you told me I couldn't sing then, I would have an argument with you. Later on, I found out how little I really knew, how bad it really sounded. I then found out that my guitar playing wasn't any good either [*laughs*]. It's funny how this happens, because at first, you believe that you *really* have it, like you're God's great gift. I mean I felt like that, I really did, and had someone told me I wasn't, well, I would just ignore them because I figured they didn't know what they were talking about. My

singing was more popular in the early years than my guitar playing. I was crazy about Lonnie Johnson, Blind Lemon Jefferson, Charlie Christian, Django Reinhardt, T-Bone Walker, Elmore James, and many, many others, and if I could have played like them, I would have, but I've got a thick head that just don't make it, and my fingers — they don't work either. Therefore, I think my playing was very, very, *very* limited, more so than my singing, because I did have a kind of style of singing at that time.

Compared to many electric guitarists, you play few notes.

I was at the Apollo Theater one time, and there was a critic there, and to me what he said was one of the great compliments that people have given me. The critic wrote: "B.B. King sings, and then Lucille sings." That made me feel very good, because I do feel that I'm still singing when I play. That's why I don't play a lot of notes maybe like some people. Maybe that's the reason why most of my music is very simple — that's the way I sing. When I'm playing a solo, I hear me singing through the guitar.

How did people like Django Reinhardt and T-Bone Walker influence you?

In the way they phrase. They still do it today. Even though they may be in different categories, even though some are jazz and some are blues, when I hear them *phrase*, each note to me seems to say something. And it doesn't have to be 64 notes to a bar. Just one note sometimes seems to tell me a whole lot. So that's one of the reasons why I like them. Same thing with Louis Jordan; even though he plays saxophone, the way he phrases seems to tell me something, and that can just stop me cold when I listen.

Did you play rhythm guitar first?

No, I never accompanied myself, still can't. I *cannot* play and sing at the same time; I just can't do it. I've always been featured from the very beginning. I still can't play rhythm worth anything,

> "Muddy Waters and John Lee Hooker and all of those guys were playing before me, and they didn't know me from Adam. I was plowin' when they was playin'."

because I never had the chance to really play in a rhythm section. But I know a few chords.

Did you invent the fingerstyle, perpendicular-to-the-neck vibrato?

Let's put it this way: I won't say I invented it, but they weren't doing it before I started [*laughs*]. I will say that I'm still trying. Bukka White and quite a few other people used bottlenecks. As I said, I got stupid fingers. They won't work. If I get something like that in my hand and try to use it, it just won't work. So my ears told me that when I trilled my hand, I'd get a sound similar to the sound they were getting with a bottleneck. And so for about 32 or 33 years I've been trying to do it, and now they tell me that I'm doing a little better.

What about the idea of hitting the fret a step lower than the intended note and bending it up — were people doing that before you?

Yes, but I'd never heard anybody do it the way I do it. My reason was that my ears don't always hear like they should. I'm always afraid that I might miss a note if I try to hit it right on the head, so if I hit down and slide up to it, my ears tell me when I get there. But also it's more like a violin or a voice; you just gliss up to it.

Were there any milestones in the evolution of your technique, specific experiences or events that made you alter your approach?

I don't think so. It was like this cancer that got hold of me and started to eat on me. Like when I heard T-Bone Walker play the electric guitar, I just had to have one. I had to play, but it's been a gradual thing, and it still goes on. In fact, if you went to my room right now you'd find a Blind Lemon tape that I've been listening to whenever I'm lying around.

Do you take many cassettes on the road?

I take quite a few in order to hear the old

things. I listen to the radio to hear the modern music, but I like to go back to some of the old things so that I can keep the same feeling. I like contemporary things with slick changes, but even if I play them I like to put in the feeling of yesterday. You're lost with either extreme, so I try to make a happy medium and do them together.

Your record collection is something of a legend.

Well, I've got over 30,000 records now. You won't believe this, but even though they're not alphabetized I can always tell if one's missing. One day I plan to get me one of these home computers and enter them all into that. Every time I go home I just tape, tape, tape. [*Ed. Note: B.B. has since donated his record collection to the Blues Archive at the University of Mississippi.*]

Do you play visualized patterns on the fingerboard, or do you hear a note or phrase in your head before you hit it on the guitar?

I hear it first, sure do. It's like some guys use an electronic tuner and just look at the needle on the meter, but I can't buy that; I have to hear it, and it's the same with a phrase. No one else can set your hat on your head in a way that suits you. I don't think I've ever seen anybody that when you put their hat on their head they didn't take their hand and move it, even if it's just a bit. Well, I'm like that with the guitar. Do it your own way. When I play it's like trying to describe something to someone; it's a conversation where you say something in a certain way. A lot of times I play with my eyes closed, but in my mind I can still see the people paying attention to what I'm doing. I can see them as if they're saying, "Yeah, okay, I get it." Playing the guitar is like telling the truth — you never have to worry about repeating the same thing if you told the truth. You don't have to pretend, or cover up. If someone asks you again, you don't have to think about it or worry about it. To me, playing is the same way. If you put yourself into it, instead of something else,

> "My ears told me that when I trilled my hand, I'd get a sound similar to the sound they were getting with a bottleneck. And so for about 32 or 33 years I've been trying to do it."

then when you get out there on the stage the next time, you don't have to worry, because there it is. It's you.

Today you're doing things on guitar that sound different from what you were doing only six months ago. Your style seems to continue to grow.

Well, I hope so, because I do study. People hold it against me sometimes. They say, "You're not playing the same thing that you played the last time." But I don't *want* to play the same thing I played last time. That would get boring. I always try to add something, or maybe take something away, to give it a little twist.

Do you play instruments other than guitar?

I try. I was doing pretty good on clarinet before I got ripped off for one. I got to where I could read faster on clarinet than I could on guitar. I know a few scales on the violin, and I fool with that a bit. I'm a little better with piano, and better than that with bass. Drums — I did some time with them, too. Also harmonica.

Does working with other instruments alter your approach to guitar?

Yes, it affects my phrasing, and it makes me a little more fluent. It's something for me to do when I'm not practicing like I should. I usually practice mentally, but when it comes to physical practice, I'm a little lazy. I don't know how it is with other musicians, but with me sometimes I don't play like I want to, and then I get a little bit disgusted and lay off for a while. Then one day, something happens, and I can't wait to get back to it.

You mentioned mental practice.

Sometimes I hear something — someone will walk by and whistle, or I'll hear it on the music in a restaurant — and I'll start to look at the fingerboard in my mind to see how I'd do it. I visualize the different ways to do it. That's a good thing to do; it helps you learn the guitar. Just don't do it too much when you're driving, or you'll forget where you're going [*laughs*].

Do you ever stick your neck out onstage, or do you usually reassemble a series of notes, a scale perhaps, the structure of which is already known to you?

In my room, you'd be surprised at all the things I try, but I never go out on a limb, not onstage, no, no, no. I make enough mistakes without it. The guys in the band always tease me. But if you're in the key of C and really don't want a *Cmaj7* — that B note — if you should hit it, you can flatten it and get the dominant 7th, which sounds all right, and if you make a mistake and hit the A, it's the 6th, so it's still relative. I learned through these many years of being out there and hoping to get everybody working with me that if you make a mistake, *please* work something into it, so that it's *not* a mistake.

There's a very unusual melody line near the end of "Chains And Things" on *Indianola Mississippi Seeds*, where...

I made a mistake. Now you're getting all the secrets. My bandleader and I have laughed about it many times, but I made a mistake and hit the wrong note and worked my way out of it. We liked the way it sounded, so we got the arranger to have the strings follow it. They repeat the phrase the way I played it. If you've got a good take going and then hit one wrong note, you don't want to stop, so I was in the key of A♭, and when I hit [hums E, D♭, E♭, E♭], which is ♯5, 4, 5, 5, we just got the rest of the band to follow right along.

Do you read music?

Reading music is what I call spellin'. I *spell*; I read slowly. If the metronome is not goin' *too* fast, I can do it pretty good.

"Three O'Clock Blues" was your first major R&B hit. How did it change your life?

I could go into the important theaters. As far as the black people were concerned, when you were getting into show business there were three places you *had* to go through to be acclaimed: the Howard Theater in Washington, D.C., the Royal Theater in Baltimore, and the Apollo Theater in New York. "Three O'Clock Blues" enabled me to go into these places, and it opened other areas, like one-nighters. I had been making about $85 a week with my playing and being on the radio and everything else I could do — $85 total — and when I recorded that first big hit, I started making $2,500 a week. I didn't get to keep all of it, but that was the guarantee.

In the early years, how widespread was racial prejudice in show business?

In the *early* years — you mean right now?

Well, I was talking about...

Well, *I* do. It still happens. A lot of things are not happening for us as blacks as they do for the whites. It's a fact. It's a *natural* fact. I've been one of the lucky few. A lot of things have happened for me, yes; a lot of things have happened for a lot of blacks. But when you compare it to what's happening for the whites, it's a big difference, a great big difference. Fortunately, though, it has gotten much better over the past few years. Blacks get better breaks. We're getting there.

Does racism exist predominantly in one field — radio, recording, club work?

You find it in all of them. I can't say which is more, one or the other. But the problem is never with the musicians themselves; it doesn't matter to them. Even when it was very segregated down South, the players always got together and had a good time. Still do. The trouble's been more with the companies, the establishment. Being a blues singer is like being black two times — twice. First you've got to try to get the people to dig the blues, and then to dig you. As a blues singer today, yes, I'm very popular. The FM radio is usually very fair with us, but you won't hear B.B. King or blues very often on AM radio. And I'm not only talking about the white stations. I'm talking about the black ones, too.

Your music is kept off of some white stations because you're black, and off of some black stations because it's blues?

Yeah, of course! I remember once I went to a black dude, a disc jockey that had a program in the South, and he said, "You know, every day we have an hour of blues." I said, "Really? Who do you play?" He said, "Well, I play you, Bobby Bland, Junior Parker, Albert King," and so on. I said, "What about Jimmy Reed, or John Lee Hooker?" "No," he said, "they don't fit my program." And that really got me uptight, you know. This guy is lord and master. He knows what everybody wants. I guess by being a Virgo, I'm a little sarcastic sometimes, so I said, "Well, how long is your station on

the air?" He said 12 hours. And I said, "And you play a *whole hour* of blues?" He says, "Yeah." I said, "Well *look* [*laughs*], why be so nice to us blues singers and give us a whole hour? Why not play a record or two during them *other* 11 hours?" He didn't like what I said, but I didn't really care, because that's the way I felt and that's the way I feel today.

Have the attitudes of black people toward the blues changed over the years?

They're chang*ing*. Today they're not ashamed of it. We've always had black people who like blues, but if I had to try and put it into categories, we had the people that were down here with me, that did the work, you know. Then you had the middle and upper classes, as we called them in Mississippi. The people that worked on the plantations, the regular working-class people — *they* understood. They were never ashamed. About 90% of them were a part of it in the beginning; they knew what I was doing. A lot of them could do it even better than I do. But then you had that middle class. A *few* of them would be down with us, and then the others would play our records, but like I said before, they'd only play them after 12:00, you dig? They felt that blues was kind of degrading a bit. They were made to be ashamed of it. They liked blues, but they weren't particular about everybody knowing about it. It's just like me. I like to eat sloppy, and I'd rather eat in my room rather than let people catch me. Among the upper class, the college graduates and the ones who had money, only a precious few would acknowledge my kind of music in the early days. That is changing today, and they're listening.

Early on, were you more popular among younger listeners?

Some of the people have stood up and been counted all along, of course. This is a funny thing to say, but it's the truth: When I was young, young people as a mass didn't dig me. When I was, say, like 20 years old, it was always people my age and older. But today, we are gaining ground because black kids will come up to me and say, "Hey, I don't dig the blues, but I dig *you*." So I think we're making progress. At some concerts we'll have all ages and colors. That I like. Lately we're starting to have not just blacks and young whites, but older whites, too. I'm surprised, but we have them.

You once complained about the notion that in order to be a blues singer you have to be in torn clothes, you can't be successful, and you've got to be high on something. Do you still encounter that attitude?

I think that that's the one thing that has been *the* big mistake about people in the blues. They seem to think that you have to be high or just completely smashed or stoned out of your head to be able to play blues, and that's *wrong*. And then I don't think that a guy has to be in patched trousers. That image that people seem to put on us is wrong. Blues music is like any other kind of music. Some of us excel, and some of us don't. Some of us are really able to please people, and some of us are not. But we all have the blues. Red, white, black, brown, yellow — rich, poor — we all have these blues. You can be successful and still have the blues. I have been fortunate, and yet now I have more to sing about than I ever did before.

You're referring to the world situation?

Yes. I look around me and I read the papers, and I see what's happening in this country and all over the world. Here, there are money troubles. Food's running low in other places. There's been price fixing, and oil problems. I go to the prisons, and I see what's happening there. Look at what's happening with the people that we pay our taxes to. Look at Asia, at Cambodia. There was bombing going on for years after the Vietnam war was supposedly over. They weren't bombing trees. They weren't bombing ditches. I think of my people, the ones I left behind in Mississippi, and *all* the people in *all* the Mississippis. We are a part of each other, you know. Those problems used to affect me individually, directly, and now they affect me indirectly. When one person is hurt, it hurts me, too. When I see their condition, I know what they feel, and I feel it, and it hurts.

Comparing the earlier years when you were playing to limited blues audiences in the South and in the black theaters in the North to your present success when you are known all over the world, have the blues taken on any new meaning for you? Do you feel the same when singing and playing as you did then?

My blues mean *more* to me now than it did then, because in the early years, sure, I wanted other people to like what I was doing. But at times, I was singing for my own personal amusement. A lot of times I'd get it in my mind that nobody understood me, to be honest with you. A lot of times, the people were there, but they really *weren't* there. The *bodies* were there, but I didn't think they were *with* me. And whenever I felt like that, I would go ahead and sing to amuse myself. I'd close my eyes and visualize all of those beautiful people out there enjoying themselves. But as I kept playing and years started to pass, I started thinking a little different from that. I started to feel that it was my *job* to make people interested in what I was doing, to make them be *able* to understand what I was doing, to make them see that I wasn't just teasing, that I was really for real, you know. And this took a while to do, and it takes time today, too.

In purely artistic terms, do you relate to your music any differently?

Yes, it's more of a creative art form now. Before, when I made a record I really didn't think that that's exactly what it is — a record of what you're doing and who you are on that day. And once it's out, it stays. I'm much more conscious of that.

What do you do differently?

It's not just music. It's kind of like a selling job, public relations. Sometimes audiences don't pay attention unless you present it a certain way. No matter how good it is, you seem to need to put a catchy title on it. A lot of people, especially blacks, won't like it if you call it blues, but if you go ahead and play it and call it a different name, they'll like it. That's the truth. So the blues are more important artistically, and also because I feel that I've got a

> "*People seem to think that you have to be high or just completely smashed or stoned out of your head to be able to play blues, and that's wrong.*"

message that should be heard.

What's your message?

Well, here I am. I'm trying to work. I'm trying to bring people together. I'm trying to get people to see that we *are* our brother's keeper. So there are many, many things that go along with it. I still work at it.

It was reported that you once deliberately chose a spot to perform that was located between black and white neighborhoods of a small Mississippi town so as to draw a racially mixed audience.

Yeah, I got 'em all. We never would have had any segregation if people would've had enough music around. If musicians from all around the world could get together, country to country, that would be a good thing. Like when I toured the Soviet Union in March of '79, the other people who got together thought about politics, but the American and Russian musicians didn't think about anything but music. It was a tremendous experience.

> *"We never would have had any segregation if people would've had enough music around."*

Do you find that your goal of using music in order to bring people together is a common attitude in the entertainment business?

Yeah, I think most of us are doing it. As musicians we feel that if we can get people together just on a social level, having fun, then they can go ahead and get to know each other in other ways, too. They can discuss their differences. We get them together and then something good can come from it, because that's when people start communicating.

What brought about your recognition on an international scale?

That has to do with many things, like the changing of times, like the marching, and like the people getting together and trying to stamp out prejudice and all of the many, many things. It seemed to bring people together. It started out to make people think, to see that everybody had something to offer, and that if you listen carefully you could learn something from others. People started searching for the truth... while I've been diggin' all

this time. Black awareness — there was a time if you called me black, it was insulting [*nods*], oh yeah, insulting. In Mississippi we always did call white people white people but we, as a whole, really didn't want to be called black. We felt that at the time it was degrading, because it seemed that the person calling you black was really saying *more* than what they said. But later on we started to think about it. If the Indian is a red man, and the Chinese is a yellow man, and you're a white man, then why *not* be a black man? Everybody got aware, and became proud of the fact that we are what we are. We began to feel that we *did* have something to be proud of.

Like when James Brown made "I'm Black And I'm Proud," this really hit a lot of us, and I think all of this has to do with the blues. There was a time when we felt that nobody else had dirty clothes in the closet, you know — the troubles of life. We were sort of made to feel like we were the only ones that had dirty clothes in the closet, and anytime somebody said something to us or about us, we always felt that we should close the door and not let 'em know what we had in the closet.

And that finally began to change?

Yes. After the early '60s and all that, it's a funny thing, we come to find out that *everybody* has dirty clothes in the closet, and if the people in Nashville and Kentucky can be proud of bluegrass music — which is real music about the way they live, and about their problems, and their happiness and all — why *not* be proud of the blues? This kind of transition caused people to recognize the blues singers. Even the people who don't dig blues come up to me and say that they respect what I'm doing.

Many guitar players discovered you by reading comments by Eric Clapton, Mike Bloomfield, and your other musical descendents.

I talked in terms of black people. Now, as far as the white part of it is concerned, when the Beatles came out, they started people to listening again. See, when Elvis came out in '54, they'd scream — *yaahhh*, you know. They never did hear half of the lyrics. If you could move or shake a bit, if you could twist a bit, rock and roll, that was it. Even though the Beatles' fans used to yell their heads off, their songs said something. People listened again for lyrics. All of this seemed to come back, to be re-imported, in a manner of speaking, because I heard many Beatles tunes that had been recorded by some of the blacks over here. They were re-imported with a different sound. Then Michael Bloomfield, Elvin Bishop, Eric Clapton, and quite a few of the other guys had been listening to myself, Muddy Waters, and many others. *Their* followers started getting inquisitive about their playing, and they said that they had listened to me. That's when the white youth started listening to us. And then another thing: The white youth never did have to feel, say, inferior when they were listening to blues, because they never did have to go through the thing that a lot of the young blacks did — things that made them feel that blues was really degrading to them.

Do you ever get a chance to jam with some of the younger musicians whose careers you've influenced so greatly?

Jamming is something that I rarely do, but we have done it, yes. I have jammed with some of the guys that say they idolize me, but most times I'm rarely around them, or if I am it's just for a short time, like playing the same job. But who knows about the future?

Did you ever jam with Jimi Hendrix?

Yes, we all jammed together at a place called The New Generation in New York City. Any guitar player in town would usually get off work long before us, so they'd come by to see if I was really like someone had told them I was. Everybody would have their guitar out, ready to cut me, you know [*laughs*]. Jimi was one of the front-runners.

Do you ever listen to any of the guitarists who have become famous by playing a style that was originally derived from you? Do you ever find that you are influenced by their playing?

Actually, I'm influenced by anybody that I hear. I don't think that I've ever heard anybody play something that didn't intrigue me at one time or another. If they have been influenced by me, I still find that they have put *their* feelings into what they did, and my things which have influenced them

sound different when they come out again. There's only been a few guys that if I could play just like them I would. T-Bone Walker was one, Lonnie Johnson was another. Blind Lemon, Charlie Christian, and Django Reinhardt: Those were the only guys I ever heard — well, there's Barney Kessel, and Kenny Burrell [*laughs*]. If I could have played just like them — not today, but when I first heard them — I would have. And there are also things that they do today that if I *could* do, I probably would, but not the way that they did it. Instead of playing it A, B, C, D, I'd probably play it A, C, D, B — not the exact same thing, because I think that there are very few people that play the same ideas identically as you would feel it yourself.

How long have you been using semi-solid, thin-body guitars?

Since the first one I saw, about '58. I have been using Gibson ES-355s for a long time because they're stereo and I like the highs. I can't hear lows too well — my ears don't tell me much — but highs I can hear very well. My new guitar, which Gibson is planning to release as the Lucille model, is sort of like a 355 but with a few changes.

How has it been modified?

It has a closed body with no f-holes, so you don't get the feedback. I used to have to put towels in my 355 to cut down the resonance, but with the new Lucille I can crank right up. Also, I can tune the tailpiece [a Gibson TP-6] at the back. I usually wear sleeves most of the time, and on the other tail-piece, because of where the strings were wound, I always snagged my sleeves, or I'd wind up hurting my hand a little. With this one, my sleeve doesn't get caught, and when I cup right on the bridge, it doesn't hit the end of the windings, so I don't hang up my sleeve and I don't hurt my hand. Also, the neck is a little bit thinner.

What kind of circuit does it have?

There's a Y cord that lets me bypass the stereo.

Which pickup do you use?

I usually go through the stereo circuitry, with both pickups working against each other. With just a quick shift of the hand I can set the volume or change the tone. To tell you the truth, I'm not even sure which pickup does what. I just put them both on and use my ear.

Did you ever use the vibrato tailpiece on the 355?

No. I think the reason people came out with vibrato tailpieces was because they were trying to duplicate the sound that I was getting with my left hand, and they forgot that I don't need it [*laughs*]. I always took the handle off. The new guitar is really something. I can't put it down, and it has really got me wanting to play again, just like when I started.

Have you had many guitars over the years?

Yes. I was in an accident once, and the insurance company gave me a Gretsch, and then I was in another accident and that one got busted up, and they gave me an Epiphone. Somebody *stole* that. Then I got some Gibsons, and about four of them got busted up. I've been in about 16 accidents. On the thirteenth or fourteenth one, an accident right outside of Shreveport, Louisiana, I remember seeing the bone in my right arm. They took me to the hospital and sewed it up, and the doctor told me that I nearly lost the use of the arm because of some nerve in there. But we drove to Dallas, and I played that night with my left hand. I still made the job.

Weren't you also injured in Israel?

Yes, I fell about nine feet and messed up the side of my face and my shoulder, and busted a blood vessel in my left hand. My teeth went right through my lip — seven more stitches. But I went swimming that evening in the Dead Sea. I couldn't miss it, man, because we were sold out in Jerusalem. The Holy City — I *had* to make that!

What kind of strings and picks do you use?

I use Gibson's 740XL set, with the .009 for the first string. I use a fairly stiff pick. Sometimes it's hard to get good amplifiers, and since I almost always play only with down-strokes, I find that I don't have to hit the strings quite as hard with a stiff pick to get the volume I want.

What kind of amplifiers do you prefer?

Whatever the promoters set up for us ahead of time on the road. I used to request Gibson SG amps, and the second choice was a Fender. Lately I've been trying the Gibson Lab Series amps, and I

think we'll be using them from now on.

Of your own records, which ones do you think are the best? Any favorite solos?

I've never made a perfect record, never. Although I'm not ashamed of any of them, there's always something that I could have done better. I know the critics always mention *Live And Well* or *Live At The Regal*, but I think that *Indianola Mississippi Seeds* was the best album I've done artistically.

How seriously were you criticized for using strings and pop songs and more sophisticated chord progressions on some of the recent albums?

I have had some people that weren't thinking. They'd come up and say something about it, but they didn't realize that I was using strings in the early '50s, with things like "My Heart Belongs To Only You," "How Do I Love You," "The Keys To My Kingdom," and quite a few things like that. We were using strings long before "The Thrill Is Gone," many years before. But those critics didn't say much about that. They thought that you were being Mr. Big or you were being jazzy. My answer is this: If the song needs just a guitar and me singing, we use that, and if you need something else to make it, then you should use that. Whether it be a full orchestra or just a harmonica and guitar — whatever's needed, that's what you should use, though I don't think that one should put a lot of stuff in there just to put it in there.

Were you criticized when you decided to have a large stage band with nine or ten pieces?

I have been criticized, yes, but again, a lot of the people who are criticizing didn't know that I had a big band back in the early '50s. It's a great thing to have a big sound from time to time. Years ago, Blood, Sweat & Tears and Chicago showed that if you've got a good band, a band that shouts and plays well, you can get a great thing going. Count Basie and them — that's all they did. They'd swing you to death, man, they'd swing you crazy, and I've always liked that.

What do you look for in a musician who comes to work for you?

A man. I look for a man first, and a musician

second. I must respect what he has to offer. I wouldn't say that a guy that can really blow the roof off a building is necessarily the best musician. He may be fiery; he's the type of guy that can really move an audience in a hurry. But an audience don't like to stand on its nose all the time. They want to get down and be something else from time to time. Then you've got another guy that has a touch when he's playing that can really move people, like in a slow groove. Well, you don't want *that* all night. Each guy is good for his one particular thing. Everybody in my group is behind me to push me. I need their cooperation. But I look for someone who's 100% man. If he's only 50% musician, that's okay; we'll turn him into 75% musician after a while. But if he is not 100% man, there's nothing I can do.

Do you have much of a problem with discipline, members not showing up on time and so forth?

I've had guys in the band that screwed up from time to time, but I feel kind of like their father or uncle, and unless they do it very bad I won't do anything to them. I may fine them today and give it back tomorrow. They can tell you such fantastic lies: "Man, the *train*, like, came by, and one of the cars ran off the track, man, and they wouldn't *allow* nobody to come across." So I laugh, and if he doesn't screw up tomorrow I don't say anything about it. All of the guys are very good musicians and very dependable. I've been fortunate to have dependable men. But I got a thing: Three days of screwing up in a week's time, and you're out. No more fines. So these guys are cool. I tell them that if I can make it, so can they.

You've toured the world and worked 300 nights a year for over three decades. What is the source of your strength and energy?

You've asked me a hard question. I guess one thing is that when I first became popular and started going to many, many places, I always felt kind of bad about stopping school in the tenth grade. I always felt that I wanted to be able to talk to people everywhere I went, to really participate in whatever

> **"I** never think of myself as King Of The Blues; I happen to be a guy named B.B. King, and he plays the blues."

was around. As I moved about, I found then that my education was really far off. I started learning how much I didn't know. That was one of the reasons why I *really* started to push myself, and I've done it through the years. Sometimes a lot of people wouldn't expect a blues singer to know certain things, and I *do* know them. I won't mention them, being a Virgo, but it just knocks me out for people to cut me short, thinking that I may not know. I work a lot of times just to have that little bit of pleasure. That might not sound like very much, but to me it kind of knocks me out for people to think, okay, the B. didn't go to college or he didn't do this or he didn't do that, and certain things they don't expect me to know — I know *about*. I pay attention, and if I hear something played or hear somebody say something, I'll put it on the tape recorder and listen to it and work with it. I wouldn't say it as he did, but I liked what he was doing and I would do it *this* way, *my* way.

How do you maintain your health and keep up the pace?

It's part of my job. It's like this story about the snake who's lying by the road all cold and muddy. This guy sees him, picks him up, and takes care of him. He gets home, around the fire, and the snake warms up and pokes his head up and says, "You know what? I ought to bite you." The guy says, "You wouldn't do that. I took care of you." And the snake says, "Yeah, but I'm a snake, and that's my job — I'm *supposed* to bite you!" [*Laughs.*] It's the same with being on the road and keeping up with the schedule. Sometimes it's a part of your job to eat, and sometimes it's a part of your job to get some sleep.

Many people call you the King Of The Blues. Does that change your outlook on your work, or make you feel obligated in some way?

Well, I guess I look at it both ways. First, I never think of myself as King Of The Blues; I happen to be a guy named B.B. King, and he plays the blues. Of course, I think I know my job pretty well. What keeps my feet on the ground is that there are people who haven't had the popularity that I've had who are just as talented, or even more so, some of them. But I have so many young fans now, white and black, that come up to me. They trust me; they have faith. You know how it is when you do something and it's appreciated by your girlfriend or your father or mother or whoever it may be. You can see it in their eyes. I can't explain it; it's a feeling that I can't tell you about. You have to see for yourself to know. Maybe like your little brother or your daughter or your son, maybe even like your pet, your little puppy or something. When you look at them, there's something that *tells* you — I know it seems a little deep, and it's hard to explain — but you know that this pet or this person or whoever is really serious about what you've done.

I wish I knew the words — now I'm really at a loss. You're hurting when you can't say what you really want, but there are times when no one else can tell you that they dig you like this special person can. This feeling has happened to me as a musician through the years. It's made me think a lot of times when I go out on the stage and guys come up and want to play guitar with me. You can look in their eyes, the young musicians, and know that you have been something that's going to help them go much further than probably what they would have without you. It's like seeing your own children or your neighbor's children. You don't want to mess up, and this makes you really buckle down and try to do it a little better. I look at my own kids sometimes, and my nephews and nieces. They won't say it around me, but I can tell that they've been whispering, "That's my daddy! That's *my* daddy!" That within itself is enough to make me really go out and try to do better. I try and live and be a certain way so that each day I meet a person, they can't help but say, well, he's just B.B. King. And that's all.

A SELECTED
B.B. KING DISCOGRAPHY

Early recordings: *The Rarest King* ('49), Blues Boy; *The Memphis Masters* ('50-'52), Ace; *Across The Tracks*, Ace; *Do The Boogie! Early '50s Classics*, Ace; *One Nighter Blues* ('51-'54), Ace.

On Kent: *You Done Lost Your Good Thing Now; Incredible Soul Of B.B. King; I Just Sing The Blues; Better Than Ever; The Unexpected Instrumental B.B. King; Boss Of The Blues; Doing My Thing Lord; From The Beginning; The Jungle; Greatest Hits Of B.B. King; Pure Soul; Let Me Love You; Rock Me Baby; Underground Blues; Turn On With B.B. King.*

On United: *B.B. King, 1949-1950; Singing The Blues* (early/mid '50s RPM sides); *The Blues* (early to mid '50s); *The Great B.B. King* (mid to late '50s); *I Love You So* ('58-'59); *The Soul Of B.B. King; Swing Low, Sweet Chariot* (gospel songs); *My Kind Of Blues* ('60); *A Heart Full Of Blues; Easy Listening Blues; Blues For Me; King Of The Blues; Let Me Love You; Onstage — Live; The Jungle; Boss Of The Blues; The Incredible Soul; Turn On; Better Than Ever; Live; The Original Sweet Sixteen.*

On MCA: *Live At The Regal* ('64); *Why I Sing The Blues; Live And Well; Back In The Alley* ('64-'67); *Blues Is King* (live in Chicago, '66); *Great Moments With B.B. King* ('66-'68); *Now Appearing At Ole Miss; Guitar Player; His Best: The Electric B.B. King; Live In Japan* ('71); *Live In Cook County Jail* ('75); *The Best Of B.B. King; Completely Well; Midnight Believer* ('78); *Take It Home* ('79); *There Must Be A Better World Somewhere* ('81); *Blues 'N' Jazz* ('83); *Love Me Tender* ('85); *Six Silver Strings* ('85); *King Of The Blues, 1989.*

Other labels: *Best Of B.B. King* (reissue of first LP), Ace; *Lucille Had A Baby* (mid '50s), Ace; *Indianola Mississippi Seeds*, ABC; *Completely Well* (reissue of Bluesway's *Live And Well* and *Completely Well*), Charly; *Spotlight On Lucille* (instrumentals, '60-'61), Ace; *Blues Is King* ('67), Bluesway; *Lucille* ('68), BGO; *Blues On Top Of Blues* ('68), BGO; *In London* ('71), BGO; *B.B. King* (Newport Jazz, '72), Accord; *10 Original Big Hits*, Fantasy; *The Feeling They Call The Blues, Vol. 1* (RPM/Kent sides), Trio; *The Feeling They Call The Blues, Vol. 2* (RPM/Kent sides), Trio; *Ambassador Of The Blues* (RPM/Kent sides), Crown.

With Bobby Bland: *Together For The First Time...Live*, MCA; *I Like To Live The Love*, MCA.

Anthologies: *Atlantic Blues: Guitar* ('72), Atlantic; *Live At Newport*, Intermedia.

Soundtracks: *For Love Of Ivy* ('68); *The Seven Minutes* ('71); *Black Rodeo* ('72); *FM* ('78); *When You Comin' Back, Red Ryder?* ('79); *Into The Night* ('85); *The Color Of Money* ('86).

On film: *Monterey Jazz Festival* ('67); *Monterey Jazz* ('68); *Medicine Ball Caravan* ('70), Warner Bros.; *En Remontant Le Mississippi/Out Of The Blacks, Into The Blues* ('71 West German/French film featuring one B.B. track); *Blues Music In America — From Then Til Now* ('71); *Le Blues Entre Les Dents/Blues Between The Teeth* ('72, four songs); *Sing Sing Thanksgiving* ('73); *Black, White And Blues* ('74); *Give My Poor Heart Ease* (William Ferris' 1975 documentary features footage on acoustic and electric guitar); *Got Something To Tell You: Sounds Of The Delta Blues* ('77); *Good Mornin' Blues* ('78, with onscreen narration by King); *Live At Nick's* ('83, Sony Video).

Freddie King

January 1977

BY DAN FORTE

ASK NEARLY ANY ROCK GUITARIST today who his early influences were, and almost as a matter of course you'll hear the names of the three "Kings" of electric blues: B.B., Albert, and Freddie. With highly distinctive approaches to the instrument, each offers the guitarist/student a different technique to master and a different code to decipher — B.B.'s hummingbird-like vibrato, Albert's long, bending phrases, and Freddie's aggressive, piercing attack.

Oddly enough it was Freddie, the youngest of the three (born in Gilmer, Texas, in 1934), who most aspiring white guitarists heard first. Back in 1961, while B.B. continued to record and tour as a top name in the all-black market and Albert split his time between driving a bulldozer by day and playing blues by night, Freddie scored a hit single that was picked up by AM stations, both black and white, all across the country. "Hideaway," an uptempo instrumental recorded a year earlier, was swept up by the wave of twangy guitar instrumentals churned out by people such as the Ventures and Duane Eddy and succeeded in getting Freddie, at least temporarily, out of the chitlin circuit.

Originally a singer/guitarist/bandleader much like B.B. or Albert, Freddie recorded the song as a flip side to his vocal on "I Love The Woman" for the Federal/King label in Cincinnati, Ohio. The pattern of success his flip sides began achieving resulted in his first LP, *Freddie King Sings*, followed by an all-instrumental release, *Let's Hide Away And Dance Away With Freddy King*. (This LP was also repackaged and marketed by King as *Freddy King Goes Surfin'*, with the only difference being some canned applause. During this period his first name was spelled with a "y.")

The Freddie King uptempo instrumental has by now become somewhat of an institution, much like the Elmore James slide guitar shuffle. John Mayall's first three Bluesbreakers albums each included one of Freddie's themes, with Eric Clapton recreating "Hideaway" on *Blues Breakers*, Peter Green plowing through "The Stumble" on *A Hard Road*, and Mick Taylor covering "Driving Sideways" on *Crusade*.

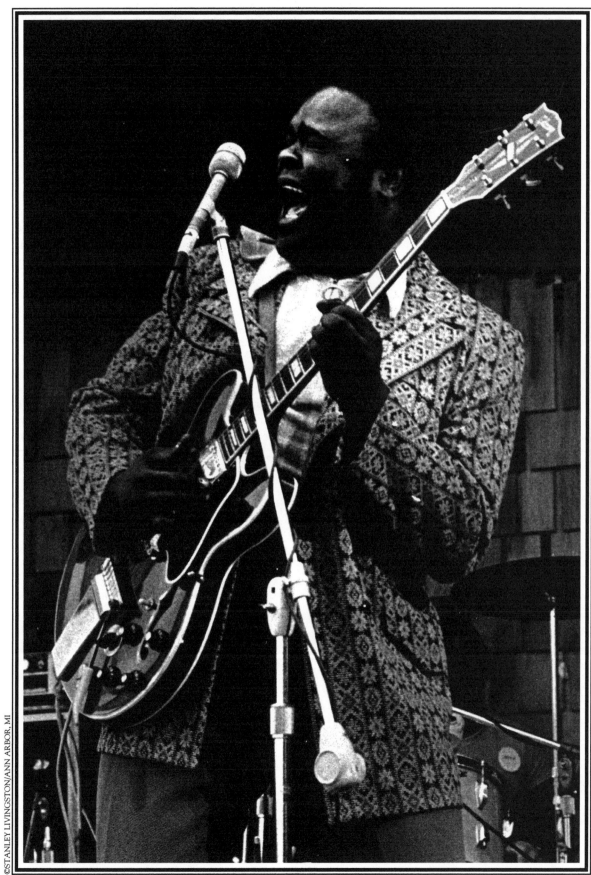

These songs and several others by Freddie are now standard warm-up or break songs for countless semi-pro bands featuring guitar. And much in the same way that organist Bill Doggett's "Honky Tonk" is in seemingly every R&B band's repertoire with all of Billy Butler's guitar licks left intact, guitarists tend to stay close to Freddie's lines in "Hideaway" — from the open-string hammer-ons to the muted bass runs to the tongue-in-cheek quotation from "Peter Gunn."

Freddie's relationship with the guitar began at age six, when he began learning some blues and gospel from his uncle and mother, who each played guitar. His first axe was a Silvertone acoustic, and the records he was listening to at this time were by the prominent blues artists of the day — people like Lightnin' Hopkins, T-Bone Walker, Muddy Waters, and John Lee Hooker.

> ## "Me, Otis, Magic Sam, Jody Williams — we'd go around and listen to each other; then we'd trade licks."

Electric guitars didn't enter the picture until several years later. As he recalls, "I finished school at 16 and went to Chicago. Carried a guitar on my back. I went there to live in 1954, but I'd been there back in '50 and in '49. Muddy Waters, that's who I was looking for. So I found him and Jimmy Rogers. Then I met Howlin' Wolf and all those cats, you know."

It was Muddy's guitar man, Jimmy Rogers, who influenced Freddie to forego flatpicks. "I never have used one," King states. "I use a steel fingerpick on the index and a plastic thumbpick. Jimmy Rogers and Eddie Taylor taught me how to play like that. Robert Jr. Lockwood can play with all three fingers." King later co-produced and played some guitar on Jimmy Rogers' 1973 comeback LP, *Gold Tailed Bird*.

Freddie's Texas roots intertwining with the Chicago blues environment made for his up-to-date musical outlook in comparison to many of the already established South Side bands. King soon became close musical kin to the younger generation of Chicago blues guitarists, including Otis Rush and the late Magic Sam, who gravitated mainly to Chicago's West Side. "We played a whole lot of stuff together," King remembers. "We'd go around and listen to each other; then we'd trade licks. Me, Otis,

Magic Sam, Jody Williams — I taught Luther Allison how to play." It was this atmosphere that actually provided Freddie with his initial hit "Hideaway." "Hound Dog Taylor played that," he confesses, "then me and Magic Sam worked it out."

Whereas Taylor played strictly bottleneck guitar, King has steered clear of the slide technique because, as he explains, "my fingers are too heavy; I play too hard. I wish I could play slide, but I can't. I do some of the same licks, though, as Elmore James, Earl Hooker, and guys like that." While his heavy right hand attack precludes the use of a slide, it is this factor which Freddie credits as his "gimmick."

During the mid '60s, between the time of his first Federal singles and the white awakening to blues music, Freddie, like virtually every other blues artist, was working hard and gaining little ground, since even the top of the blues heap was still at the bottom of the popular music market. His tunes began turning up on LPs from the English blues scene, and two sessions for Atlantic's Cotillion subsidiary let listeners know that one of the originators was still around.

But it wasn't until rock pianist Leon Russell signed King to the Shelter label that Freddie got his second shot at the masses. "We met," he recounts, "and I told Leon that I wasn't with Atlantic no more. He said, 'I'm starting a company. Would you like to come with it?' So we tried it. And everybody knew me from 'Hideaway,' so the Fillmore circuit wasn't really too hard for me."

The association with Russell did more than merely bring some old tunes out of the closet. Freddie's vocals (something he'd never actually stopped doing) again came to the spotlight. As Freddie states, "It's taken me a long time to get back into the vocals. Everybody wanted to hear the instrumentals. I always did do both, but they wouldn't push the vocals. When I really started singing again was with Shelter."

King is quick to credit the Leon Russells, Eric Claptons, and John Mayalls for reviving interest in blues. "These young whites started people looking at me, B.B. King, and all the rest of them," he declares. "If it wasn't for them, I think the blues would still be in the same old black market. But now it's a bigger market. Johnny Winter, John Hammond, Paul Butterfield, Mike Bloomfield — he hung around us as a kid in Chicago. They're really blues cats. It went okay for me."

Freddie's equipment consists mainly of a Gibson ES-355, wired in stereo and fed into a Fender Quad amplifier. Both pickups are employed, with all controls set at half bass, half treble. The string set is split between Ernie Balls (.010, .011, .012) on the top three and Gibson medium gauge for the bass strings. Freddie favors Gibson guitars and in addition to the 355 owns an ES-335, an ES-345, a Les Paul, and two Firebirds. "I used to use Fenders, but not anymore," he says. "Fender is a good-sounding guitar, but for the way I play I think Gibson is the best."

He sums up his technique, saying, "I play my guitar like Louis Jordan used to play his horn. That's the same sound I get."

Though he has at times easily transcended the boundaries of categorization, and dabbled with funk numbers and tunes like Bill Withers' "Ain't No Sunshine" and Dave Mason's "Feelin' All Right," King is quick to give credit to "all the blues players" for his extensive background. Still, judging by a brief list of contemporary guitarists he enjoys listening to, Freddie is anything but narrow-minded. "I like other guys, too: Steve Cropper, Kenny Burrell, Chet Atkins — he plays with his fingers, too. I listen to a whole lot of people, but the thing I'm into is the blues."

[Freddie King passed away in 1976.]

A SELECTED
FREDDIE KING DISCOGRAPHY

Solo albums: *Freddie King Sings*, Modern Blues (reissue of superb King sides, '60); *Let's Hide Away And Dance Away* ('60-'61), King; *Takin' Care Of Business* (Federal sides, '60-'64), Charly; *Freddy King Gives You A Bonanza Of Instrumentals* (King, '62-'64), Crosscut; *Just Pickin'* (King/Federal instrumentals), Modern Blues; *Freddy King Goes Surfin'*, King; *17 Original Greatest Hits*, King; *Girl-Boy-Girl* (with Lulu Reed), King; *Freddie King Is A Blues Master* ('69), WEA; *My Feeling For The Blues* ('70), WEA; *Getting Ready* (recorded at Chess Studio, '70), Shelter; *Texas Cannonball*, Shelter; *Woman Across The River*, Shelter; *The Best Of Freddie King*, MCA; *Burglar*, Polydor; *Larger Than Life*, RSO; *Live In Antibes, 1974*, French Concerts; *Rocking The Blues — Live* (Germany, '74-'75), Crosscut; *Larger Than Life* ('75), Polydor; *1934-1976*, Polydor; *Live At Texas Opry House, April 20, 1976*, P-Vine; *Hideaway*, Gusto.

With others: Jimmy Rogers, *Gold Tailed Bird*, Shelter.

Anthologies: *Atlantic Blues: Chicago* ('68-'72), Atlantic; *Ann Arbor Blues & Jazz Festival 1972*, Atlantic.

Eddie "Guitar Slim" Jones

March 1984

BY JEFF HANNUSCH

TWENTY-FOUR YEARS AFTER HIS DEATH, Guitar Slim's extroverted, passionate blues guitar playing can still send chills down one's spine. His highly personal compositions, including the R&B standards "The Things That I Used To Do" and "The Story Of My Life," are still staples in the repertoires of blues, rock, and even zydeco bands. And anyone who ever saw the man perform, be they player or listener, has vivid memories of one of the most colorful figures in the history of New Orleans rhythm and blues.

Fellow New Orleans guitarist Earl King remembers seeing Guitar Slim at the peak of his all-too-short career: "Gatemouth Brown, T-Bone Walker, Lowell Fulson, and Guitar Slim were all performing one night at the White Eagle in Opelousas. Slim was headlining, because 'The Things That I Used To Do' was a scorcher. They were all sitting in the dressing room, and Guitar Slim walked up to 'em all and said, 'Gentlemen, we got the greatest guitar players in the country assembled right here. But when I leave here tonight, ain't nobody gonna realize you even been here.' Well, they all laughed, but that's exactly what happened.

"Slim came out with his hair dyed blue, blue suit, blue pair of shoes. He had 350 feet of mike wire connected to his guitar, and a valet carrying him on his shoulders all through the crowd and out into the parking lot. Man, he was stopping cars driving down the highway. No one could outperform Slim. He was about the performinest man I've ever seen." King's description coincides with virtually everyone else's who saw Guitar Slim onstage, or knew him personally. Though he's been dead for over two decades, Guitar Slim's legend continues.

When I was researching the Guitar Slim story, I got the telephone number of a guy who supposedly had been his tailor — because Slim was famous for the outlandish suits he wore. I called the number, and an older black lady answered, and I told her I wanted to ask her husband about Guitar Slim. He got on the phone, and I introduced myself, and he proceeded to tell me this story about taking the bus downtown in New Orleans. They got in front of the Dew Drop club on LaSalle Street, and traffic was

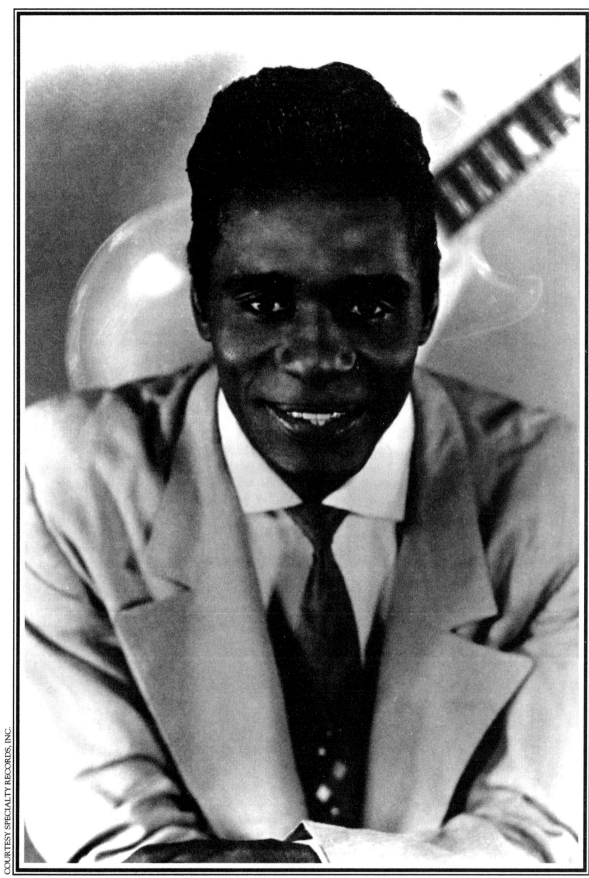

lined up on both sides of the street. So he got out of the bus to see what was going on, and Guitar Slim was playing out in the neutral ground on the boulevard, walking over the tops of cars while his valet was spooling out his big, long guitar chord to him. Then I asked the guy to tell me about the suits he made for Slim, and he said, "No, I'm no tailor; I'm a carpenter. You must have the wrong number." In New Orleans, even the wrong numbers have at least one Guitar Slim story.

Even though his music has remained popular all these years, many details concerning his life are still shrouded in mystery, so much so that putting together a concise biography is like completing a complex jigsaw puzzle. Guitar Slim was born Edward Jones on December 10, 1926, and he's known to have at least one sister. Though Slim claimed in his Specialty Records biography that Greenwood, Mississippi, was his birthplace, Hollandale, Mississippi, has also been suggested. No matter, Slim was raised in the Greenwood area, a rural region of intense cotton production in the heart of the Mississippi Delta. Times were probably tough, and likely Slim did his fair share in the fields, visiting Greenwood on weekends.

The first mention of Guitar Slim (he was six feet tall, 160 pounds, so he easily fit the colorful alias) in the *Louisiana Weekly* was during September 1950. It stated: "New Orleans' newest gift to the show world is Guitar Slim, held over at the Dew Drop. The New Orleans blues sensation has made a terrific impact on blues fans in New Orleans. Acclaimed to be an exact carbon copy of Gatemouth Brown, the singing guitarist includes 'My Time Is Expensive,' 'Gatemouth Boogie,' and several other performances made popular by Brown."

The comparison between Guitar Slim and Gatemouth Brown is indeed apt; it is interesting to note that he would draw his greatest influence from the Texas guitar school, rather than the guitar players from his own state, Mississippi. "Gatemouth's 'Boogie Rambler' was Slim's theme," adds Earl King. "He listened to all of them and compiled bits of their style — Gatemouth, T-Bone, B.B. King. But

he took a different approach; he had a lot of melodic overtones in his solos. He used to play a solo that had a marriage to the rest of the song, rather than just play something off the top of his head."

Earl also chafes when others suggest Slim was a poor instrumentalist and unable to even play without the aid of a capo, or as Slim referred to it, "a choker." "Slim tuned standard, but he used that capo to get the effect of open strings. You can't do that without a choker. I've seen Slim play many a time without it. He just used it for effect."

> "*Guitar Slim just blew me away . . . period.*"
> — Stevie Ray Vaughan

Percy Stovall, who booked Slim during his early career, remembers: "I used to worry him sometimes and hide his choker. He'd be runnin' around saying, 'Stove, where's my choker at? I can't find my choker.' I'd say, 'I ain't seen it, Slim,' and he'd be running around trying to find it everywhere. Then just before he would go on, I'd pull it out of my pocket and hand it to him, and he'd say, 'Stove, I knew you had it all the time.'"

Stovall is the first to admit that Slim was his favorite artist, but also points out he had his share of headaches with him. "Man, he loved to drink," says Stovall, shaking his head. "If I didn't watch him all the time he'd miss his job. If he had a job over in Florida, I'd have to ration him. I'd make sure the valet gave him only a fifth of wine when he left New Orleans, another fifth in Biloxi, and one more by the time he got to Mobile. And don't nobody fool with Slim's wine or he'd be in trouble."

One of Stovall's favorite stories concerning his early days of booking Guitar Slim took place in Monroe, Louisiana. "Fats Domino and Slim played a Battle Of The Blues," he recalls, "at the Monroe Civic Auditorium. Man, the place was packed. Slim had told Fats before the show, 'Fats, I'm gonna run you offa that stage tonight.'

"So Slim went on first because Fats had hit records out. Slim just tore 'em up. The place was goin' wild. Slim walked off the stage with his guitar and went out the back door of the place and got in a car, still playing. Everyone wondered where Slim had gone. When it came time for Fats to come on, Fats just told the people, 'Ain't gonna be no battle tonight. You just saw it.' So Fats just played his regular show."

By 1951, the record companies had been hearing about this wild guitar player in New Orleans. Imperial approached first, and Al Young produced four sides by Eddie Jones at the J&M Studio. The session was rather chaotic, originally producing "Bad Luck Is On Me" and "New Arrival," which sold poorly. Imperial wouldn't ask Slim back to the studio, but still issued the remainder of the session when Slim hit the big time, using his alias instead of Eddie Jones.

Slim's next record was a different story. Percy Stovall arranged a session with Jim Bullet in Nashville, producing the popular "Feelin' Sad" in 1952. David Lastie played sax on the tune and remembered the circumstances that surrounded the session: "We was working at the Kitty Cat Club in Nashville, and me, Huey Piano Smith, Little Eddie Lang, and Willie Nettles did the session with Slim. 'Feelin' Sad' was a good little record; it had a church sound to it. We worked pretty good off it."

When Slim came in off the road, he stayed upstairs at the Dew Drop. "Slim liked to be where the action was," chuckles King. "In fact, you knew Slim was back in town, because early in the morning, around seven or eight o'clock, if he was tanked up, you'd hear them amps and PAs going off. People'd be calling the police because you could hear Slim three blocks away! And here's Slim up in his room with his shorts on, going through his stage routine.

"And Slim's room was something else, man. If you went up there, there'd always be about seven or eight different women up there. He'd have his songs written with eyebrow pencil on pieces of paper tacked to the wall."

King also recalls that Slim bought the first Les Paul guitar in New Orleans: "Slim was playing one of those big hollow boxes like T-Bone had. But when the solid boxes came out he got one right away. Slim said the hollow boxes were too big, and they didn't give him enough room on the stage. He couldn't control the feedback that was coming out of them. So he dealt with the Les Paul."

By 1953 Guitar Slim was one of the biggest draws on the southern R&B circuit. The responsibilities of managing and booking reverted to Slim's landlord, Frank Pania, who owned the Dew Drop, while Percy Stovall concentrated on building up a larger roster of performers. Pania also took it upon himself to find Slim a new band. He hired the Lloyd Lambert band from Hosea Hill's Sugar Bowl in Thibodaux, Louisiana. Hosea was a friend and business associate of Pania, and paired Slim with the band for a series of road dates. Bassist Lambert claims that Pania was responsible for introducing Slim to Johnny Vincent, then a Specialty Records A&R man. Vincent was impressed enough to convince his boss, Art Rupe, to sign Slim to a recording contract. "Slim was supposed to sign with Atlantic," Vincent recalls, "but this was one artist I just had to get. He was fantastic. Slim wouldn't let anyone outperform him. I wouldn't let him out of my sight until he signed with Specialty."

On October 16, 1953, Slim entered the J&M Studio to record what was to be the biggest record of his career, "The Things That I Used To Do." According to Lloyd Lambert, the personnel on the session was pianist Ray Charles, Gus Fontenette, Charles Burbank, and Joe Tillman on saxophones, Oscar Moore on drums, Frank Mitchell on trumpet, and Lambert on bass, with Jones playing his goldtop. Vincent claims he had to bail one of the musicians out of jail to play on the date.

When Vincent says, "Slim was hard to record," he has lots of support. Tales of Slim's recording sessions are many. Vincent claims that it took "all night" to record "The Things That I Used To Do." Engineer Cosimo Matassa says "all day," and Lloyd Lambert reports it took "two days." Nonetheless, the musicians were obviously gratified when it was over, because Ray Charles is clearly audible yelling "Yeah!" in relief in the last bars of the song.

According to Earl King, the idea for the tune came to Slim in a dream. Slim related to King that in the dream he was confronted by a devil and an angel, both of whom held the lyrics to a song. Naturally, Slim chose the devil's song, and it turned out to be "The Things That I Used To Do."

Vincent sent the tapes of the session to Rupe, who was less than impressed with the result. According to Vincent, "He told me it was the worst piece of shit he'd ever heard. He said, 'I'm gonna put it out, but if it don't sell, you start looking for a job.'"

The public disagreed with Rupe, to say the least. Immediately after its release, both *Billboard* and *Cash Box* made it the pick of the week. *Cash Box* called it "a slow southern blues rhythmically chanted by the blues shouter . . . great vocal with the proper blues styling, and this side is headed for sales. Top notch."

"The Things That I Used To Do" stormed the charts. It topped the R&B roster for six solid weeks and ended up the biggest selling R&B record of 1954. The lyrics, sung in Slim's impassioned gospel-like style, struck a chord in the public's imagination. For many, the real appeal of "The Things That I Used To Do" was the novel guitar approach that Slim took. As Earl King explains: "Slim was gettin' a fuzztone distortion way before anyone else. Believe it or not, Slim never used an amplifier. He always used a PA set, never an amplifier. He was an overtone fanatic, and he had those tiny iron-cone speakers and the sound would run through them speakers, and I guess any vibration would create that sound, because Slim always played at peak volume. That's why it was hard to record him — because of the volume he was accustomed to playing at. Let's face it, if Slim was playing you could hear him a mile away."

Lloyd Lambert agrees that Slim played as loud as he could. "He had this tinny sound," says Lambert, "that he'd get by turning all the bass controls as low as they would go, and turning up his treble controls as high as they'd go."

Although Slim was most associated with his gold-top Les Paul (after switching from his hollowbody electric), some pictures show him playing a white Fender Telecaster. The piercing tone Slim achieved was similar to that of Clarence Gatemouth Brown and Johnny Guitar Watson, and derived in part from the fact that he, like the others, played guitar with his fingers, pulling at the strings. ZZ Top guitarist Billy Gibbons concurs: "Eddie Jones definitely played with his thumb and his fingers. A lot of people could never figure out why R&B had such vicious guitar tones. They forget that most of the rooms that they played in were so loud anyway. I mean, can you imagine going into a black blues

joint in 1954 and having it quiet and sedate? They'd just turn those old Fender amps up all the way, man, just to be heard. Slim would, like, aim for 'patent pending' and just blow!"

New Orleans songwriter Al Reed, who backed Slim, Earl King, Smiley Lewis, and others, also credits Jones with pioneering the distorted electric guitar sound. As he told John Broven in *Rhythm & Blues In New Orleans* [Pelican]: "A lot of the electric guitar sound has been attributed to Chuck Berry, but many people aren't aware of the type of guitar that Guitar Slim played. Guitar Slim was a most profound musician. He had an electric sound like you never heard. They would open the club doors wide so that the sound could just go in and out of the club, and he would draw people off the street. Big passing automobiles would stop, and the people would just listen to this guy play and watch him walk. I think he had a greater impact on the electric guitar sound than any other guitarist because he used the electric sound very much as it is used today. And Chuck Berry was not using that sound at the time. Guitar Slim was the finest and about the first. He was a great guy to be around. He was a man you could learn from — not what you heard, but what you saw. Because he could exhilarate you. Man, he would lift you above and beyond the clouds as he played. He could create sensations within your body that really played tricks with your mind. He was the first man to do this."

> "*Guitar Slim's solo on 'The Story Of My Life' is one of the best early distorted guitar solos; it really sounds like he's mad at somebody.*"

With the #1 record in the country, Frank Pania booked a full itinerary for Slim through the South, and bought him a brand new Olds Delta 88. Slim promptly got drunk one night and ran into a parked bulldozer, wrecking the car and ending up in the hospital. "Slim weren't too good a driver," laughs Lambert. "He didn't hurt himself too bad; the doctor just told him to take it easy for a month."

Pania decided to send Earl King out to impersonate Slim on a number of dates, and apparently got away with it. Even though King went along with the charade, he admits he was scared to death:

"When I got back to town, the first person I saw was Guitar Slim," laughs Earl. "He was walking down LaSalle Street with a hospital gown on, a guitar under one arm and an amp under the other, yelling 'Earl King, I heard you been out there imitatin' me. If you wreck my name, I'm gonna sue and I'm gonna kill you!'"

Slim was soon back on his feet and ready to hit the road for a tour of the northern theater circuit. Since Lambert's band already had Lawrence Cotton on piano, Slim had to split with Huey Smith, an event which likely saddened both of them.

Eventually Slim's popularity became too much for Frank Pania to deal with, so he turned over Slim's management to Hosea Hill, who ran his own popular nightspot in Thibodaux, the Sugar Bowl. Consequently, Slim spent a good amount of his time in Thibodaux, which nestles Bayou Lafourche, Louisiana.

Guitar Slim's next release, "The Story Of My Life," was a powerful follow-up and came from his initial Specialty session. Once again *Cash Box* spotlighted it by giving it its weekly award and calling it "another powerful item. His mournful tale is accentuated by the chanter's stylings and impressive guitar work."

His guitar work was indeed impressive, less lyrical but more visceral than his solo on "The Things That I Used To Do." Frank Zappa, one of Guitar Slim's biggest fans, ranks it as one of his favorite guitar solos of all time. In the February '82 *Guitar Player* he elaborated: "It's got that 'I don't give a fuck about nothin', I'm gonna play whatever I want in here, and you guys can hang it in your ass' kind of primitive abandonment."

Lambert still relishes the days of the mid '50s, barnstorming the country. "We had the best band out there," he affirms. "Fats, B.B. King, even Lionel Hampton — we could cut 'em all. We had trouble following Slim at first, because he'd always jump meter, but it got to where we'd just jump right with him and it would sound fine. Slim was a showman and a musician. He'd have purple suits, orange suits, green suits, with shoes and hair to match. He'd

> "We had trouble following Slim at first, because he'd always jump meter, but it got to where we'd just jump right with him and it would sound fine."

make motions and faces that would drive people berserk. You couldn't hardly get into the place when he was playing."

Earl King agrees: "Slim could play at the Dew Drop and get a mob of people, and the next night play in Shrewsbury [in adjacent Jefferson Parish] and get the same mob. Even the people who knew him to say 'hi' in the streets would think nothing of driving 100 miles to go see him that same night."

When the first electric Fender basses came on the market, Slim wanted one for his band and talked Lambert into buying it. Although Lambert became one of the first electric bass players, Earl King says that it took a lot of convincing on Slim's part to prod him into buying the new bass. "When he saw that B.B. King's band had one, that was it. Slim wanted everything electric. If Slim would have seen all the gadgetry that's out today, it would be ridiculous. When the Cadillacs came out with all that gadgetry he was just like a little kid. He just marvelled over that — seats moving, water shooting." Slim stayed so busy that Specialty had to arrange to record while the group was touring. Lambert recalled that the second Specialty session took place at Chess Studios in Chicago, and produced "Sufferin' Mind" in 1955, with Art Rupe flying in from L.A. to produce.

Rupe, however, took it upon himself to bury Slim's guitar way down in the mix, and even added a Hammond organ. The session lost a little of the New Orleans feel, but it was identifiable Slim just the same. His final Specialty session took place in early 1956 and was recorded in Los Angeles, before he switched to the Atlantic/Atco label.

Even though Slim's record sales began dipping, he was still a top attraction. He and the band crisscrossed the country, playing to overflow houses. When he came in off the road, he would spend the days in a lazy manner, usually drinking with friends at the Dew Drop or the Sugar Bowl.

Atlantic recorded Slim both in New York and at Cosimo's in New Orleans, according to Lambert.

There was little departure from the last Specialty sessions (although voices were occasionally added and the horn section beefed up), largely due to the strength of Lloyd Lambert's tight band. However, on a previously unissued track, "Along About Midnight" (available on *Texas Guitar — From Dallas To L.A.*), Slim is backed by a host of New York jazz heavyweights, including bassist Percy Heath, saxophonist Johnny Griffin, pianist Elmo Hope, and drummer Philly Joe Jones.

Atlantic must have been somewhat disappointed, though, in their attempts with Slim. They had visions of crossing his records into the teenage market on the same scale Chess had done with Chuck Berry, but had little success. As it would turn out, his last Atco session in 1958 would produce the prophetically titled "When There's No Way Out" and "If I Had My Life To Live Over."

Despite doctors' warnings about his heavy drinking, by 1958 Slim was really sick and getting weaker, so much so that he was unable to travel and forced to stay in Thibodaux. "I wouldn't say he was a pretty good drinker," says Lambert. "He was the best! Slim just wouldn't take care of himself. He lived fast; different women every night. I'd try and tell him to eat good and get his rest, but he'd say, 'Lloyd, I live three days to y'all's one. The world won't owe me a thing when I'm gone.'"

Earl King gives some insight into the last days of Guitar Slim: "Slim got ruptured [from riding the guitar onstage], and I think that's what caused him to drink more than he ever had. Man, when he came in off that last tour, he almost had to wear a truss. I went over to visit him in Thibodaux when he was sick, and he had empty 100 proof bottles laying all over his room. The doctor told him to stay off that hard liquor, but what are you gonna tell a guy who drinks a pint of gin and chases it with a fifth of black port every day?"

Strangely enough, Slim had quit drinking the last months of his life, according to some. "Slim was getting ready to go on another tour," continues Earl. "Slim sat in the Dew Drop one night and was talking very straight and serious. He told me, 'Earl, all this liquor I been drinkin', all the wrong things I

> ## "*I* live three days to y'all's one. The world won't owe me a thing when I'm gone."

been thinkin', you know my body's been slowly sinkin'.' That's when I went over and asked Hosea Hill, 'Is there something wrong with Slim?' He said, 'No, he's fine. He just got out of the hospital, and he's not even drinking. Why do you ask that?' I said, 'Because Slim talks too straight tonight; he's not funny. He's never under the weather about anything.' That was the last time I saw him."

In February 1959, the group embarked on a tour of dances and nightclubs in New York State. "We went up to Rochester," recalls Lambert, "and Slim came up to me and said, 'Lloyd, I'm tired, I don't think I can make it no more. Y'all got a good band; you can get another singer.' I said, 'Come on Slim, you can make it. You just been with a broad or something.' He said, 'No, Lloyd, my time is up.' So we played the dance, and when it came time for Slim to come on, he could only do part of the first song and couldn't finish.

"We drove to Newark to play the next night, and Slim played the gig but he collapsed right after. One of the valets ran and got a doctor, and the doctor looked at Slim and said, 'Check this man into a hospital; he's really sick.' We were gonna stay in New York, because that's where our next date was. So we drove up to the Ceceil Hotel, and I sent the valet across to take Slim to the doctor while I checked into the hotel. When I got to the desk, there was a telephone call waiting for me from the valet. He said, 'Lloyd, Slim's dead.' I didn't believe it, because I'd seen him not more than five minutes before. We got in the station wagon and drove 'round the corner to the doctor's. But sure enough Slim was layin' up on the table, gone."

Word of Slim's death was slow getting back to New Orleans. The *Louisiana Weekly* was a full week late in its announcement. "Somebody knocked up on my door and said 'Slim's dead,'" remembers King. "I said, 'Man, that can't be true. People like Slim don't die. They're still here when I'm gone.'"

"It wasn't liquor that killed him," specifies Lambert. "The doctor said it was bronchial pneumonia. Today, they might have saved him, but all that drinking and hard living brought his resistance down." Slim's body was kept in New York by authorities to see if drugs were involved in his death. Hosea Hill eventually paid the fare to fly Slim's body back to Thibodaux for a massive funeral at the Mt. Zion Baptist Church. Guitar Slim now lies in an unmarked grave next to his benefactor, Hosea Hill. He was buried with his gold-top Gibson Les Paul.

So ended the all-too-short life of the 32-year-old Guitar Slim. He is survived by several common-law wives, and a number of children, one of whom plays guitar in the small clubs around New Orleans and who keeps Slim's name alive. Hardly a year has passed since his death that someone hasn't rere-corded one of his songs. Earl King's 1982 version of Slim's anthem, "It Hurts To Love Someone," only reinforces the timelessness of his work.

Almost everyone is adamant about what would have happened if Slim were alive today. "He'd have been on the scale of a B.B. King or a Ray Charles," says Earl King.

Lloyd Lambert states simply, "No question about it. Guitar Slim would have been the biggest."

A SELECTED
GUITAR SLIM DISCOGRAPHY

Solo albums: *The Things That I Used To Do* ('54-'56), Specialty; *Guitar Slim & Earl King: Battle Of The Blues* (nine Specialty sides), Ace; *Red Cadillacs & Crazy Chicks* ('51-'58), Sundown.

Anthologies: *Atlantic Blues: Guitar* ('56-'57), Atlantic; *Texas Guitar — From Dallas To L.A.*, Atlantic.

Buddy Guy

April 1990

BY JAS OBRECHT

I T'S ALMOST MIDNIGHT AT LEGENDS, Buddy Guy's popular Chicago blues club, and our host is two-and-a-half hours into his set. He whoops, shouts, and sings with the passion of a country preacher faced with the fires of perdition. A quick jerk of his left hand, and his band drops to a *whisper*. He raises his eyebrows, grins charismatically, and careens into a solo like a runaway Mack.

The crowd roars wildly as Guy leaps from the stage to prowl the house. Surrounded by fans, he wails from the aisles, the pool tables and video machines, even from *inside* the ladies' room. His band pumps hard as he journeys outside the front door onto the icy corner of 8th and South Wabash, never missing a lick. A nearby El roars past, momentarily drowning out the band. Guy looks up and laughs: "That train is messing my time up!" He rushes back inside to finish his solo on tiptoe, his back against a wall as overhand runs and choked bends segue into a patented Muddy Waters lick.

Long before the sweat dries, you're sure of one thing: Like hurricanes, tornadoes, and earthquakes, there's no holding back Buddy Guy.

Jimi Hendrix sat at his feet. Eric Clapton insisted in *Musician* magazine that "Buddy Guy is by far and without a doubt the best guitar player alive. . . . If you see him in person, the way he plays is beyond anyone. Total freedom of spirit." Jeff Beck recalls the night he stopped by Legends with Stevie Ray Vaughan: "That was just the most incredible stuff I ever heard in my life. We all jammed, and it was *so* thrilling. That is as close as you can come to the heart of the blues."

Opened in 1989, Buddy Guy's Legends has become a mecca for rockers and bluesmen. During our visit, saxophone great A.C. Reed got up to sing a dirty blues, and B.B. Odum plowed through a set of his namesake's best tunes. Other famous drop-ins include Hubert Sumlin, Robert Jr. Lockwood, Eric Clapton, Bill Wyman and Ron Wood, Joe Walsh, Jimmy Vaughan, and Buddy's longtime playing partner, harmonica ace Junior Wells. (Blues-approved players preferred! Staffers still smirk about the night a batch of puffheads from the nearby NAMM Show

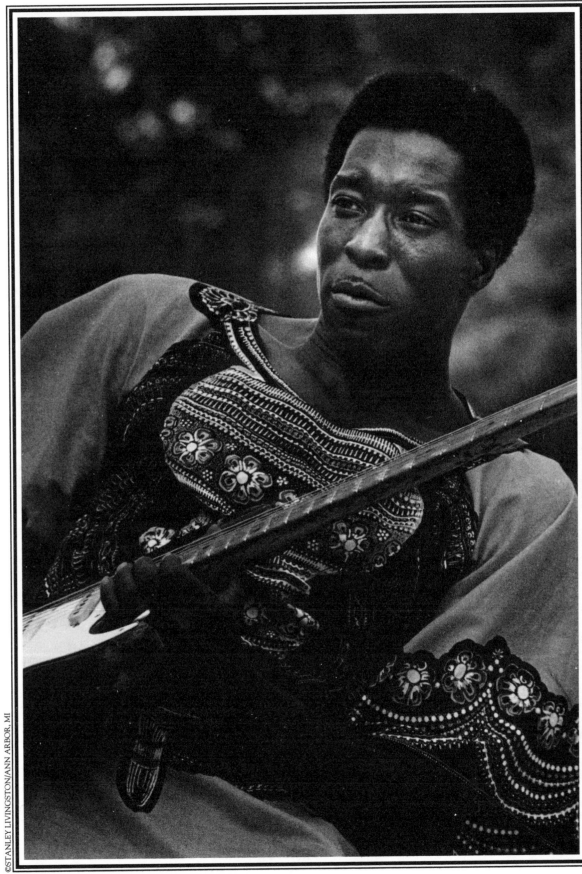

stopped by and cleared the stage — and audience — with pyrotechnic blazing.)

What's going to happen on any given night is anyone's guess. Greg Rzab, a 30-year-old bassist who cut his teeth with James Cotton and Otis Rush before becoming the mainstay of Buddy's band, explains: "We've had this particular group about a month; Buddy just hires people and we play. I've seen him do this many times, like a snake moulting. In fact, during the four years I've been with him, there hasn't been one rehearsal — ever. And with all the bands that have been here, I've never heard him direct any musician. There's no script. Buddy comes onstage and just starts playing. Sometimes it's like he's plugged into a 240-volt socket—all of a sudden, he'll burst into some stuff, and no one knows where it comes from! He plays some things with the same tone and feel, but there's no pattern in his playing, so we just wing it. I keep the groove happening, so he keeps me around. It's a great gig, and a lot of fun."

At 53, Buddy Guy still looks remarkably young. Face to face in Legends' small, bare-bulb back office, he sometimes bears an unnerving resemblance to Jimi Hendrix. Despite his supreme talent, he's criminally under-recorded. Raised in Louisiana, he cut his first sides in Baton Rouge in 1957; within a year, he was recording in Chicago with Otis Rush and Willie Dixon sitting in as his sidemen. He became a house guitarist for Chess Records in the early '60s, backing Muddy Waters and Howlin' Wolf, among others, but didn't release a full-fledged solo album until 1968's *A Man & The Blues*. His solo sessions escalated in the late '60s and early '70s, when he was frequently paired with Junior Wells. Since the mid '70s, though, he's been poorly represented on vinyl, except for portions of *Stone Crazy* (recorded 12 years ago in France) and a few live tracks released by Antone's Records. His ambition, as you'll see, is to someday record an album of the *real* Buddy Guy.

You're really a gentleman towards other players.

> "*I* was taught by the greatest musicians that ever lived. And that was Muddy Waters and the Wolf and Little Walter and them."

You move to the side of the stage when they solo. You play great chords behind them.

[*Smiles.*] Yes. You know, I was taught by the greatest musicians that ever lived. And that was Muddy Waters and the Wolf and [Little] Walter and them. And they never did *dominate*, although they were, in my book, dominating musicians. I had a chance to come up there with them. Junior, James Cotton — we all taking lessons from those people. And in order for someone else to carry on, we have to just say, "Okay, here's your shot." I didn't get that. There's this young kid I got, Scott [Holt]; he's out of Tennessee, and his dad and his mama thanks me now, because I had to *fight* my way up. There was so many guitar players when I came to Chicago, you were just one out of the bucket. And there was so many places.

Your bandmates claim that you never try to cut other guitarists.

No, I don't, but I don't hold back. I was shy all of my life, up until I really got here [in Chicago], and Muddy Waters slapped me in the face. Him and Wolf and Walter and them told me there ain't no such thing as that. I'm going to tell you exactly like they said: "There ain't no such thing as that shit." They said, "We know you can play, and you gonna play." Because I didn't want to get in their way. That's why I got a chance to make quite a few records with those guys. And I was so nervous at them asking me to play, I would lose a lot. I was afraid to even play what I knew, because I'd say, "How can I show who *I* am, sitting behind Muddy Waters, Wolf, or Walter," or any of the other greats that I played with — John Lee Hooker, Big Mama Thornton, just to name a few. And it all flashes back to me now when I'm playing onstage with these young kids. Sure, I feel proud letting them see what I'm doing, because I'm self-taught. It's a God-gifted talent that I have, because I've never been taught guitar by anybody.

John Lee Hooker says that a lot of young players can play flashy solos, but have trouble keeping a groove.

Music is just like the automobile: You get in it, you look for air-conditioning, you look for heat, and you look for that thing to almost take care of you. These young people are saying, "I'm playing what's gonna take me to videos and MTV," whereas I suppose John Lee — and I'm not speaking for him — I suppose John Lee and myself and Muddy and all of us were just playing for what we like. When I learned how to play guitar, I wasn't looking forward to making a decent living at it, because there wasn't no such thing as that. We were playing for the love of blues. And the kind of blues that John Lee and I play, young people are going to take it and improve it. This is what they're doing. Our music don't take us into bigger spotlights as these young kids' music do. You know, the record companies are looking for young, good-looking, talented musicians doing something different, and the young people are record buyers. And the way they're playing those guitars is being sold to those young people, and that's what it's all about.

I would like to be commercially successful, but the love I have for blues sometimes makes me forget about how successful I could be — or wealthy, should I say — at my music. A lot of great friends have did a lot for me just by speaking about me, or speaking about my playing, which has helped me a lot. And I owe them a lot of big thanks for that.

> "*I* would like to be commercially successful, but the love I have for blues sometimes makes me forget about how successful I could be — or wealthy, should I say — at my music."

Does having people like Clapton claiming you're the greatest living guitar player cause any pressure?

I feel good about him saying that, because it helped me with who I am. I don't have albums out that compare to Stevie and Eric and Beck and the rest of those people. My albums come seldom and *very* seldom, because I'm not with a company or anything now. I haven't had an album out in going on 12 years. And when someone like Eric makes a statement like that, it's great, but I don't want to pat myself on the back and try and live up to that. I don't let that cross my mind. I still just want to be Buddy Guy. I thank him for saying something like that, but man, you've got him for number one, Stevie, and quite a few more. That's a big question mark there — how good I am, or the best one alive. Now, I don't know about that. Because if you go catch him, he can make you almost forget about what he said, because he can play.

You own Legends, where you could control your sound. Why not tape a live album here?

I wish I could. I'd jump in Lake Michigan on a night like tonight and swim if someone would come say, "I want to do an album on you live." I just want to be treated right. I want to be Buddy Guy on an album. The closest I've ever come is *Stone Crazy*, and I had to do that in France. The guy I did it for named the label after my mother, Isabel, and he said, "I want you to do what you've wanted to do all your life." I said, "What's that?" He said, "Be Buddy Guy." I said, "I'd be glad, then, to do an album for you."

I guess this is why I don't have a company giving me a shot at it now, because I really wants to be Buddy Guy. I wants to play the things that never came out of me that I know I have. And if I get that opportunity next time I go into the studio, I'm going to give it. If it sells, fine. If it don't, I will please myself inside because I know what I *can* do, and I'm not going to be shy with it anymore. I don't want anybody teaching me how to play when the tapes are rolling; I've had that happen to me a lot in the past. I've got to play what I already know.

You do have your own style. No one plays like Buddy Guy.

Thank you, but that leads back to being self-taught. I've got some bad habits in the way I play. That's the way I taught myself, and I can't get away from it.

What bad habits?

I play a stiff hand. My right hand is very stiff;

it's not relaxed. My picking is very hard. I tears up a lot of my Ernie Ball strings at night. I have to keep them by the stack. I tears into my guitar with my whole heart, soul, and body. When I decided in 1967 to go professional, traveling as a leader, I left a day job driving a tow truck. And my boss told me, "Whenever you feel like coming back, you don't have to ask for a job. Just come in here and punch your time clock." And I do my guitar the same way. I feel towards my music just like I did when I was working. If I'm going to do it, I want to do it to death.

Was that your last day job?

Yeah. I went on vacation in 1967, and the manager I had then, Dick Waterman, told me, "The people love you out there." I said, "How could they love me? They don't know who I am. I just want to make sure I don't starve." My mother and father were living then, and I wanted to try to help them. I didn't trust myself on the road, as sometimes now I doubt my playing, even though Eric and them make those statements about it. But I think it's proven itself now. When I go places, quite a few people will be there saying, "I want to hear you." That lifts me a lot. And when I left on vacation that time, I went to Ann Arbor, Michigan. I had three pieces. I started playing some of my wild licks, and you could hear the kids between songs saying, "He's been listening to Hendrix." And then another guy would say, "No, that's who Hendrix got his influence from." So, they got to me and said, "You listen to Hendrix?" And I said, "Who is Hendrix?" And this kid looks like, "You've got to be crazy if you don't know who that is." So I said, "I've got to find out who this is."

So I go to Toronto, my next stop, at an outdoor festival called Mariposa. There was about 30,000 people there, and naturally I got shaky nervous. A.C. Reed said, "Man, go burn them. If they don't know you now, they'll know you when you finished." So I said, "Okay, man, if you say so, I'm going to *try*." And I decided to jump off the stage. I thought there was a brace to brace myself back when I leaped off, but there wasn't nothing there

but a curtain. But it so happened that I didn't fall; the curtain saved me. So I said to myself, "The best thing to do is don't stop playing." When I came from under there, there was 30,000 people hollering, "That's Buddy Guy. That's the real Buddy Guy."

Did you ever meet Hendrix?

Yes, I did. I've got a film of it now. The night Dr. Martin Luther King got assassinated, I saw a kid come in with a big hat on and ease up to the stage with a tape recorder. And some amateur cameraman was spotting his video on him. This was in New York City, and they were yelling about him being Jimi Hendrix. I was just doing what I had to do, and he said, "Pay them no mind. I've been trying to catch you. I canceled a show in London just to come see you play, because I'd never seen you. But I heard you, and I stole a lot of licks from you." As a matter of fact, a kid just came in the club and said, "I've got a tape I want to show you: Hendrix on his knees, taping your licks and watching you play with your mouth, with the guitar under your feets, and different things like that."

Did you get some of that from Guitar Slim?

I got all of it from Guitar Slim. I don't want to make a comment about what some other guitar players would say, but Guitar Slim and T-Bone Walker are some of the people I copied for *showmanship*. B.B. King, he don't have to do nothing but just shake his left hand and everybody will listen. But the first time I saw Guitar Slim, a guy brought him in on his shoulders like a little baby. And he had on a red suit — I got one back there now for tonight — with some white shoes. And when I heard him, I said, "My God! This is the way a guitar should be played."

If you're not going to give it all you've got, you shouldn't play anymore, because you owe this to the people. Your fans are your supporters. Don't hold nothing back from them. You owe them everything that they come to see. And strangely enough, since I've been professional, I haven't missed a gig yet. I had the flu last night enough for the average guitar player to say, "Get somebody in my place," and stay

> *Jimi Hendrix told Buddy, "I stole a lot of licks from you."*

at home. But I think somebody was sitting there last night saying, "I wants to see Buddy. I wants to see him play." And I owe that to him. I'm going to come if I have to come on my knees and play.

What should a Buddy Guy solo be all about?

Muddy Waters, T-Bone, Guitar Slim, and B.B. King, and Eric Clapton. I could name them for an hour.

And yet you don't sound like any of them.

I guess that's the Buddy Guy coming out in me then, but I be hitting the same strings, the same fingering of the board, that they do. And the same thing goes for them. You know, I can't be a B.B. King. I can't be an Eric, even though I try a lot. I wonder a lot — what's my problem about not getting records out? So I try to be everybody up there at once — even John Lee Hooker and Lightnin' Hopkins. And please believe me, I'm not lying: Even before I go out tonight, all of these people will cross my mind just as I pick up my guitar. It looks like they're telling me, "Go get it, Buddy. Do it!" Because without those people, I don't even know if I would be playing. Yes, they were sending a message to me while they were alive, and I think they're still sending it to me now, saying, "You've got to play. We left this load on your shoulders, and you've got to carry on." Matter of fact, Muddy told me that two weeks before he passed. I heard he was sick, and Junior Wells and I called him. I said, "We're on our way to your house." He said, "Don't come, because I'm doing fine. Just don't let the blues die." And the next time I heard, it was the international press saying, "How do you feel about Muddy passing?" And I couldn't say nothing for a day. I just sat there. I just couldn't believe it. You know, those things are going to happen to all of us.

Do any conversations with Muddy stand out in your mind?

Yes. I was very shy when I started. I wouldn't sing, but I would play if you'd corner me off, and I'd play well. And Muddy went out there one night and

> "**M**uddy slapped me and said, 'I don't want to hear that from you. You gonna play.'"

said, "Gee, that guy can play," but when he called me out of the room, I just shied back in the corner and said, "Pay him no mind, man. He's just talking like that." And he just turned around and slapped me, man! And it was hard enough for me to say, "Why are you doing that?" He said, "I don't want to hear that from you. You gonna play." After that he just took over like a daddy to me, man.

As a matter of fact, Muddy was the one.... I was going on my third day without eating in Chicago, trying to borrow a dime to call my mom to get back to Louisiana. And Muddy Waters bought me a salami sandwich and put me in the back of his 1958 Chevy station wagon. He said, "You're hungry, and I know it." And talking to Muddy Waters, I wasn't hungry anymore; I was full just for him to say, "Hey." I was so overjoyed about it, my stomach wasn't cramping anymore. I told him that, and Muddy said, "Get in the goddamn car." Yes, he's dead and gone, and that's exactly what he told me. This happened at the famous 708 Club, and he was parked in front of the club. And then he said, "Sit down and eat." I said, "Yes, sir!" [Laughs.] I wish he were here now. I thanked him many times before he passed away, and told him how much better I felt after he slapped me and made me eat that sandwich that night.

And then later he just walked up to Junior [Wells] and grabbed him in the collar and went to slapping him. Junior said, "Why are you doing that to me?" And Muddy said, "Remember you used to stay at my house? And remember you pulled your knife on me?" Junior had pulled a knife on him because the whole band was staying at his house, and he found out that the drummer or somebody didn't pay him rent, so Junior felt that he shouldn't pay no rent. [Laughs.] Muddy said, "I got you where you don't have the knife now, and I'll whoop your ass!" And he starts spanking Junior all in the face. Junior wasn't saying nothing, just holding his head down. I said, "You going to fight back, Junior?" He said, "No, I ain't going to fool with that old man." [Laughs.]

Yeah, good old man. He could spank me now if he was here. I wouldn't say nothing but laugh and go drink me some beer behind that man. [*Laughs.*] Yeah, I deserve a spanking from somebody that great, man, because those people paved the way for the electric music that we play now. I don't know if anybody else would give them that credit, but them, and the Chess Records, left a great trail for us to follow. Yes, they did.

You recorded with Muddy early in your career.

Yes, I did. He had heard about me because I'd played a set or two with a horn player by the name of Rufus Foreman, and Magic Sam had seen me play. And the word was just getting around: "This little black guy from Louisiana can play, man. He's playing these Muddy Waters tunes." Naturally, that's what I was playing — B.B. or Muddy or Jimmy Reed. It just caught on, and they took me in like a kid. For instance, for one of Muddy's albums, Leonard Chess said, "I want to go way back and have an acoustic album," and I got to play on that [*Folk Singer*]. As a matter of fact, I'm fixing to do some things with Eric Clapton the first week in February [1990], and from then on I'm going to do two or three songs each and every night with my acoustic. Because it takes me back to the sound that you can't take away from the guitar.

Is *Folk Singer* one of your favorite albums?

Yes, but everything I did with Muddy Waters is my favorite. Everything I ever did with that guy, man, was like an experience to me. I often tell young people right now that those are some shoes that never will be fulfilled. I used to listen to that guy sing "Got My Mojo Working," and it was like my mother sewing on a sewing machine. She would make her feet make the stitches, and she never would stick her finger when she pushed under that needle. And that's just the way he would sing "Mojo Working." And whatever he sang, he could make me sit there all night. During those days, there wasn't hardly a club in Chicago that didn't stay open until 5:00 in the morning. And you better believe they had to kick me out of it, because I

couldn't miss a lick of it. [*Laughs.*] My manager gave me an album of everything he ever recorded [*The Chess Box*], and I can go lie down on my floor now and put them one by one, and don't miss nothing he said or what he played.

Do you own a lot of records?

Not so much of the new stuff. Not much of my stuff. But him, and B.B. King, and the Wolf.

What records do you treasure the most?

"Sweet Little Angel" by B.B. King, and Muddy Waters' catalog. And I got everything Eric ever played, him and Stevie, and all of the guys. I think we listen to each other a lot. And when we meet, that makes us communicate better, too.

Stevie Ray covered your "Leave My Girl Alone" during his tour with Jeff Beck.

Yeah, he's a great friend of mine. Matter of fact, he came here as a special guest on my birthday. He walks in the door, and these people just go crazy. And now he tells me just call him; anytime he's available, he will come sit in here with me to help keep the club going.

Your version of "Leave My Girl Alone" has one of your characteristic sounds—the double-stop with a constant high note over a hammer-on in the lower voice.

It's kind of like an octave with two fingers. You pick the two strings at the same time, but they're different notes. I could probably show you better than I could explain it to you. I don't have long fingers, but I can stretch over almost five frets. I can play the A note on the E string, and take the G string and go five frets down and drag the little finger back up and play those octaves all the way back up until the fingers go together, plucking two strings at the same time.

What's the secret to playing those Buddy Guy wildman bends?

> "*I* got everything Eric ever played, him and Stevie, and all of the guys. I think we listen to each other a lot. And when we meet, that makes us communicate better."

I use my third finger. It seems to be the strongest one. It's hard for me to explain what I'll be doing, but when I'm up there trying to please that audience, I can bend it from here to the front door of this place [laughs]. Eric mentioned something about that once. I just will bend it until it breaks. I'll make the little E kiss the big E. Yes, and if it sounds good, I'll keep getting it. And if it sounds bad, I just try to make it sound good.

Do you back that third finger up with other fingers?

I don't have to. You just have to practice and get your fingers real strong. I'm not the best guitar player. I've got a lot I should learn, or could learn, but I always thought that other finger has to be ready for something else. I can't just depend on it on that string, because if you stay on that one string, you'll wear your welcome out. So I have to stretch it, make it kiss the E, and go grab another one and take it somewhere else. I try to make the best that I can out of it.

Describe how you add vibrato.

You mean with the left hand? It's similar to what B.B. King does, rocking back and forth with the hand, but I'm not as good as him. I don't think anybody can do that as well as he can, and we talked about that. As a matter of fact, last year was the first time I opened the show for him — twice — and you better believe I had to hurry up and get my front-row seat so I could try to get some tips on that man. This guy invented the squeezing. T-Bone was playing the neck of the guitar, but when B.B. started squeezing that guitar, we *all* started squeezing that thing. I have to give it to him, because I got more into guitar than I'd ever been. I was just so in love with playing blues, I would play Lightnin' Hopkins and T-Bone. And then when he squeezed the guitar, I said, "Jesus Christ! Who is this?" And when I saw him, I thought I had a lot to learn. And I'm still like that [laughs].

How far back does your knowledge of blues go?

"When B.B. squeezed the guitar, I said, 'Jesus Christ! Who is this?' And When I saw him, I thought I had a lot to learn."

Are you familiar with players from the 1920s?

Yes. Strangely enough, I'm one of the luckiest blues guitar players alive, in that respect, because I had a chance to play with Arthur Crudup in Australia. We went on tour together. I had a chance to play with Fred McDowell. And Son House, who just passed a year-and-a-half ago; I understand he taught Muddy. [Ed. Note: Buddy appeared with Son on a 1960s television show called Camera Three.] So what else can you ask for if you're a guitar player and had a chance to sit down with *this* guy and play? Those are the kind of things that keep us all going.

When do you play your best?

When I'm not trying to be my best. When I'm not pressing myself to try to make this audience get into what I'm doing. I feel like I'm not doing a good job if I don't see them smiling or saying, "Yes." For example, when we first started going to Europe playing blues, the Europeans were like, "We take this as a *serious* music, almost like opera." Nobody said anything or patted their feet — nothing. I was thinking, "Oh, Jesus. I'm not doing nothing right now. Maybe I got to flip out or do something." Then I got booed. I talked to Muddy again, and he said, "Don't feel bad. It happened to me." When [promoter] Chris Barber took Muddy back to England for the first time, they booed him for playing this loud stuff through the amp! They invited him back the next year, and he left the amp and took the acoustic guitar, and they booed him for not playing the amp! [Laughs.] The same thing happened to me in Germany. I had to go stepping out in front of Roosevelt Sykes, John Lee Hooker, and Big Mama Thornton, and they would just boo every time they'd see me. I said, "Oh, my God!" Me being shy, man, I was just like going under the table. And then when I went back, I said, "I know what I'll do. I'll get me a chair and sit down like John Lee and them and play." I went back, and they got me the same way they did Muddy. They said, "No, no. You've got to get out there and move around. That's what we're looking for now." It takes you so long to figure out what they're saying, unless someone comes up and translates it for you.

You're said to be one of the first Chicago blues guitarists to play standing up.

When I came to Chicago, everybody was sitting down: Muddy, Junior, the Wolf, Walter, and all of them were in chairs playing this beautiful music that still is the best blues you ever heard of. And we used to have the Battle of the Guitars. I was the poorest, and I told them I needed the more-est [laughs]. Most of the bandstands used to be behind the bar, and Muddy, Wolf, or Walter would play in their chairs. So I said, "Oh, jeez, these guys is playing way more than I can play. I got to figure out something else to do to be a winner." The winner got a bottle of whiskey, and at that time I didn't drink whiskey. I had a little friend who weighed about 300, and he said, "I'll make you win this whiskey, because I don't have a nickel." It was snowing, and he said, "You remember that thing you told me Guitar Slim used to do?" I had this 150-foot lead wire, and he said, "I'm going to take this wire outside, and you sit in the car. I'm going to plug it in while you're in the car. You come out of this car playing and sliding in the snow, and we got the whiskey." I said, "That's not going to win it, but I'm going to do it."

And when they called me, I stepped out of the car. He opened the door and said, "You all want to see him, come out here." The place was packed, and I had the streets full. So when I walked in, there was Magic Sam and a few more guitar players — including Earl Hooker, who is the greatest guitar player that I ever saw. They had the bottle of whiskey, and it was empty. They told me, "You won it, but we done drinked it all!" [Laughs.] The club owner came out and picked me up and stood me on the bar, and I walked straight down the bar. And then he said, "Here's another bottle of whiskey." And that little guy looked at me and said, "Let's go to the bathroom." And I went in the men's bathroom and played for about 45 minutes solo!

Wasn't that called "headcutting"?

Yes, but I don't think I would outplay anybody. It was just like a winner in a contest. We didn't have just one judge saying, "Buddy, you won it." The audience would clap, and it was kind of like something on TV a long time ago, when they'd show a gauge needle move according to how loud the audience clapped. After a while it got to the point where they'd say, "Well, I don't care who wins it, we're going to drink it anyway, because he doesn't drink!" [Laughs.] So I learned a lot from that, and I got a lot of experience from it. Those guys like Earl Hooker, man, they couldn't jump around and run up and down the bar like I did, and that's the advantage I took of them.

No one ever played slide like Earl Hooker.

No. I found one of Muddy's tunes in this collection I've got, and he had Hooker playing on it. As it struck, my guitar player said, "Listen to Muddy!" I said, "That's not Muddy; that's Earl Hooker. Nobody plays it that clean, and you don't hear nothing but the strings."

What did he use for a slide?

I got it! I got his slide in my pocket at home, and I sleep with that thing. It's just a piece of pipe like anybody else used.

You're not usually associated with slide guitar.

I learned a little of Muddy's slide, but it don't ever come out. I'm embarrassed to come out with it. After I heard Earl Hooker play slide, I put that thing I was using in my pocket — it was a bottleneck — and I said, "I don't even want to see that no more, the way this guy plays."

> "After I heard Earl Hooker, I put my bottleneck in my pocket and said, 'I don't even want to see that no more, the way this guy plays.'"

Did you ever play in open tuning?

No, I never did. When I finally met B.B. King, he took me to his hotel room — I didn't even use a straight pick then, I was using fingerpicks — and he told me, "If you want to get a little faster, you have to start practicing with a straight pick." And from him telling me that, I would have one ever since.

You hold the pick with your thumb and two fingers.

Because I can switch it into my palm, and you won't miss it. All of a sudden, I'm picking with my fingers. My pick's like a small triangle. I have to buy them by the thousands because I break them. [*Pulls a Gibson medium rounded-triangle from his pocket.*] That's a heavyweight; the thin is the one I use mostly. I also have a [coffee-colored] Buddy Guy pick that I give away to people as souvenirs.

Do you always know what you're doing in musical terms?

No.

Do you know the names of chords?

A few. F, F#, and flats, and so on like that. You learn that through the years.

Do you always know what key you're playing in?

Yes. You have to know that. But if you'd asked me what did I just play before I left the stage, each note — no, I couldn't tell you. But I could go back and get the guitar and find it and tell you what note I played.

If you're in the key of A, for instance, will you automatically solo in a certain area of the fingerboard?

Yes. I know exactly where I want to be. On all of the new guitars — except the acoustics — you've got several places you can play A. I play A in the middle of the neck on the 5th fret, and then you can go to the high A, which is *way* up there. You start all over again at E when you get higher [at the 12th fret]. It goes, E, F, the same as it is at the beginning of the neck. I don't run enough in the different positions on my guitar like a lot of people do. For instance, George Benson is one of the greatest I've seen; he can do that from top to bottom. I have a tendency to stay there and wear a hole in the neck of my guitar [*laughs*] and just play one sound. Oh, that sounds so good! Someone stole my first Strat from me, and Eric had asked me about buying it. I had wore that neck almost through, and I didn't want to get it redone because I wanted it to stay

> *"I have a tendency to stay there and wear a hole in the neck of my guitar and just play one sound."*

original, just like it was.

You're now endorsing Fender and Guild.

Yes. I started with a Strat in the beginning. Guitar Slim was tearing 'em up every time I saw him — that's just the kind of wild man he was — and I wanted to be like him so much, I just went into that. And that guitar was built to take it. I finally went to Newport in 1967, and the owner of Guild offered me an endorsement. What else could I ask for? He walks up and says, "You come over to the factory tomorrow; we're going to give you a guitar." And I started playing the Guild guitar. Then B.B. King walked in in New York and said, "I see you got a little Lucille." [*Laughs.*] It was red, and that was enough to make me stick with playing that. It was a semi-hollow Starfire. Now I have a Nightingale. They made one for Eric and one for me. Mine is number 002.

I pop so many strings from playing so darn hard that I have to keep two or three guitars up there to make sure the few fans I got don't miss anything. When I break a string, I don't want to take that time in between and have them missing that note. My guy just hands me another guitar while he puts the string on the other one.

What's your favorite guitar?

The two I'm playing, the Fender and the Guild.

Does your tone change when you use a wireless?

Yes, a bit. Actually, a cord is as true as the acoustic guitar. It gives you the truer sound.

What's your favorite setup from the guitar?

I'm using a Marshall amp. Different clubs will call for you to do different sets on the amp. Sometimes you can be too loud, and normally I will ask the audience, "Am I too loud, or am I too soft?" because I do play very soft sometimes. And then you get the mixed emotions. Some will say, "You're too loud," and then the other half will say, "You're not loud enough." So then I just back up from the mike and tell a big lie, like, "I'm going to do it my way anyway!" I usually use a Marshall 800 amp, but they just sent me the new two-piece head. My soundman hooked it up for me last night and said, "Go for it!" I kind of liked it, but I've got to learn it and play with it for a while. Then I'll be able to get my different sounds and things that *I* like best out of that myself. I play for the people, and if it calls for it, I'll use a wah-wah or an octave [divider]. I'm not trying to be like anybody else.

Do you modify your Strats?

No, this one I have now is special-made for me. They made one for Eric Clapton, and they called me in there to pick out the neck and the kind I want. And without even knowing what he had, I just went for this. They said it was too close to put out a Buddy Guy model or something like that, but it's a bit different from what he picked out.

Some players insist that old Strats are the best.

Well, I've talked to quite a few of the engineers, and they will tell you it's just like the car now compared to the cars in the '40s and '50s. You could run one of those old cars into these things we got now, and that car out of the '50s is going to have a scratch and the one we're riding in now is going to have the grille knocked out because it's plastic. So what they told me is that it's the same thing as talking about guitars. The material's not the same. The wood that they're making them out of now is not the same. And why is that? I don't know.

Actually, I was in Africa in 1969 with my original Strat. We were riding in a station wagon, and it was tied on the top of the station wagon. They was driving 85 and 90 miles an hour, and the guitar flew off and fell out of the case. We backed up to get it, and a car was coming. I laid in the street to make sure the car would go around. The guy said, "African people will run over you, man! They don't care nothing about it." And the only string that was out of tune was the E. [*Laughs.*] It got scratched all up, but it was still in tune.

That guitar got stolen?

Yes, some kid broke into my house when I was living here in Chicago, and I guess I cried as long as I did when my mother passed. The lady next door was a nice old lady, which was the kid's mother, and I guess he was so embarrassed. I even asked him why did he sell it — I would've bought it again. I would even give the guy more than what he got for it. He left his mother's keys in the apartment, and the police said, "Whoever broke into here left the keys," and his mother said, "Those are my keys, and my son did it." Her husband was very sick, and I was loaning her money every month, and she owed me. She said, "Well, I'll have to pay you," and I cried more then. I said, "There's no way you could pay me." I wouldn't even accept it from her, because she didn't do it; she was a very nice lady. As a matter of fact, I talked to her a couple of days ago.

> "*I* just have this good feeling about blues music and what I'm doing, and I feel like I should try it, man, try it."

Do you have a guitar at home?

Yeah, a lot of them. I got one in the bed with me now, 12-string acoustic. I use heavier strings at home; that keeps the muscles in my fingers a little stronger.

What do you play when you're by yourself?

I will put the slide on sometimes. If you catch me practicing at home, I hit a few licks that I hit here onstage. And to be honest with you, a lot of stuff you see me do onstage, I've never done it before. Everything I do onstage comes to me right then. I just have this good feeling about blues music and what I'm doing, and I feel like I should *try* it, man, try it. Actually, a lot of the sustained notes that you hear us all doing now — and Hendrix said he was getting this from me — I was doing out in the public early on. Chess Records called it *noise*; they wouldn't let me cut it. They was telling me, "Who's going to listen to that noise?" And where did I get the idea from? Once I took a break and forgot to cut my guitar off, and this lady passed by with a wide skirt. The jukebox was going with a tune I liked — I had punched it — and her dress tail hit the G string, and this guitar just stayed there, humming in G, the whole time that record was going. I got the idea from that to just hold this sustained note. That had to be '59, or something like that. If you love it like I do, boom! I can just be sitting there listening, and all of a sudden somebody will hit something, and I'll jump and say, "What was that?" It's just like a good-looking woman will pass, and you can't keep your eyes off.

What's the best band you ever had?

If I had to name the best people that I ever played with in my life, I would name the guys traveling with me in about 1967: A.C. Reed, [tenor saxophonist] Bobby Fields, who passed away, a bass player named Jack Meyers, and a drummer named Glen McTeer. But I would have to put Fred Below and Otis Spann in, too. Those guys taught me a whole lot, just about being a musician. Below used to look up and curse at me, and he would be counting. You could hear him playing drums, "A-one, two, three...." And when I'd make a mistake, he would tell me right then [laughs]. A funny story: When we used to be recording at Chess, they built a pen to put Below in, because Below would interfere with the other musicians, telling them what to play! Oh, man, how I wish nobody had to die, when it comes to something like Below and Otis Spann. Otis Spann would set a bottle of whiskey on a piano and tell me, "If you don't take a drink of this, you ain't going to let the soul out of you." Yeah, they was the best I ever seen, man. They corrected me in so many *wrong* things I was doing in my earlier days. If I was playing a bad time, they would tell me, "You got to clean that up."

Is that where your good sense of rhythm comes from?

I don't know if that's the case. I would listen to them. And right now, I listen to these kids if they tell me something. I've never gotten to the point of, "You can't tell me nothing!" In anything I do, I'm listening. There's people working for me in the club right now. If they tell me something, I don't jump up and say, "Oh, no, this is *my* club. I want it this way; I want it that way." They'll hear, and I've got to listen. That's the way it should be.

You never rehearse your band.

[*Laughs.*] You know, that's a bad habit. But I like for my guys to be free. I don't hold anybody *down* back there behind me. And tonight I'm going to do the same thing. Let them go, let them loose. On a given night, they're going to give me the best that they can. I didn't ever rehearse with Muddy or any of them. They would tell me, "Go get it, Buddy." Matter of fact, I was playing with B.B. King at Bill Graham's Fillmore West one night, and he said, "I'm going to play, but I want *you* to put on a show."

Do any of your children play guitar?

I got one son, 19 years old. He came to me about a year-and-a-half ago and said, "Daddy, give me one of them guitars. I'm going to play Prince." I gave him a big amplifier and a guitar, and two weeks later I went over, and this guy was playing this thing about the doves on Prince ["When Doves Cry"]. And he looked at me and laughed. He's as much shy as I was when I was a youngster. He said, "I got Prince, now who else should I listen to, Daddy?" I said, "Well, if you like Prince that well, you better find Hendrix. I'll look out for some stuff for you." And before I found anything, he had found a Hendrix show on an educational channel. He came back; he was crying. He said, "Daddy, you know the first thing Hendrix said?" I said, "What?" He said, "He said he learned something from you. I didn't know you could play that." I said, "You didn't ever ask me, son. If you had, I could've told you I gets wild." He never could just see me in person, and I don't have anything on television that he could see. I finally sneaked him in a club and he saw me play, and he cried a little more. I done wrote a song like that, too: My child don't know who I am, so how could I expect other young people to know who I am? That's because I don't have records out.

I just hope to hit something one of these days. Maybe somebody will get back to some record company and say, "You better listen to him, and give him another shot at another album." I don't know. If I knew what my problem was, I would correct it. I would like to do a little better financially, because I'm not getting any younger. I want to play as long as I'm alive, and there'll come a time when you need something to carry you as a musician. I've been lucky enough to buy a couple of raggedy buildings, and I pay a retirement-type insurance, because I don't want to be a burden on nobody if I live long enough to survive this. I don't want nobody to say, "We got to take care of him," make collections for me, and different things like that. And in order to do that, you have to make it while you're in good health and try to save some of it for a later day. My mother used to tell me, "Son, always put up a dry stick for a wet day." A blues player like myself has so many ups and downs — more downs than ups.

Despite this, you seem to love your work.

I love it so much, man, I even forgot what down is like. Even when I'm down, I think I'm up. If anybody in the business loves it better than me, they must eat it! [*Laughs.*] All my life, I've been doing what I love, and I'm not going to change that for nothing in the world. I'm having a lot of fun, and I've never been angry enough to do something to somebody in a way that would hurt them. All of my life, I've been in between people. When I'm in clubs and two people are disagreeing and it looks like it's going to get physical, I can get in between them and say, "Why? What do you gain by doing this to each other? Tomorrow you could be best friends. Tomorrow he could do something to save your life. But if you hurt him or kill him, who knows what he could have done? He's not there to do it."

The world is so tangled with so much craziness. I think we need to be loved a little more than we do. That's why I'm so thankful for my music. At least I draw people together and try to put smiles on their faces. I'm so tired of frowns and fighting. One day I hope the whole world could just look and smile. Yes, especially when I play a note on my guitar!

A SELECTED
BUDDY GUY DISCOGRAPHY

Solo albums: *A Man & The Blues*, Vanguard; *Hold That Plane*, Vanguard; *This Is Buddy Guy*, Vanguard; *I Was Walking Through The Woods*, Chess; *Left My Blues In San Francisco*, Chess; *Buddy Guy*, Chess; *First Time I Met The Blues*, Chess Japan; *In The Beginning*, Red Lightnin'; *The Dollar Done Fell*, JSP; *Breaking Out*, JSP; *Buddy & Philip Guy*, JSP; *D.J. Play My Blues*, JSP; *Live At The Checkerboard Lounge*, JSP; *Ten Blue Fingers*, JSP; *Stone Crazy*, Alligator.

Buddy Guy & Junior Wells: *Buddy Guy & Junior Wells Play The Blues*, Atco; *Buddy And The Juniors*, Blue Thumb; *Drinkin' TNT, Smokin' Dynamite*, Blind Pig; *The Original Blues Brothers*, Intermedia; *Going Back*, Isabel (acoustic); *Live In Montreux*, Black And Blue.

With Junior Wells: *Hoodoo Man Blues*, Delmark; *Southside Blues Jam*, Delmark; *It's My Life, Baby*, Vanguard; *Chicago/The Blues/Today! Vol. 1*, Vanguard; *Coming At You*, Vanguard; *Live Recording*, Bourbon.

With Muddy Waters: *Folk Singer*, Chess; *The Chess Box*, Chess; *Baby Please Don't Go*, Chess France; *The Super Super Blues Band*, Chess Japan.

With Howlin' Wolf: *Chester Burnett A.K.A. Howlin' Wolf*, Chess; *The Real Folk Blues* (Buddy plays bass on "Built For Comfort" and "Three Hundred Pounds Of Joy"), Chess.

With others: Big Mama Thornton, *In Europe*, Arhoolie; Sonny Boy Williamson, *More Real Folk Blues*, Chess; Koko Taylor, *Koko Taylor*, Chess.

Anthologies (on Chess, except as indicated): *The Blues, Volume 1*; *The Blues, Volume 2*; *Folk Festival Of The Blues*; *Chess Masters*; *Blues From Big Bill's Copa Cabana*; *Chicago Blues Anthology*; *Chess Blues Rarities*; *The Golden Age Of Chicago Blues*; *Second Time I Met The Blues*; *The Best Of The Chicago Blues*, Vanguard; *Chicago Blues*, Red Lightnin'; *Atlantic Blues: Chicago*, Atlantic; *Guitar Workshop*, Pausa; *Tenth Anniversary Anthology, Vol. 1 — Live From Antone's*, Antone's; *Bringing You All The Best In Blues*, Antone's.

On film: *Supershow* ('69, three cuts); *Chicago Blues* ('70, solo and with Muddy Waters); *En Remontant Le Mississippi/Out Of The Blacks, Into The Blues* ('71 West German/French film featuring "Ships On The Ocean"); *The Blues Alive* (with John Mayall's '82 Bluesbreakers reunion tour; RCA/Columbia Home Video); *Rainin' In My Heart* (PBS documentary, '87).

J.B. Hutto

March 1979

BY DAN FORTE

PAUL OLIVER'S BOOK *THE STORY Of The Blues* is probably as close to a definitive source as has been written about the idiom. But almost as valuable as the painstakingly comprehensive text is the extensive selection of photographs — each offering a rare insight into the lifestyle and environment surrounding the people who played or listened to the blues. For example, there's a 1966 glimpse of slide guitarist J.B. Hutto playing at Turner's Blue Lounge on 39th and Indiana in Chicago's South Side, a club which Oliver describes as "a rough joint."

Judging by the picture, the late author must have been a master of understatement. Hutto, in short sleeves and sunglasses, sits on a tiny stage barely a couple of feet higher than dance-floor level. The reason he's not standing is obvious: If he did, his head might bump the low ceiling. Next to him a middle-aged black couple, dressed as informally as the musician, are boogie woogie-ing. On the stark back wall hangs a burned-out Schlitz sign next to some crude ventilation system. Hutto doesn't seem to be too excited about whatever he's playing on his cheap Kay electric; his expression is more like that of a graveyard-shift fry cook flipping hamburgers — just someone doing his job. But in spite of his weary countenance, J.B. Hutto was and is one of the most inventive and individual slide guitarists to emerge from the school popularized by his chief mentor, the late Elmore James.

The blues has been J.B.'s occupation off and on for nearly 30 years. Born Joseph Benjamin Hutto in Blackville, South Carolina, J.B. was raised in Augusta, Georgia, from the age of three. With his three brothers and three sisters, J.B. formed a gospel group, the Golden Crowns, and sang at the local Galilee Baptist and Holy Trinity churches; J.B. sang lead or second lead.

As far as the blues was concerned, Hutto recalls, "I listened to the majority of the blues records out then, but I wasn't playing that. I guess I was too young, anyway. I listened to them and liked them, but I wasn't really attracted to no kind of music until I hit Chicago." This is evidenced by the fact that J.B.'s resultant style sounds basically like

electrified Mississippi Delta blues — whining guitar, percussive attack, and hollering vocals — and reflects none of the qualities found in the sort of ragtime blues played on the Eastern Seaboard.

When J.B.'s father died in 1949, the family moved to Chicago, and it was there at the age of 20 that Hutto became involved with the blues. "I was kind of young," admits J.B., "and I didn't know about people playing in clubs and things of that nature — so I was still looking for house parties, fish fries, and things like that. But there wasn't nothing happening. I began to make a few friends and began to talk, and they showed me around, and I started going to the clubs, seeing bands."

Hutto's first instrument was drums, which he played with Johnny Ferguson And His Twisters. "I played drums, but I was singing, too," he reminisces. "Johnny was the leader, and he had a guitar. But when he'd lay it down I had it." J.B. met one-man band Eddie Hines, better known as "Porkchop," and the two (with Hutto on guitar) played on Maxwell Street at the open-air flea market known as Jew Town.

From the very start, J.B. played strictly electric guitar. Asked to describe his early style, he shrugs, "I can't explain it; I'll have to show you. [*He plays a dirge-like blues in standard tuning using a lot of open strings and sounding a bit like Lightnin' Hopkins.*] I didn't know how to come up here and maybe bend a string, then get back down here to catch it. But that's where I was coming from."

After hearing Elmore James, Hutto became enchanted with the sound of the electric slide guitar and set out to play it almost exclusively. "He was the cat who made me see what I wanted to do," declares the pupil. "He raised me. He could pick some, but he didn't do too much picking. I think he was like me — he liked that slide. If I could make this thing slide and cry like I want to, maybe I wouldn't do so much picking."

Hutto and Porkchop soon formed a band, and during the early '50s they played clubs like the Globetrotter and the 1015 Club. As Mike Rowe describes it in his book *Chicago Breakdown*: "J.B. blew upon the Chicago scene with one of the noisiest and toughest bands ever. Singing in the fierce, declamatory style of his idol, Elmore James, and backed by the heavily amplified guitar of Joe Custom, the crude harp of George Maywether, and

the elemental percussion of Maxwell Street's Porkchop, they sounded ready to devour anything in sight!"

J.B. spent a lot of time with James, listening and learning, but while virtually every blues slide player owes a huge debt to Elmore, Hutto soon found his own voice — with a more varied single-note guitar approach and a more primitive, wild vocal style. In 1954 Hutto got his first opportunity to record, for the Chance label, under the name J.B. And His Hawks, a moniker his various groups have carried over the years. With his first 78, "Now She's Gone," the guitarist established himself as a powerful bandleader and a highly personal lyricist.

But almost as quickly as he had appeared on the scene, J.B. vanished from it around 1954 after recording a mere nine sides for Chance, only six of which were ever issued. The reason for his hiatus can perhaps be found in an anecdote related in Mike Rowe's book: "J.B. lost his guitar when a woman broke it over her husband's head, and he quit music for the quieter life of an undertaker."

Not until the mid '60s did Hutto re-emerge, but he seemed none the worse for the 10-year layoff. Producer Sam Charters recorded the Hawks — Hutto, bassist Herlan Hassell, and drummer Frank Kirkland — in 1965 for Vanguard Records' *Chicago/The Blues/Today!* The session featured J.B.'s composition "Too Much Alcohol." Recordings for Testament, Delmark, and other independent labels followed, and the early '70s found Hutto touring blues festivals across the country and overseas (where he also recorded a couple of albums).

A number of different guitars have gone through J.B.'s hands over the years, and he doesn't seem overly concerned with model names and numbers. Until recently J.B.'s main axe was a Fender Telecaster with the finish worn away at the top frets, near the cutaway, due to Hutto's habit of riding the slide up past the neck (near the rhythm pickup) to obtain higher notes. That problem was partially alleviated with J.B.'s most recent change in guitars, when he purchased a solidbody Epiphone with a longer neck and deeper cutaway. The two-pickup model is usually set with just the treble pickup or both pickups on.

After some experimentation, Hutto settled on an open-*D* tuning. "I used to be a one-key man," he confesses. "Tuned it in open *E* [*E B E G# B E*, low to high], and for anything else I used a clamp, a capo. But I had to tune it *up* to E, so now I tune it down to *D* [same as open *E* but one whole-step lower on each string]. I don't like my action too high; I don't move the strings up or down. If they're too high, I get a kind of grating sound; if they're too low, naturally you're going to hit the frets."

J.B.'s current amp is a Fender Super Reverb, and as for his slide, he explains, "I used to cut off a piece of pipe with a hacksaw. Now they're selling slides all over in music stores, so I bought one. I tried playing with a glass slide, but it didn't work. I play with it on my little finger, and now I've got two metal slides, a thin one and a heavier one that has a great tone — that really brings the sound out; it almost sounds like two notes. I can't find any as heavy as this one."

Unlike Elmore James, who used a flatpick, Hutto plays with a plastic fingerpick on his index finger, along with a thumbpick. "Elmore played with a flatpick," J.B. explains, "but he could use anything — flatpick or finger and thumb. But I think playing slide is good for playing with the thumb — Hound Dog Taylor used to play with the thumb. You can always catch the strings better. If I play very long without a pick, a knot will swell up on that finger. One night overseas our stuff was late, and we had to play a college gig with new instruments — no picks, no nothing. The next day I had to stick my finger in alcohol to cool it off."

J.B.'s current repertoire includes many of his old favorites, new tunes (which he's writing all the time), and blues standards — all played with Hutto's indelible stamp. "I learned to play like nobody," he boasts. "And anything I play, I have to play my way because that's how I learned. Now, you can play just like the other man — that's fine — but in this open tuning it ain't gonna sound the same.

So I just kick off my songs in my beat. Like 'Thrill Is Gone' — it's a beautiful song by B.B. King, and I can do it B.B.'s original way, or I can do it in my version. I'll tell you something about me — I just do my thing. Now, when I play with someone else, what the other man do, I got nothing to do with that. I don't try to outdo him, because we're playing together, making music for the public. When you get over-anxious trying to outdo somebody, you always mess up."

Since the death of Hound Dog Taylor, Hutto has been one of the leaders in a very select group carrying on the Elmore James tradition. Of J.B.'s admiration for Hound Dog Taylor, there is no better indication than the fact that for a time after Taylor's death, Hutto inherited his band, the Houserockers, which was the only time J.B. traveled under a name other than the Hawks.

As for current favorites, though, and younger blues-rock sliders, Hutto sighs, "You hear one, you just about heard them all — the way they're playing now. Black musicians are trying to slip into the disco, trying to put the blues into something else and give it another name. They're carrying the same beat, the same sound, and you got nothing. The older blues, you can hear the changes and feel the changes, you know."

As for J.B. trying to update *his* style or cash in on current trends, purists have little to worry about. Today Hutto is playing the blues in the same loud, raucous, beautifully simple style that has been his trademark since the beginning. "When I got this here guitar," he states, "I loved it. This is what I liked; this is what I wanted. I have to have it with me. Sometimes you can wake up in the morning, and you'll find it laying right there on the pillow beside me."

[*J.B. Hutto passed away in 1983.*]

A SELECTED
J.B. HUTTO DISCOGRAPHY

Solo albums: *Hawk Squat* (1960s and '70s sides), Delmark; *J.B. Hutto & The Hawks* ('66), Testament; *Blues For Fonessa* ('76), Amigo; *Live, Vol. 1* ('77), Charly; *Keeper Of The Flame* ('79), Baron; *Boogie With J.B. Hutto And The Houserockers*, Baron; *Slidewinder*, Delmark; *Slideslinger*, Black And Blue; *Slippin' And Slidin'* ('83), Varrick; *Bluesmaster*, JSP.

Otis Rush

October 1987

BY DAN FORTE

IRONY IS AN ESSENTIAL INGREDIENT of the blues, be it Muddy Waters belting out "You Can't Lose What You Never Had" or Robert Cray singing "Right Next Door." But Otis Rush's career has had more than its share of ironic twists.

After storming onto the Chicago scene in 1956 with "I Can't Quit You, Baby," Rush recorded a short but impressive string of classics for the Cobra label, including "All Your Love (I Miss Loving)," "My Love Will Never Die," and "Double Trouble." Anyone familiar with the work of Eric Clapton or Stevie Ray Vaughan will recognize that this handful of sides cut for Cobra over a two-year period sealed Rush's status as a major influence. Clapton's milestone *Blues Breakers* album with John Mayall included a version of "All Your Love," and he later recorded "Double Trouble," the song after which Vaughan named his band. Otis' influence goes much further, however; just listen to Peter Green's composition "Black Magic Woman" with the original Fleetwood Mac on *Black Magic Woman* — not to mention the playing of Robert Cray, Jimmie Vaughan, Ronnie Earl, Anson Funderburgh, Luther Allison, and the late Magic Sam. As Allison once told *Guitar Player*, "I'll put Otis Rush next to any guitar player or any vocalist in *any* bag of music."

Although Rush was signed to the mighty Chess label, home of Bo Diddley, Muddy Waters, and Chuck Berry, the company had its hands full with its established early-'60s hitmakers and recorded only eight songs by Otis in the three years he was under contract — most of them unissued until much later. Rush moved to the Duke label, which had done well for Bobby Blue Bland and Junior Parker, but it released only *one* single — "Homework" — in three years. In late '65 Otis recorded five stunning tracks for Vanguard's fine *Chicago/The Blues/Today!* series, including a more dramatic arrangement of "I Can't Quit You, Baby," which served as the blueprint for versions by John Mayall (the *Crusade* album, with Mick Taylor on guitar) and Led Zeppelin's self-titled debut, with Jimmy Page copping Otis' solo note-for-note. As the British blues movement was coming on strong, one

of its biggest influences didn't even have a recording contract — in fact, had never even released an album under his own name.

Atlantic's Cotillion subsidiary remedied that situation in 1969 with the release of *Mourning In The Morning*. But while it had its moments, the album served to frustrate Otis and loyal fans even more, due to rather heavy-handed production and songwriting by Mike Bloomfield and Nick Gravenites. In 1971, though, Rush signed with Capitol and went into the studio with a liberal budget and a well-rehearsed San Francisco band. The results amounted to his highest points since his Cobra days, with even more consistency. The trouble was, Capitol never released *Right Place, Wrong Time*, which didn't see the light of day until 1976, on the small Bullfrog label. In the liner notes to that package, blues enthusiast Dick Shurman wrote, "His ability as a vocalist and instrumentalist are each remarkable enough separately; the combination of the two is devastating."

A handful of Otis Rush albums were recorded in the following decade, with respectable if not overwhelming results, and in the early '80s frustrations got the better of Otis, who quit performing for nearly two years. Upon his return it was immediately apparent that even while inactive professionally, he had continued to practice and search for new sounds.

Born in Philadelphia, Mississippi, in 1934, Otis began fooling with an acoustic guitar at age 10. "I had an uncle who I used to see play — for his own amusement, not in clubs," he recalls. "I'd be happy when he picked the guitar up. I'm left-handed, see, so I'd take the guitar and flip it over." Like Albert King, Otis crafted his mind-boggling style playing upside-down with the guitar's low strings closest to the floor. He made a couple of attempts at switching to a standard left-handed instrument, but was met with "a lot of confusion."

If Otis has been underrated as a guitarist, it's only because his singing is so powerful. Oddly enough, the gut-wrenching blues singer first sang country music as a child. "I would listen to other

people sing on the radio," he points out, "like Eddy Arnold, the country music singer, and Bill Monroe And The Blue Grass Boys. I'd sing that, too. Maybe I'll record some of that one day, but for now I'm trying to find *my* way. My mother was a church lady, so I sang in church a little bit, and I played guitar in church, too."

A few years after moving to Chicago in 1948, Otis began checking out the local club scene. "Muddy was the first guy I saw — with Elgin Evans on drums, Jimmy Rogers on guitar, and Junior Wells or maybe Little Walter on harmonica. I said, 'Whoa! I got to do that.'"

Eventually he lucked into a steady gig of his own. "I'd just be practicing," he relates, "and the neighbors would lean out the window and say, 'Would you please get out of here with that noise?' But I was really progressing, practicing, and learning — stuff like Muddy Waters, Howlin' Wolf, Jimmy Rogers, John Lee Hooker, B.B. King, T-Bone Walker. I was just listening to everybody back when I was trying to play. One night some guy came and said, 'Who's that guy making that noise up there? I need a guy to come and play at my club tonight. My band stood me up.' So he offered me four or five dollars, and I went and played — at 2711 Wentworth in Chicago. It was by myself, just stomping my foot and playing. He said, 'Come back tomorrow night.' And I came back three or four nights. I was working a day job in a warehouse, and I wasn't getting any sleep, playing nights and working days, so I just turned to the blues. I'd been making a couple hundred dollars a week, and I gave it up to make forty or fifty — just to play."

In 1956 blues songwriter Willie Dixon hooked Otis up with Cobra Records. "He was scouting for them," Rush explains, "and I was playing at the 708 Club with Louis Myers as the Four Aces. Matter of fact, Junior Wells was a part of it for a while. We were playing together two or three years before I cut 'I Can't Quit You, Baby.' A lot of good things happened at that club; that's where I saw Robert Nighthawk."

Otis' first several recordings found him backed by Dixon, pianist Lafayette Leake, and guitarists

> "*I'd been making a couple hundred dollars a week, and I gave it up to make forty or fifty — just to play.*"

Wayne Bennett, Reggie Boyd, or Jody Williams, but for the session that yielded "Double Trouble" he was teamed with the Ike Turner band. "Ike was up there trying to get Cobra to let him do a record. He was there, and I needed musicians to record. They made a little money — helped me out." On "Double Trouble" Turner's exaggerated wang-bar vibrato contrasted with Rush's own distinctive hand-vibrato technique. "He played lead and I played lead, in different places," Otis clarifies.

After recording Dixon's "I Can't Quit You, Baby" and "Groaning The Blues," in Otis' words, "I said, 'Damn, if the people accept that, I can write one better than that.'" He was inspired to write "Double Trouble" after overhearing a woman use the phrase in line at a grocery store. Of his anguished vocal, Mike Rowe wrote in *Chicago Breakdown*, "He approaches the harrowing poetic terror of a Robert Johnson."

From the very start Rush had a more modern, urban sound than the status quo of Chicago blues — Muddy Waters, Howlin' Wolf, and Little Walter. "I was listening to Albert King and B.B. King, really," he shrugs, "and I just sort of went that way — between that and T-Bone Walker and Gatemouth Brown." Songs such as "My Love Will Never Die" anticipated '60s soul ballads. "That was pretty much a church sound," says the guitarist, "a sad sound." Even more progressive was "All Your Love," with its shifting rhythms — from bastardized calypso to shuffle.

After Cobra came a frustrating period of inactivity with Chess, although at least one classic, "So Many Roads," was released. "Chess didn't really need me when they signed me up," he states. "But they get you and handcuff you, you know, where you can't be making records for no one else. They weren't too interested in pushing me; they just wanted control. That's America. After three years with Chess I signed with Duke. I didn't know what I was doing. They promised me the moon and only put out one single. Now I don't sign nothing — just one LP at a time."

Vanguard's three-volume *Chicago/The Blues/Today!* series, with three artists presented per disc, still ranks as one of the best by-products of the mid-'60s blues resurgence. With stellar performances by J.B. Hutto, Homesick James, James Cotton, Walter Horton, Johnny Shines, Johnny Young, Junior Wells, and Otis Spann, Otis Rush's five selections easily rank as the lineup's most progressive and modern. Of particular interest is his instrumental arrangement of Ike and Tina Turner's hit "Think It's Gonna Work Out Fine" (here dubbed "Everything's Going To Turn Out Alright"), with Luther Tucker on rhythm guitar, a position he held with Otis for 10 years, off and on.

Asked about his progressive leanings, Otis downplays his groundbreaking efforts. "That's for people like you to decide," he laughs. "I just play, and I've got sounds — I hear things onstage — and I go home and try to figure them out. I know I'm gonna mess up in places, but sometimes I get away with it. To me, I'm trying to learn how to play. I'm not ashamed to let people know I'm trying to learn. I'm scuffling, trying to find something new, trying to make it off the ground. I'll be reaching for sounds — right onstage. I know I'm going to get caught; that's why you hear a lot of bad notes. I can't just play straight. If I hear something, I go after it. Sometimes it works out; then again, you get some bad collisions [*laughs*], so I try to cover it up. Just like a boxer: You get hit, you got to try to recuperate. I've got some sounds coming around. I got some other things that sound like piano. I'm not bragging; I've just been working on them."

Unlike a lot of "upside-down" players who are strictly soloists, such as Albert King, Rush commands an impressive chord vocabulary. "That's true," he says with uncharacteristic pride. "I went to school a little bit, you know, for chords — just to make me understand my thing. But the guy who was teaching me, Reggie Boyd, wanted to teach me country, which wasn't what I wanted to learn. So I walked out. But he did

> "*If I hear something, I go after it. Sometimes it works out; then again, you get some bad collisions, so I try to cover it up. Just like a boxer: You get hit, you got to try to recuperate.*"

show me some things." Probably Otis' most distinctive stylistic elements are his full-chord bending and his fast, shimmering vibrato, which Jimmie Vaughan dubbed the "singing string" sound. Both techniques were developed from listening to slide players. "I practiced to get that sound without using the slide," Rush explains. "I'm still trying to develop it. I get out a slide in the hotel room sometimes and do a little. My favorite slide players were Earl Hooker and Robert Nighthawk. There were a lot of them, but I listened to those guys' touch. I don't have the touch they had with a slide, so in order for me to get that sound, I'm trying to just get it with my hands." Otis' instrumental "Easy Go" from *Right Place, Wrong Time* is reminiscent of the Earl Hooker slide approach, and onstage he often performs Hooker's "Will My Woman Be Home Tonight?"

Even though he sometimes plays tremolo-equipped guitars, such as a Stratocaster, Otis prefers to achieve wang-bar-like effects with just his hands. "I use the bar a little bit, but would shake my strings [with my hands] if I wanted to. I can shake them without the bar. I can shake a whole chord. I guess by me being left-handed, it's a little bit of an advantage for that style, and then there's other advantages for a right-handed player. No one has it over the other."

To demonstrate some of the advantages, Otis gets out his guitar. "If I hear a chord, I can play it," he begins. "There are some chords that a right-handed player can finger that I can't — because it might have a note I can't reach — but there are other chords I can do that a right-handed guy can't do. It works both ways." He plays a Jimmy Reed shuffle, arching his fingers to stay out of the way of the lower adjacent string, and then launches into Kenny Burrell's "Chitlins Con Carne" in several different positions. "I thought that was one of the most beautiful things I ever heard," he smiles. "I'm working on these piano runs now, and Oscar Moore

> *"There are some chords that a right-handed player can finger that I can't — because it might have a note I can't reach — but there are other chords I can do that a right-handed guy can't do. It works both ways."*

and Johnny Moore things. As a kid I listened to 'Driftin' Blues' and 'Black Night' by [pianist] Charles Brown. You don't listen to one person, though; you listen to everybody." He then proceeds to play note- (and rhythm-) perfect T-Bone Walker lines. "T-Bone had his shit very well-placed, playing all those horn parts. I just put 'em all together — even Ray Charles," he concludes, playing a pianistic lick obviously indebted to Brother Ray.

One technique that definitely sounds different because of Otis' upside-down approach is his bending — grabbing and pulling *down* on the strings, instead of pushing upwards. Physics might suggest that bending a string in either direction would yield the same sound, but with Otis it's definitely not the case. "Pulling down is easy for me," he states. "I pull the high E all the way down to the other E. Sometimes I push mine up, too — even the G and the B."

Although he employs fairly light-gauge strings these days, Otis accomplished the same effect in the old days with heavy strings. "I used to use the heavy strings, with a wound G," he smiles. "Then they came out with .010s and .009s and all these different strings, so why suffer, you know? I use .010s now, and I can squeeze them quite a bit. With .009s, I break them." (Of his picking-hand technique, guitarist Derek O'Brien of the Lou Ann Barton Band, who has backed Otis on numerous occasions, says, "The first time I worked with Otis, he played the first night all with a pick, and then he played the next night all with his fingers." "It just depends on how I feel," says Rush.)

Referring to his belated debut album as "good-intentioned," the guitarist feels "it was a little bit too much of Bloomfield's and Gravenites' ideas and not enough of mine. I don't think the public accepted it, because it wasn't me. They'd prefer I was going back to the stuff that I usually did." Recorded at Fame Studios in Muscle Shoals, Alabama, the project featured such studio luminaries as Duane Allman and Jimmy Johnson on guitars,

Jerry Jemmott on bass, Barry Beckett on keyboards, and Roger Hawkins on drums, although Otis points out, "The leads are by me."

The appropriately titled *Right Place, Wrong Time*, with its title track reminiscent of Albert King, marked Otis' maturation as singer, songwriter, guitarist, and producer. Although songwriter Nick Gravenites was credited as co-producer, Otis stresses, "I put that stuff together — Nick don't know that stuff. I also put [1975's] *Cold Day In Hell* together, although I was high as a kite — drinking heavy at that time. It was okay, but I wasn't getting a good sound. *Right Place, Wrong Time* wasn't a bad album, as far as sounds. We did some gigs in San Francisco with the studio band first, to get our confidence up. I'll give Nick credit for that — setting up the gigs. That stuff really wasn't even mixed; it was just straight playing and straight playback. It's just like we recorded it, because Bullfrog just took the masters and released it." Resigned but still frustrated over the years that the album remained in the can, Otis shrugs, "And in the meantime Dr. John came out with a song called 'Right Place, Wrong Time' and got a gold record for it. All the time my record was laying up on the shelf. If I had come out with that record when I first recorded it, I'd be in better shape today. I'd be more popular."

Although his old promo pictures from the Cobra days show him with a Stratocaster, Otis has used a wide array of guitars. "First I recorded with an old acoustic Gibson with a pickup on it," he begins. "I played a Kay also. After some records came out, I switched to a Strat. I watched Earl Hooker; he had every gimmick or gadget that came out. He had a Strat, so I bought one. He had an old Fender Bassman, so I got that, put them together, and developed a hell of a sound. I used to sing *and* play through that amp; it takes a lot of punishment. My old Strat got stolen, so I got a Fender Jaguar, and then I used an Epiphone Riviera. The Epiphone got broken, and somebody gave me another Strat.

Then I switched to a Gibson ES-345. I still use my Strat for different things. [Vintage guitar authority] Danny Thorpe gave me a 1965 ES-355 and a 1962 *left-handed* ES-355 [with the nut and strings reversed], so the controls would be out of the way. That's a problem with the right-handed models. I can get by, but I have to keep reaching up and resetting the knobs onstage.

"There's a lot of Strats out there, but all of them don't sound good. I'm always searching for a better tone. I still occasionally play my white Strat that was given to me about three years ago. It sounds good. A Telecaster also sounds great. Magic Sam had one, and I used it. I play the blues on the Strat; if I want to play some Jimmy Smith stuff or some Kenny Burrell chords, I use the Gibson."

These days Otis is still looking for the right amplifier. "I'm searching for an amp, because the last time I was in the studio, I didn't like the sound. I cut some new stuff for Rooster Blues, but the sound was too fuzzy. I'd like to try a MESA/Boogie. I've got a Fender, but you can only turn it up so loud, and then it doesn't get any louder. The old Twin Reverb comes through pretty good, though. I try to play with a clean sound. I can do a little bit of that Chuck Berry stuff, but not like some guys, who can use that fuzzy sound. I'd rather mine be clean. Like when you make a chord, man, you've got to hear it."

1986 marked Otis' first, albeit long overdue, meeting with one of his most devoted disciples, Eric Clapton. "I met him when I was in England," he says. "Great guitar player." What did it feel like when the struggling Chicagoan first heard a young English kid playing his songs and style? "Well, everybody plays like somebody. It's good to know that somebody's listening. To me, I'm just a guitar player. I'm not trying to influence nobody, I'm just trying to play, and play well. And hopefully I can sell some records. I've got a better chance now — I'm in a better position — than 10 or 20 years ago. People are listening. Blues

> "Everybody plays like somebody. It's good to know that somebody's listening. To me, I'm just a guitar player. I'm not trying to influence nobody, I'm just trying to play, and play well. And hopefully I can sell some records."

today is mostly white people. A lot of black people passed it over. That's strange, I swear. I hear people say, 'I don't like blues.' Well, I be looking under the table at their feet — to find something to get them going. Because blues is the foundation of *all* music."

During his self-imposed hiatus, Otis was never far from his guitar. "I listened to records a lot, listened to sounds, and practiced," he says somberly. "I've sat up 24 hours with it. You've got to get it mentally, and you've got to get it mechanically. It's just like the Lord's Prayer: You've got to know that and get that from the heart. I've been down and up.

I quit for two years, and I suffered. These companies screw you around, and I got to the point where I was real angry. To be that angry is not good, so I quit for two years. I had to figure out if I wanted to play or not. I needed to get myself together and either accept what's going on or quit.

"But what I have, He gave it to me. 'You gonna quit, huh? What are you gonna do?' [*Laughs.*] So, yeah, I suffered. I'm back at it — for good or bad. I'm not gonna quit no more. I just want to play the guitar the best I can and survive."

A SELECTED
OTIS RUSH DISCOGRAPHY

Solo albums: *Groaning The Blues* (Cobra sides, 1956-'58), Flyright; *Cobra Alternates*, P-Vine; *The Classic Recordings*, Charly R&B; *Otis Rush And Magic Sam — The Other Takes, 1956–'58* (includes separate tracks by each), Flyright; *Mourning In The Morning*, Cotillion (dist. by Atlantic); *Albert King/Otis Rush: Door To Door*, Chess France; *Blues Masters, Vol. 2* (also issued as *This One's A Good 'Un*), Blue Horizon/Polydor; *Cold Day In Hell*, Delmark; *Little Walter & Otis Rush: Live In Chicago* (mid '60s), Intermedia; *Right Place, Wrong Time* ('71 sessions), Bullfrog; *Screaming And Crying* ('74), Black And Blue; *So Many Roads* (live in Japan, '75), Delmark (issued in Japan as *Blues Live!*, Trio); *Troubles, Troubles* (live in Europe, '77), Sonet; *Live In Europe* (France, '77), Isabel; *Tops* (1985 San Francisco Blues Festival), Blind Pig.

With others: Eddy Clearwater, *Flim Doozie*, Rooster Blues; Willie Dixon, *The Chess Box*, Chess.

Anthologies: *The Story Of The Blues, Vol. Two* (one Cobra side), CBS; *Otis Rush And Little Walter — Live At The Chicago Blues Festival* (includes separate tracks by each), Cleo; *Ann Arbor Blues & Jazz Festival 1972*, Atlantic; *Chicago/The Blues/Today!*, Vanguard; *Atlantic Blues: Chicago* ('69 sessions), Atlantic; *The Great Blues Men*, Vanguard; *Tenth Anniversary Anthology, Vol. 1 — Live From Antone's*, Antone's.

Jimmy Reed

December 1976

BY DAN FORTE

THIS NATION'S BICENTENNIAL YEAR was relentlessly harsh on one of America's few unequivocally indigenous musical forms, the blues. The year started off with the deaths of three of the idiom's longtime leaders in rapid succession — Howlin' Wolf, Jesse Fuller, and Mance Lipscomb. All this while the deaths of T-Bone Walker and Hound Dog Taylor a year earlier were still fresh in the blues fan's mind. Still, Wolf had been suffering from kidney trouble for several years (in fact, his death had been reported prematurely more than once), and Fuller and Lipscomb were 79 and 80, respectively.

But perhaps the worst shock came on August 29, when the blues world lost a veritable institution, Jimmy Reed. Born in Leland, Mississippi, Reed was not quite 50 years old and seemed to be at the beginning of a strong comeback when he died of respiratory stoppage apparently caused by an epileptic seizure during his sleep.

After having spent several years hospitalized due to problems of epilepsy compounded by alcoholism, Jimmy had returned to performing with regained health and an optimistic attitude. By this time the Reed repertoire sounded like a "Greatest Hits" album (or two or three). Songs like "Bright Lights, Big City," "You Don't Have To Go," "Baby, What You Want Me To Do," "Take Out Some Insurance," "Caress Me Baby," "Honest I Do," "Going To New York," "Ain't That Loving You, Baby," and "Big Boss Man" poured out, one after the other, all with that immediately identifiable shuffling, walking bass — relaxed but heavy on the backbeat. (As guitarist Albert King, who played drums behind Reed for a short time, once said, "All I could play was a shuffle with a back-beat" — which was about all that was required for the gig.)

Jimmy's guitar playing was primitive to say the least — but nonetheless bluesy, and as recognizable as his whining, nasal vocals. While repeating his usual song formula, in every possible variation, Jimmy Reed provided countless rock, jazz, pop, and R&B artists with a good portion of their material. The Rolling Stones, Elvis Presley, Count Basie, Muddy Waters, the Animals, Chuck Berry, Johnny

164

and Edgar Winter, Charlie Rich, the Grateful Dead, John Hammond, Jerry Lee Lewis, the Blues Project, James Cotton, the Persuasions, Sonny James, Hot Tuna, Jimmy Witherspoon, Etta James, Bill Cosby, Ike and Tina Turner, Aretha Franklin, and others all turned to Reed's simple but effective music.

Here, in an interview taped just two months before his death, "The Boss Man" reflects on his early development on guitar, his recordings, his career-long partnership with blues guitarist Eddie Taylor, his years in a V.A. hospital, and his subsequent short-lived comeback.

Didn't nobody teach me how to play the guitar. I just started off trying to fool with a box ever since I was about 9 or 10 years old. I wasn't making too much progress at it then, but I just kept on trying to do it. Eddie Taylor and me were raised up in the cotton patch together in Mississippi, and we'd fool around with guitars when we got off work in the fields.

But I really didn't get interested in it till after I'd done been up in Chicago. When I was 18 I went into the service, and when I come out, at about 20, I wanted to try it all over again. I was working in the steel mill and listening to that old Muddy Waters, Little Walter, Howlin' Wolf, the Aces, all of them. There was a tavern — it wasn't no "club" — across the street from my house when I was living out in South Chicago. I never did worry about going in the place or nothing; I would stand out there and listen to them playing a little while — but I couldn't play nothing. I said to myself, "Well, if these guys can play in here — I don't see too much that they're doing — I think I could do some of the same thing."

I went and bought me an old piece of guitar and just sat out in the alley right in back of my house. I bought me a little amplifier and plugged it in on the patio where I could hear myself.

And at that time you could buy them old 78-size dubs [blank recording discs] that didn't have nothing on them; and I bought one of these old record players where what you was playing on the

> **"I** didn't know anything about cutting no records; I just wanted to hear myself either over the radio or in the jukebox."

guitar, you could take this dub and turn it over, and it would play back to you what you had just got through playing. I tried a couple of those, and it seemed like the junk sounded pretty good to me. But it didn't sound like I was getting enough in there — you know, just *me*. So this friend, Willie Joe Duncan, had this piece of wire. Him and me used to get together and just fool around in the alley, drinking and going on.

Then it got around to the point where after I cut about two or three of these old crazy dubs into records, I took them down to Leonard Chess [of Chess/Checker Records]. I asked him what he thought about them. He said, "Well, I tell you what: They sound nice. But I'm so tied up now with Muddy Waters and Walter and Wolf, I can't accept nothing else right now. You're going to have to catch me again later." This was around 1953.

And Vivian Carter was a DJ in Gary, Indiana, and she had a record shop on 16th and Broadway in Gary. Her old man, Jimmy Bracken, was working for Leonard Chess, and he was taking all this in when he heard those dubs, and he told her what he'd overheard. She sent me a telegram that I had an appointment with her for that coming Sunday. So I went over there and took these dubs along with me and my little piece of guitar and little old amplifier, too. I played a couple of the records for her and got my guitar and amp, so she could see me do it. She said, "How would you like to cut some records for me if I could get you started?" I didn't know anything about cutting no records; I just wanted to hear myself either over the radio or in the jukebox. So we arranged to do a session, but I didn't have no band. She said she'd get the musicians to play behind me and asked me if I wanted pianos or horns or what in there. I never did bother about having piano on no records; it just didn't sound right to me. At the speed of the background I had, it seemed like it was always betwixt and between — wasn't fast enough or slow enough, either.

And when I got to the studio the next week, she had Eddie Taylor there to play background behind me! So on some of them records there was him, me, [guitarist] Lefty Bates, a drummer — and my son [Jimmy "Boonie" Reed, Jr.] had been fooling with my guitar and got pretty good himself. So I had something like four guitars, and the drums made five, and I was blowing harmonica, too, just like I do it now. The one that made me want to get a harmonica was old man Sonny Boy Williamson — the original [John Lee Williamson], the one that did "Good Morning Little Schoolgirl." He could play some stuff! I was fooling with it in Mississippi and started playing with a harness in about '52.

So we did the session, and it sounded pretty good. The first record was "Found My Baby Gone." They named the company Vee Jay — "V" for Vivian and "J" for Jimmy Bracken. Their first records was mine. When I first started making records I thought everything was going to be all right. And everything *was* all right until the thing started making money. I was supposed to be getting royalties, but I didn't get none. But I been thinking about cutting some more records, and a lot of people have been on me to do some more.

But anyway, back in 1954 Vee Jay put out this thing I had cut about "You Don't Have To Go" with "Boogie In The Dark," a stone instrumental, on the reverse side. One evening I was coming home from the Armour Packing Company — I'd quit the iron foundry and was working as a butcher — and I heard this old number about "You Don't Have To Go" over the air. The guy on the radio said, "That's Jimmy Reed; he's going to be out in Atlanta, Georgia, this Friday and Saturday night" — and this was Thursday evening! I didn't know that I was booked in Atlanta. I headed home, grabbed my junk, headed to the studio to cut a couple of numbers, and told Eddie Taylor, "Eddie, I'm supposed to be in Atlanta, Georgia. You going down there with me?" He said, "Yeah, wherever you want to go!" So we bought a little jug and struck out driving to Atlanta.

And I never did go back to the packing company to even give them back my knife or my clothes or to get my check or nothing. That was the first time I had went on the road or played *anywhere* before the public. I'd just been playing up and down the alley or at friends' houses. I went to see *other* guys in Chicago playing in clubs — go by just to holler at them. I didn't want to play or see the show either; I just wanted to speak to them. Muddy

Waters, B.B. King, all of them big cats — "Oh, you're Jimmy Reed? I'm so glad you come down here to see me. How much they charge you to come in?" "Oh, they let me come in for nothing." "Well, come back in the dressing room." And I'd go back and listen to them talking about this, that, and the other, but it didn't mean too much to me; I didn't know nothing.

I was working one-nighters mostly in Texas, Alabama, Florida, Louisiana, Georgia, and out on the West Coast — while I was still living in Chicago. I might be playing in California one night and have to be in Washington, D.C., practically the next night. I had a little stage fright about playing before the public, but I was drinking liquor at the time. I wasn't never no pot smoker, and I never did fool with any of that cocaine or junk or crazy pills, but I'd drink me some liquor.

Then in the '60s some time I started having these [epileptic] seizures. I remember one time I went on the stage, and I didn't even know when I came off. I must have collapsed on the stage, and they carried me off. After they found out I had been in the service, the V.A. hospital in Downey, Illinois, accepted me in 1969.

The doctor said my nerves had got shook up, and the liquor I was drinking just kept *pushing* me. He said he thought it would be a good idea for me to quit playing music for a while, quit cutting records and everything. He said, "You need to just lay down and rest a while; let your nerves get together." Used to be I could feel those things coming on, and I'd go sit down. But then they started coming on me in my sleep; then I'd have a heck of a time. Because you're capable of coming out from under them things, and you're capable of not coming out. If there ain't nobody there to stick something in your mouth, you might swallow your tongue or something.

Then I left the hospital and lived in one of these registration [convalescent] homes until the doctor said, "Jimmy, you can go home when you get ready." So they'd mail me a supply of medicine about once a month after I left in '72. I gave up music for about four or five years; I didn't cut no records or do nothing.

I played guitar a lot in the hospital, though. They had a big old music center up there where I would go and get me a guitar and amplifier and just

167

lock up in a room all day. And I didn't have nobody to help me out and back me up. See, during my first two or three records I wasn't doing nothing but blowing the solo on the harmonica and starting off the intro on the guitar. Then the rest of the band would haul off and head into it. But after I got in the hospital, my style changed in a way: I started trying to play my intro part, as much of the lead part as I could get in, do my singing part, blow the solo on the harmonica, and play the bass part all the way through, too. I started doing all that myself, which was a pretty hard thing. But it got me to the place where if I *ain't* playing the lead part, it don't sound right now, since I been doing it a few years.

I used to do all my numbers with a B♭ harmonica, which would cause the guitar to be in F. But after so long it started to strain my voice, so I started playing A harmonica, which caused the guitar to be E. I put a clamp [capo] on the 5th fret when I blow on the high part of the harmonica, and the band will be playing in A then. Of course you don't *have* to put a clamp on it — there's a whole lot can be played up there without one. Eddie Taylor, he don't fool with a clamp. He's played with everybody, and you don't ever catch him putting a clamp on. I imagine if I hadn't tried to play the harmonica and done nothing but play guitar with everybody, I'd probably have been like him. Eddie, I don't care how many records he's made or who he's played with, when he plays somewhere with me, he don't worry about playing nothing he ever did on anyone else's junk. He helped me on all my records but about two.

I can't play behind anybody else. I have to start my own thing and let everybody push me. You can put me up there with somebody else playing, and I can't get in tune or keep up with them. But let me start *my* stuff, and I can go ahead on.

My son also played on all my records, except the first couple and the last couple. He's a stone musician. I ain't nothing, but he can play music, write music, read music, arrange music — he's just long gone with it. But he can't sing worth nothing, and he don't like the blues. He's a rock and roll type. He learned the guitar just from being around

me — I ain't taught him nothing. Sometimes I'd go down in the basement and be up all night, trying to see what I could play on the thing. He wasn't nothing but a little kid, and he'd sit down there with me till him and the dog would fall asleep in the corner. I think he was, I should say, 10 or 11 years old when he first played on a record of mine. He plays rock and roll, but me, myself, I play the blues. I don't play no rock and roll stuff, but my records made it on the rock stations, because the background just had some kind of a beat to it that just got everybody to moving.

When me and Eddie used to fool around in Mississippi, they wasn't making no electric guitars. I started off with one of those "folk" boxes with the hole in the middle. But when I got to recording I had me an electric. I played some of everything — I never did have no special brand. Then in '72, after I got out of the V.A. hospital, I was at a music shop getting some picks and strings, and I saw this guitar [a Japanese Les Paul copy made by Ariel]. It had the type of feel I like in a box. So the guy let me have it for $42 or $52 — I thought it was a pretty good deal.

My amp is an old Fender Concert; I think it was one of the first ones they made. I had a newer Fender amp, but I got this Concert for $90. The average cats on the bandstand, they turn their box wide open and have them blasting. I don't call that music; you can't hear what the other guy's doing. I can see them doing that if they're reading everything off sheet music, but when you're just playing by ear, you have to listen to who's doing what.

When I started out, I used a flatpick. But with the straight pick, in my style, the wrist will get tired. So then I started using the fingerpick and thumbpick, so there ain't nothing to get tired out but just my thumb. If I wanted to come off the bass with the lead notes, that's when the index finger comes in. This song I made about "Big Boss Man," I've tried to show a lot of guys who was stone musicians, pretty well professionals, how to play the intro to that, and they can't do it so it sounds right.

I just do my one straight thing. But it seems to work out pretty good like it is.

A SELECTED
JIMMY REED DISCOGRAPHY

Solo albums (on Vee Jay): *I'm Jimmy Reed*; *Found Love*; *Now Appearing*; *Just Jimmy Reed*; *Blues Is My Business*; *Jimmy Reed At Carnegie Hall*; *The Best Of Jimmy Reed*; *Jimmy Reed Sings The Best Of The Blues*; *Jimmy Reed At Soul City*; *The Legend, The Man*; *T'ain't No Big Thing... But He Is*. Other labels: *Down In Virginia*, ABC/Bluesway; *The New Jimmy Reed Album*, ABC/Bluesway; *Soulin'*, MCA; *I Ain't From Chicago*, ABC/Bluesway; *Jimmy Reed*, Archive Of Folk; *Cold Chills*, Antilles; *Upside Your Head*, Charly; *High And Lonesome*, Charly; *Got Me Dizzy*, Charly; *I'm The Man Down There*, Charly; *Big Boss Blues*, Charly; *Wailing The Blues*, Tradition; *The History Of Jimmy Reed, Vol. 1* and *Vol. 2*, Trip; *Boogie In The Dark*, Aura; *Shame Shame Shame*, Krazy Kat; *Cold Chills*, Krazy Kat; *Jimmy Reed Is Back*, Roots; *Street Talkin'*, Muse; *The Best Of Jimmy Reed*, GNP/Crescendo.

Anthologies: *All Them Blues*, DJM.

Michael Bloomfield

April 1979

BY TOM WHEELER

ICHAEL BLOOMFIELD'S LEGEND won't go away. Though he is passionately committed to discovering, dusting off, and reinterpreting the dozens of musics in virtually every corner of America's post-Civil War folk heritage, his audiences are often unaware of that fact, or are more interested in hearing him recreate the sounds of the records that made him one of the world's preeminent blues-rock guitar superstars in the late '60s, albums such as *Super Session* (with Al Kooper and Stephen Stills), and LPs recorded by Bloomfield's various groups, including the Paul Butterfield Blues Band and the Electric Flag.

"It's a real problem, a *big* one," he explains. "The records I have recorded in the last few years are very poorly distributed, or if they are well-distributed there are no print ads, or the company doesn't have enough money to promote them the way I'd like them to." These records include *Analine, Count Talent And The Originals, Michael Bloomfield*, and an album produced by *Guitar Player* magazine and nominated for a Grammy in 1977, *If You Love These Blues, Play 'Em As You Please*.

"On a recent Canadian tour," Mike continues, "I talked to hundreds of people, and only *two* had heard of those records. This is the bane of my existence, because a lot of times people come to see something from 10 years ago — *12* years ago — they're coming to see *Super Session*, the Flag, I don't know what. They're coming to see Butterfield or whatever. It's because they aren't aware of the more recent stuff. I always make a disclaimer. I say, now listen, you're not going to hear what you heard 10 years ago, although you might hear bits and fragments of it. If I could recreate it, I would. I wouldn't mind it. But I hope that you will take it for what it is. Try to remove your prejudgment, and take it for what it is. If you like it, great; if you don't...."

In the eyes of the late-'60s record-buying public, Mike Bloomfield was tall in the saddle. After all, he was an onstage accomplice The Day Dylan Went Electric at the 1965 Newport Folk Festival, and after several albums and tours with various bands he turned on thousands of guitar play-

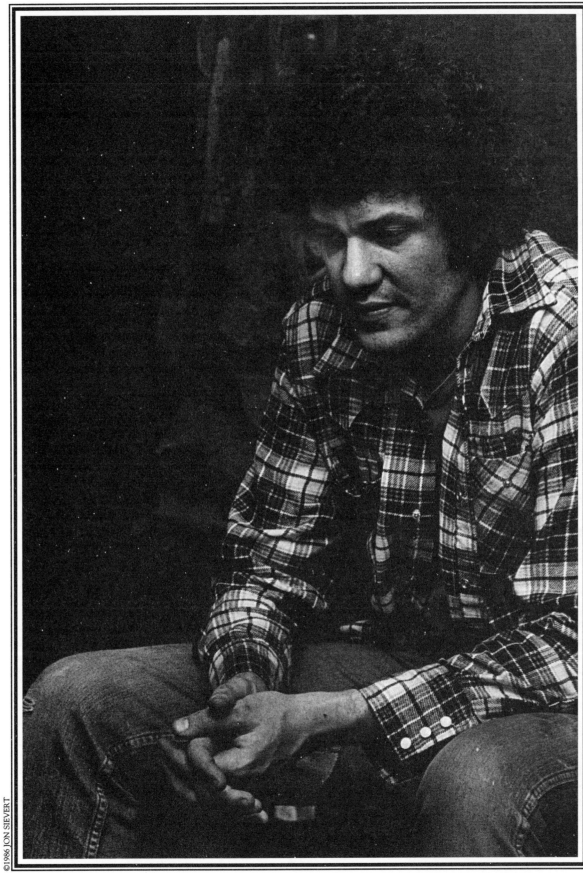

ers and countless other fans to Chicago-style electric blues.

Unlike the music of Jimi Hendrix and Eric Clapton, whose blues roots were one step removed and sometimes obscured by the smoke and sparks of the acid-rock milieu, Bloomfield's blues were unadorned, accessible, assimilable. His guitar technique churned with such soulfulness that he broke a color line of sorts, demonstrating a blues sensibility uncommon among white instrumentalists and earning respect from the sacred heroes of his youth. "Without a guitar," he once said, "I'm a poet with no hands."

For the most part Bloomfield shunned the conspicuous hallmarks of hot-licks, '60s-style electric guitar — distortion, feedback, and special effects — and instead, like the purist that he is, chose a bare-knuckles, plug-in-and-blow approach that continued a tradition discovered and embraced in the blues clubs of Chicago's seamy South Side. His consummate skill as a string bender (plus a fascination for the microtonal capabilities provided by bending) allowed him to extract the blue nuances of pitch. His dynamic pick attack, natural sustain, lyrical tone, and savory vibrato combined to infuse his art with a street eloquence, and his spontaneous but purposefully directed solos were charged with plenty of tension/release and call-and-response, comparing favorably with the best of the high-drama blues heavyweights like Albert King. In other words, as Michael himself might say of a favorite guitarist, he played his ass off. In recent years he has devoted more time to acoustic music, and his popularity among guitar players remains high.

Michael's personal quirks reveal contrasts, though not inconsistencies. For example, when it comes to worshiping Ray Charles, B.B. King, or his other blues heroes, he is an idolator to the core (or, as he puts it, to the tits). And yet during the 1960s he never related to being the star that he was, and in fact — as he discusses in the following interview

Unlike the music of Jimi Hendrix and Eric Clapton, whose blues roots were one step removed and sometimes obscured by the smoke and sparks of the acid-rock milieu, Bloomfield's blues were unadorned, accessible, assimilable.

— he considers popular hero worship to be potentially detrimental, perhaps even vaguely immoral. He is much more interested in current work than past glories. He played guitar on Dylan's "Like A Rolling Stone" and on *Highway 61 Revisited* — both seminal recordings monumentalized by pop historians — and he's referred to the latter as "that album *Highway 61* or whatever it's called."

Michael's roomy, single-level house is jammed with the tools and accoutrements of a hardworking performer and a music lover — dusty guitars with grime-caked strings, a Fender Twin in the hall, another in the kitchen, stacks of jacketless albums, photos of musicians and other friends, tacked-up clippings, an inexpensive stereo that sometimes works — but there are no rock-star trappings, no pretenses.

Bloomfield's musical credentials are the real thing. He has taught musicology at Stanford University. He is a blues historian, a curator of sorts. He loves music for its own sake. And yet he has participated in commercial ventures which he describes below as "amazing scams, filthy lucre," one of which was the historic *Super Session*. Another contrast: Even though Mike's choices of instruments helped ignite popular rages the world over — for Telecasters (during his Butterfield days) and especially for Les Pauls, both gold-tops and sunbursts — he is not equipment-oriented at all in the materialist sense. His guitars are there to be played — and played *hard* (abused, some would charge) — not to be ogled, coveted, bragged about, or traded like so many baseball cards.

Mike, 35, lives atop a steep hill in Mill Valley, just across the Golden Gate Bridge from San Francisco, and he seldom leaves; the less he tours, the better he likes it. He never made much money on the road with previous bands, and although he'd like to reach people all over the country who want to see him, he cannot tour very profitably without a hit single. Even if he could, he wouldn't hit the road very often anyway. Away from home he is an almost hopeless insomniac, a self-described displaced person. He once checked into Stanford's sleep clinic, where optimistic doctors promised to help. They wired him up to machines and hunkered down, waiting for him to fall asleep. He didn't. He stayed awake almost all of the time, occasionally lapsing into what's known as a hypnogogic state but never experiencing real sleep. After 14 days the doctors, now defeated and depressed, threw up their hands, advised him never to travel, and gave him a lifetime prescription for unlimited downers. When he's home in Mill Valley, though, he's okay. Sleeps great.

Over the past few years one of Mike's primary interests and sources of income has been the scoring of films, including *The Trip*, *Medium Cool* (photographed by his cousin, Oscar-winner Haskell Wexler), *Steelyard Blues*, *Andy Warhol's Bad*, and a wad of porno movies including *Sodom And Gomorrah* and the Mitchell brothers' *Ultra-Core* series. Michael plays northern California clubs, and income from these dates, movie scores, records, and songwriting supports him comfortably, though not luxuriously.

Mike Bloomfield is an especially animate interviewee. He'll talk at length to almost anyone who cares about music, and his conversations bulge with vivid anecdotes about hundreds of figures from musical Americana. He is both colorful and quotable ("Heroin gave me pimples"). He is a well-read, thoughtful, and serious student, and yet his eye still has the gleam, his mouth the grin, of a kid who would not only dare to show his young fat white face in a South Side club, but who would also have the gall to practically force himself into an onstage jam alongside the baddest guitarslinger in town.

Are your audiences sometimes surprised to see Michael Bloomfield the fingerpicker, the acoustic guitarist, the solo performer?

Yes, sometimes they are. There are certain places where they know me and they come to hear me play the solo thing, but at most gigs I'll get someone out there who screams, "*Super Session.*" When someone yells that I really can't imagine what's going on in his mind. I mean, here's a guy who's sitting up there onstage alone, fingerpicking — how's he going to do it? Where's the organ going to come from? The horns? What are you supposed to do, man [*laughs*], play the *changes* or something? Play the solo?

That's what they know; that's "Michael Bloomfield."

I know, I understand it. I swear, I remember when I was at a certain age I'd just want to hear the solo or something myself.

During the '60s, were you stimulated by all the attention?

Well, I don't need ego fixes. I'm sort of embarrassed by adulation. As much as anyone else, I enjoy energy transference. Like in its highest form I guess you would see it in a church, where you have a good preacher who goes nuts, and the audience has orgasms, and they have to carry out the big fat women over the heads of the crowd. That's all well and good, but I am just not a compulsive junkie for mass ego glut. Bob Marley explained to me that he found it emasculating and demeaning to play in front of people sometimes. He didn't mean that it was feminine or anything, just that it was depersonalizing. It takes away some of your personal store of self, because the audience doesn't know who you are, and you're exhibiting some of your innards in front of strange people. Playing in front of strangers leads to idolatry, and idolatry is dangerous because the audience has a preconception of you even though you cannot get a conception of them, really. You have to look upon them as a herd. Every time I get together with anyone, I try to break it down quickly, this herd situation.

So that the other person does not look at you as a fixed image, an inflexible symbol?

Yes, exactly, so that they are not experiencing just a face on a record cover that maybe they smoked their first dope to. Instead, they're talking to me, a person, doing what I do now. People resent it sometimes when we move on and we don't fit their preconceptions. I'm the same way, really I am. I'm an idolator to the tits, man. When I go to see somebody, I want to see them onstage the way I see them in my mind. I want to see B.B. with a processed hairdo.

But you didn't relate to being a rock star yourself?

No, I didn't, not at all, even when it was happening. I couldn't even conceive of myself as a rock star. I had no idea it was happening. I was into researching old forms of music and belonging to folklore societies and meeting old players and going to folk festivals. I'd been playing bluegrass and country blues for years, and I just never pictured myself as a big electric guitar hero. I would buy someone else's record and picture them as a rock star, but I could never see it in myself.

You didn't see yourself as the American Eric Clapton?

No, never. Clapton, I thought, now *here's* a guy, here's a *rock star*. Boy, did he play. I thought, if I could only do what he could do. I thought that he had taken the blues just absolutely as far as it could go. And when Hendrix came along I just wanted to burn the guitar. I'm sure Eric felt the same way. So I didn't relate to being a rock star at all. I read a lot of stuff about all that, but it wasn't real for me. All of those social implications and ramifications of a rock star trip — I was never into it.

Tell us about the record you made for *Guitar Player* magazine, *If You Love These Blues, Play 'Em As You Please.*

Everywhere I go, man, everywhere, someone asks me where they can get that record. It's crazy. I'm not that big a seller, but that album would be my biggest of all time, no doubt about it, if it were better distributed. I know it's my best record, me at my hottest.

Are there particular cuts that you think are especially good?

Yes, the playing is just so hot on some of the songs. Not only just for me, but also for blues playing in general. There's one called "City Girl," and one called "WDIA." It's just great blues playing, that's all I can say.

It also contains authentic reproductions of old-time recorded sounds.

> *"I didn't relate to being a rock star at all. I read a lot of stuff about all that, but it wasn't real for me. I was never into it."*

That's right. I was striving to get the sounds of various old records, and that came through. I was trying to look at not just different guitar styles, but also the whole setting, the feel, the persona, the ambience of certain musics — sort of a musicological period movie. I mean, I wasn't just copying licks. And now I really like to hear it. The other records that I did — I hear them now, and I hear clunkers here and there. But the *Guitar Player* record I really like to hear over and over again.

Do you have any special recording techniques?

Well, no, except I like to put that little Kay amp in the bathroom at the studio. It sounds wonderful, especially if the bathroom has a shower stall. That gives it a wonderful tone and echo.

Do you use fingerpicks?

No, usually I don't. I use the thumbnail, or bare meat. With lap guitars, though, I do use a plastic thumbpick and metal fingerpicks. But on a regular guitar, I can't get agile enough if I'm wearing those things. For flatpicks, I like the really hard kind, a Fender hard. Actually, I hardly use a flatpick when I'm playing electric. I used to use one, but lately I've just been putting it in my mouth, and I leave it there. I find that I get a much funkier blues sound with my thumb or my nail. The strings I use are the Fender Rock And Roll set.

Do you lose speed by forgoing a flatpick?

Yes, I'll never be as fast with my fingers as I am with a pick, but the tone is worth it.

How do you bend so far without the other strings getting in the way?

You bend underneath the other strings. That's the way I do it.

Was *Analine* your first predominantly acoustic album?

For sure. And I play a bunch of guitars, a banjo, bass, drums, piano, organ, ukulele, tiple — all sorts of things.

One cut on *Analine*, "Peepin' An' A Moanin' Blues," is about voyeurism. Where did that song come from? What was your influence?

One of the very biggest gospel publishers is a guy named Thomas Dorsey. He's in his seventies now, lives in Chicago, a rich old black man. He wrote "Precious Lord Take My Hand," "Peace In The Valley" — he's one of the truly great gospel writers. In his youth, though, he wrote obscene songs. He recorded as Georgia Tom. It was Tampa Red and Georgia Tom; Tampa Red played guitar, Tom played piano, and they recorded a lot of filthy songs. There was a whole school of double entendre tunes, like "I've Got A Hot Dog For Your Roll" and "Long John The Dentist." Oh man, there was "Copulatin' Blues" — all sorts of stuff. That was my influence for "Peepin'."

One of the song titles on *Analine* is "Mr. Johnson And Mr. Dunn."

That was named for Lonnie Johnson and Eddie Lang. Lang changed his name to Dunn. They made a bunch of race records for black audiences. Everything was real segregated, and Lang didn't want to mess up Lonnie Johnson's trip — they were both real successful jazz guys — so he changed his name to Blind Willie Dunn, and the two of them made some fabulous records under those names. Lonnie Johnson played a very unusual 9-string guitar on a lot of those tunes.

The *Michael Bloomfield* album has a particularly sleazy quality.

Yeah, that worked out. It was exactly planned that way by Norman Dayron — who's my producer — and me. It was to be as raw and as sleazy as possible. Two of the cuts were recorded live in a club, and I think those are the best tracks: "Sloppy Drunk" and "Women Loving Each Other."

You're not going to hear "Women Loving Each Other" on Top-40 AM radio.

Why not? If I am ever on *The Tonight Show* or something, that's definitely one tune I'd like to do.

> *"I'll never be as fast with my fingers as I am with a pick, but the tone is worth it."*

That's an old song, man, from the '30s, I think. It was written by a guy who's still alive. I told the record company to give him credit on the liner for the song, but something happened — there was some reason why he wasn't credited. His name is William Borem.

But could you get away with performing that tune on the air, on TV?

Maybe I couldn't get away with it. Maybe it is offensive, I don't know. But it's one of the tunes about lesbianism that I really like. There's a ton of them, and there's old songs about transvestites, about transsexuality, about hermaphrodites — actual songs by hermaphrodites, blues about them. There's a guy named Guilford "Peachtree" Payne who had breasts and a penis and made records about that — "Switch-Hit Loving" and all this really strange stuff. As a matter of fact, on the song "Peach Tree Man" [*Count Talent*] — that's where I got the title.

There's another song on *Michael Bloomfield* called "See That My Grave Is Kept Clean."

That's an A.P. Carter song, but I sure didn't know it was by him until I looked it up.

Where does the song come from? What's the genre?

Are you kidding? It was a hit by Blind Lemon Jefferson, one of his two or three biggest hits. He was a star — chauffeured around in a limo — a real star. He died in the most ridiculous circumstances. In 1929 he froze to death in the gutter trying to get from one part of Chicago to another. His chauffeur had split. One story has it that his guitar froze right to his hand. Very odd. He was a freaky guy, blew his money like mad. Being blind, I think he was gypped a lot. Who knew—was it a five, a ten, a hundred? But his records really sold. Anyway, I didn't know A.P. Carter wrote "See That My Grave Is Kept Clean." I learned it from Blind Lemon Jefferson a long, long time ago. It seems like I've known it all my life. It's strange. Blind Lemon's grave is *not* kept clean. I've been there. You should see it. Boy, his plea was not at all answered. His grave is a mess, weeds all over.

He was one of your early influences?

Yes, when I was a kid. You ever seen a picture of him? He was so fat that he had to play a small ladies' guitar on top of his sumo wrestler's belly. And he was really a great player, very fast, very strange. Blind Lemon didn't play with a beat — you couldn't dance to his music. I don't know how he got so popular. He also had a very high, emotional, whiny voice — really a blind man's voice.

How long have you been playing this kind of music?

Much longer than I've been famous for playing rock and roll. These people played this music for dances. One guy with his guitar would play for a whole roomful of people to dance to in the '20s and '30s, and I started discovering these old blues records when I was 13 or 14, and I've been playing it that long, though not on record. Audiences don't always know. They think, I don't know — maybe they think I just saw Leon Redbone on *Saturday Night Live* and just got into it or something [*laughs*].

Who was your first rock and roll influence?

Scotty Moore, Elvis' guitar player. Also Cliff Gallup, who played with Gene Vincent's Blue Caps. See, when I was around 15, I couldn't really differentiate between rockabilly and blues. It all sort of sounded the same to me. I lived in the suburbs of Chicago, and all I knew was that it all had a lot of energy. I still do some of that rock and roll stuff in my gigs, like "Fool" by Sandford Clark. I've often wondered what happened to that guy. I do "Endless Sleep," too, by Jody Reynolds. It's in F. I don't know what happened to him, either.

But a lot of the blues and rock sounded alike for a time?

Yeah, it all had this sort of outlaw quality to it that I was *dying* to get into any way I could. There was an outlaw group of kids in the suburbs — greaser sort of hoodlum kids — and I used to look at

"One guy with his guitar would play for a whole roomful of people to dance to in the '20s and '30s."

them and I wanted to be sort of like that, a Presleyesque, greasy guy. I couldn't really tell which I wanted to be more — a Presleyesque greasy hillbilly or a jivey blues singer.

Where did you first encounter the blues?

On the radio. As I searched the dial at nights when I was a little kid I found that Chicago had seven or eight black stations, and about three of them catered to Southern blacks and played nothing but blues. *Then* I heard the difference. The rockabilly was fabulous, and I loved it, but then I started hearing nothing but endless B.B. King records, endless Magic Sam and Muddy Waters and Howlin' Wolf and so on, and I was thinking, oh my *God*, this is . . . this is another world, another realm, the jungle, the city. And when I found out that these guys all lived right there in my town, and that all I had to do was to take a subway and I could go hear them — I could actually go *see* them — that just killed me.

Were you also going to see the rock and roll shows?

Yes, but they were different. They were sort of depersonalizing, which is the way I wanted it, because they were like idols, you know. They had records, and they were up on the stage, removed, with the bright lights and all that. That's how it should be. But man, when I went to blues clubs it was a whole different story. There they were, the guys I would hear on the radio, about an inch from my face. The clubs were open until 4:00 in the morning, and they'd be there for seven sets a night, 40 minutes a set, working their buns off. And they were in their prime, a lot of them.

How many white people in the audience?

One. Or sometimes I'd go along with a pal. Gradually I discovered others, like Nick Gravenites and Paul Butterfield, with whom I eventually played in various groups.

Did you sit in much with these players?

I sure did. I never thought much about it — I

knew I was a guitar player; I knew I was fast and hot. I'd started playing in rock and roll bands when I was 15, and I was good then, and I was about 16 or 17 when I started going to blues clubs. I knew that at the time I couldn't play blues, but I could play something similar to it — bluesy guitar — and I was dying to sit in. I came in with my guitar, and there wasn't anybody who was going to stop me. I would walk onstage, literally from out of nowhere, uninvited [laughs], and just say, "Hey, mind if I sit in?" while I was going ahead and plugging in my guitar. Many times it would be like a freak show to the audience. They'd like it—this fat little Jewish child plugging his guitar in and doing whatever he did. And I didn't get the notes out correctly, as blues, but it was near enough.

Who did you jam with?

There was no one I didn't jam with. I played with every living musician who played electric blues. The only guys I didn't play with were the ones who stayed in their regions. If someone never left Louisiana or Texas, then I wouldn't get to jam with him. Everyone else, though.

Muddy Waters?

Muddy, Magic Sam, [Howlin'] Wolf, Otis Rush, B.B. King, Albert King, Freddie King, Little Milton, Junior Wells, Little Walter, Chuck Berry — I played with most of these guys dozens of times — plus a lot of more obscure guys like Eddie King, a guy named [Eddie] Clearwater, a guy named Brewer Phillips, Mighty Joe Young, Otis Spann, Lee Jackson. Then I started getting scholarly about it and began to study it, and I found out that there were guys who had made records in the '40s who still lived in Chicago, guys who were big stars in their day. Like there was Washboard Sam; his real name's Robert Brown—he wrote "I'm Going To Move To The Outskirts Of Town," "Mama Don't Allow No Guitar Pickin' Around Here," and other things. I would find out where these guys lived and check them all out, too. I'd visit with them, learn from them. Everyone I could think of, I looked them up. There was Jazz Gillum — he wrote "Key To The Highway." There was Tommy McClennan, who wrote "Guitar King," which is on my album [Michael Bloomfield]. Endless guys.

Aside from history and folklore, how do all of the many musical forms you play come together? Is there a common thread, some basis for artistic integration?

I know what you're talking about; yes, there's a way in which I relate to all of these blues and folk forms. There's sort of a macrocosmic integration, a general artistic influence on me. I like simple sonorities. I have no present interest in spaced-out electric stuff; I admire it, but it doesn't tug at my heart. I like simpler things. I am a musicologist by bent. I am rooted in American music of all sorts — Cajun, Mexican, all the jazz players up to Django Reinhardt, like Teddy Bunn and Eddie Lang, plus all the blues and folk forms, music you play on all the fretted instruments.

And they all influence what you are trying to do now?

Yes. I began to realize some time ago that if all of these many hybrids could flow through me, then that would be what I was looking for. I wanted to innovate, rather than imitate, and yet I was doing old material. To innovate, you have to bring enough of yourself to the reinterpretive process, so that imitation becomes innovation. As Elvis tried to sound like the Ink Spots or Big Boy Crudup or various blues singers, he ended up sounding like Presley.

Do you see yourself as a musical caretaker of sorts?

Well, a lot of these songs are dying. I don't know many people our age — even black people — who play blues or care about blues. Where are the young bluesmen? Freddie King's dead. Magic Sam's dead. I have some black friends who are music teachers and folklorists, and I'm teaching them. Culturally it's so weird, a Jew teaching a black about blues. I would like to help keep those forms alive, so that people will know: This is how America played.

Was there ever a period when you were musically inactive?

There was a period when I didn't play guitar at all, around '70 or '71. I was really down and out, and I lived in this little dive. The Flag had just broken up. I had cut Super Session, and then I got really into shooting junk.

What were the effects of heroin?

Heroin gave me pimples. And I put the guitar down, didn't touch it. See, a junkie's life is totally, chronically fucked. You either eat and move and be productive, or else you're a junkie. There's no choice. Or at least there wasn't for me.

What were you doing besides shooting junk?

Well, shooting junk is very full-time. You've got to get out there and get that dope, hustle — sell televisions or whatever. If you're into being passive and nonproductive, that's one thing, but I knew that it'd hurt me. Shooting junk made everything else unimportant, null and void, *nolo contendere*. My playing fell apart.

Were you able to work with other musicians?

Not at all. Being on junk can immediately disintegrate a good band. Like I knew one guy, a great musician, really a sweet guy, and everyone loved him, a soulful little guy. But he was the worst junkie I'd ever seen in my life. If he was one millimeter away from death by overdose, he was content. He'd be at a recording session and go into the bathroom for 20 minutes and come back almost purple, different shades of blue, various shades of loss of oxygen. That's where he wanted to be, and he would *play* like this. His hands would still move, but they would move... *slow*. It was very strange watching him play. Just from a practical standpoint, a musician like that who was heavily into dope was not a very good guy to have in a band — someone you knew might die at any minute. I mean, we'd have a rehearsal and he'd hit coma.

So you couldn't play when you were on junk?

Oh *God*, no. Some people can do something behind it — they can play, they can go to the gig, they can control their motor functions. I'd just lay there and watch TV and smoke cigarettes and nod off or whatever. I couldn't keep my act together, I couldn't function. Actually, there was no prolonged period like this — it was more of an on-and-off type of thing.

What made you decide to quit?

It was a very moving experience; it affected me deeply. I'll tell you about it. Some of the best San Francisco Bay Area guitar players came to see me — Terry Haggerty from the Sons Of Champlin and Carlos Santana and others. And they said to me, man, you ought to be ashamed of yourself to charge admission at the door to see you, because you're a fucking joke, you're a laughingstock. We used to *learn* from you. When Butterfield came to town we all came to see you. We *loved* you, we loved what you did. How can you be who you are? How can you put your name on a marquee and charge money to see this ludicrous exhibition of what Michael Bloomfield used to be? You're a fraud. You can't even *hold* a guitar anymore.

How did you respond?

Well, I just said, hey, I'm not into that anymore. I'm into watching the *Tonight Show* and shooting dope. I'm into stoned leisure.

And did they leave?

No, they stayed. They wouldn't let up. They sat down, and they said, now listen to us play, man. And they *played*. Hag started playing, and, oh my God, he was better than I ever was. It was unbelievable. From then on I vowed: never again. If you're going to get up there in front of people, God *knows* you better be good. That those guys would do that, to come over, to come down on me so hard, to get the balls to do that... it so moved me that these people wanted to see me playing again, it affected my heart tremendously. What nice guys, what gentlemen. That got me back into guitar.

[Mike Bloomfield died of a drug overdose in February 1981.]

A SELECTED
MICHAEL BLOOMFIELD DISCOGRAPHY

Solo albums: *Bloomfield: A Retrospective* (two-record set including "Born In Chicago" from Newport '65), Columbia; *Live Adventures Of Mike Bloomfield And Al Kooper*, Columbia; *Super Session*, Columbia; *If You Love These Blues, Play 'Em As You Please*, Kicking Mule; *Between The Hard Place And The Ground*, Takoma; *Analine*, Takoma; *Michael Bloomfield*, Takoma; *Living In The Fast Lane*, Waterhouse; *Count Talent & The Originals*, Clouds; *Michael Bloomfield & Woody Harris* (instrumental gospel), Kicking Mule; *It's Not Killing Me*, Columbia; *Junko Partner* (live, late '60s), Intermedia; *Cruisin' For A Bruisin'* (last recordings), Takoma; *Best Of Mike Bloomfield*, Takoma.

With the Paul Butterfield Blues Band (on Elektra): *Paul Butterfield Blues Band*; *East-West*; *Golden Butter*.

With the Electric Flag: *Long Time Coming*, Columbia; *Best Of The Electric Flag*, Columbia; *Best Of The Electric Flag*, Back-Trac; *La Grande Storia Del Rock*, Curcio (Italy).

With others: Janis Joplin, *I Got Dem Ol' Kosmic Blues Again, Mama!* ("One Good Man"), Columbia; Bob Dylan, *Highway 61 Revisited*, Columbia; Muddy Waters and others, *Fathers And Sons*, Chess; James Cotton, *Two Sides Of The Blues*, Intermedia; John Hammond and Dr. John, *Triumvirate*, Columbia.

Anthologies: *Live At Bill Graham's Fillmore West*, Columbia.

Soundtracks: *The Trip* ('67); *Medium Cool* ('69); *Festival* ('70, with Bob Dylan at Newport); *Steelyard Blues* ('73); *Andy Warhol's Bad* ('77); *Sodom And Gomorrah* ('77).

Hubert Sumlin

April 1980 & February 1987

BY DAN FORTE & JAS OBRECHT

WHEN IT COMES TO THE UNSUNG heroes of the blues — of which there are hundreds — Hubert Sumlin would have to be among the main contenders for top honors. For 23 years he played guitar behind Howlin' Wolf, the scariest blues singer of all. His classic parts in "Spoonful," "Smokestack Lightnin'," "Wang Dang Doodle," and "I Ain't Superstitious" influenced a generation of blues-based rockers, including Peter Green, Frank Zappa, the brothers Vaughan, and the Rolling Stones. Jimi Hendrix once cited him as his favorite guitarist, and Eric Clapton told *Guitar Player* in 1976: "For a long time I'd really wanted to meet Hubert because he did some things that freaked me out when I was picking up the guitar — that stuff on 'Goin' Down Slow,' just the weirdest playing. He's truly amazing."

"Weird" and "amazing" are good summations of Sumlin's style. His staccato attacks, extroverted slides, and unique use of fills, bass lines, and mantra-like riffs interspersed with only an occasional chord were perfect complements to Howlin' Wolf's rhythmic style and penchant for songs with no chord changes at all. Wolf's gravelly, demonic growl coupled with Sumlin's hypnotic riffs and occasional solo outbursts could only be described as haunting. Today, more than a decade after Wolf's death, Hubert is keeping the spirit alive on his well-received solo albums and in the film *Hubert Sumlin — Livin' The Blues*.

One of 13 children, Hubert was born on November 16, 1931, in Greenwood, Mississippi, and raised in Hughes, Arkansas — a town about 35 minutes from West Memphis, Arkansas. He started playing drums at age 10, and took up the guitar a year later with an $8 acoustic his mother bought him. "I got an older brother named A.D. Smith on my father's side," Sumlin recalls, "and he was playing way before me. So I tried to get him to learn me how to play. But he wouldn't learn me a tune or nothing, and we got to fighting four or five times because of that. Of course, I got whupped every time because I was small [*laughs*]. So I watched what he was doing and got me one tune. Then my mind started getting together, you know, so I ended up

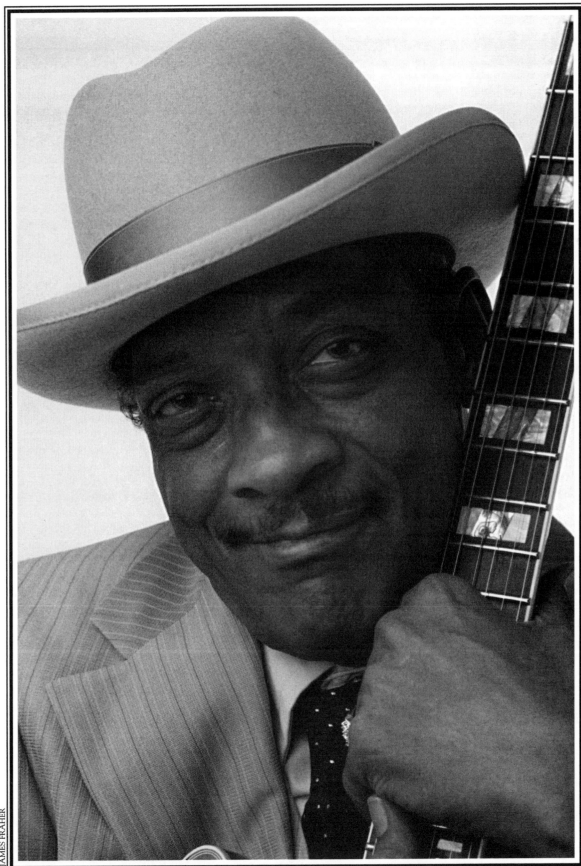

with four or five tunes."

Although the first musicians he listened to were jazz players such as Louis Armstrong, one of the first guitarists Hubert was exposed to as a child was the man he would later spend 23 years of his performing life with. He remembers, "When I first went to see Wolf, he put me out of the place. I'd crawl up under people's legs and get thrown out the door. That didn't stop me, though; I got some Coca-Cola crates as tall as I could get them, and I was sitting up there, rocking and reeling, until somebody pulled the crates out from under me [laughs]. I was just a little dude who wanted to play and hear. I was maybe 12 years old when this started. I did this around Wolf for about two or three years. Finally he knew who I was. He said, 'Let him alone.' He set me in a chair beside [guitarist] Willie Johnson, the drummer, and him. I just sat right there, boy, rockin'. He made me sit in the chair where I wouldn't see no booze or nothing.

"One night he said, 'How'd you get out here tonight?' I just thumbed me a ride, you know. Then he said, 'Does your mama know you're out here? I'm gonna take you home.' I knew if I went back home I'd get two whuppings, but I loved the Wolf anyway. He took me back to my mama and talked to her, so I didn't get no whupping. Then I went back the next Friday night! I asked the lady at the door to ask Wolf if I could come in, and he said okay. Got a chair and sat up there with him. Stayed with him for more than 20 years later on."

A plantation field worker by day, young Hubert got in the habit of taking his guitar with him when he went to work. Ultimately, he remembers, this led to his getting a better instrument: "I'd put my guitar on my back, get on the tractor, and go down to the field. I'd plow about maybe two acres, then I'd just cut the tractor off and sit and play [laughs]. So this guy caught me playing the guitar behind the wheel. And he was so mad because I didn't plow but two acres, he took my guitar and broke it across the tractor. I got so mad I hit him upside the head, but that didn't do no good — he was bigger than I was. I was only about 14 years old. So I wasn't gonna work no

more until I got me another guitar. Later my mother told this guy, 'What did you do that for?' He said, 'He should have been working.' My mother was sanctified, you know, really religious. And that was the first time I ever heard her *start* to cuss. So then this guy went and bought me a $20 guitar, but I had to promise that I wouldn't play it on my job. I still got the guitar; the strings are way up on it now. You can't even play it — I just look at it."

By the time Hubert was a couple of years into learning the guitar, he considered himself a jazz player. Circumstances, however, prompted his move to the blues. "I found I couldn't get jobs," he explains, "and I had to eat and sleep. So this is when I started thinking about playing something else." At age 18 he found his first professional job, playing second guitar for James Cotton. Cotton's first guitarist at the time was Pat Hare, who later in the '50s was part of Muddy Waters' Chicago-based band. Hubert spent close to three years in the Cotton band, touring Arkansas and Tennessee. He accompanied the harmonicist on a session for the Memphis-based Sun label, recording "I Ain't Gonna Pick No More Cotton" sometime in 1953 or '54.

In early '54 Sumlin joined Howlin' Wolf's band for three weeks, playing in Louisiana, Mississippi, Tennessee, and a stint at the Silkhairs Club in West Memphis. "These guys he had working with him, such as Willie Johnson, was his regular band," he recalls. "I didn't know at the time that they was quitting. My first night of playing with him was in New Orleans. Then we played another job, still with his same old band, down south in Mississippi. We stayed in Memphis and then went through Tennessee. Then Wolf come by in this big old long limousine. He said, 'Hubert, I'm fixing to go to Chicago. I sold the band boys all my equipment. When I get to Chicago, if I need you, can I send for you?' I said yeah, but I didn't believe it. I went on. Sure enough, about two weeks later he sent for me."

On his arrival in Chicago, Sumlin was greeted by Wolf and Muddy Waters. He soon met many of the best-known bluesmen around town, including

> "*When I first went to see Wolf, he put me out of the place. I'd crawl up under people's legs and get thrown out the door.*"

pianists Eddie Boyd, Memphis Slim, and Sunnyland Slim, harmonicist Little Walter, and guitarists Big Bill Broonzy, Elmore James, and Johnny Shines. Hubert became the second guitarist in Wolf's band. The other members included Jody Williams, a lead guitarist who could also double on bass, piano, or drums; tenor saxophonist Abe Locke; drummer Early Phillips; and pianist Hosea Lee Kennard. At the time, Hubert remembers, Howlin' Wolf mainly sang and played harmonica, although he did pick up a guitar from time to time to teach the band new material.

Howlin' Wolf had signed a long-term recording contract with the Chess label, and in May 1954 Hubert accompanied him on "All Night Boogie," "Mr. Highway Man," "I'm The Wolf," "No Place To Go," "Baby, How Long," "Evil Is Going On," and several other sides. For a brief period later on in the year, Sumlin attended the Chicago Conservatory of Music: "I went to school for my scales and to know where I was on the guitar, to find out if I was right or not. The Chicago Conservatory was the only place I could find when I got there. They taught everything — jazz, blues, rock and roll, and so forth. I was kind of taught by different people before I made it to this school. So I went there and I really knew a little bit too much about guitar. I was sitting there playing and the teacher said, 'What did you come down here for?' I said, 'Well, I come down to learn my scales.' It didn't take too long, about four months. Then I just went back in my bag. I did learn how to read music, so I can read now if it's necessary. If it ain't necessary, I don't [laughs]. It's a thing that comes to any musician if he's interested and wants to go the right route — just like you're driving a car: You don't want to go two blocks down when you could go right through where you are."

With Wolf, Hubert found he needed to modify his playing approach: "With the straight pick, I was running all over myself. I was playing some stuff that I think was before my time, and so I put it down. I sat down in the basement one day and said,

> "*I* sat down in the basement one day and said, 'Well, I gotta find Hubert; I gotta see where I am.' I had to get me a tone. It seemed like it come to me just like I was dreamin'."

'Well, I gotta find Hubert; I gotta see where I am.' I had to get me a tone. It seemed like it come to me just like I was dreamin' — I found out that I could get a feeling with my fingers better than I could with a pick. I found out that I had more soul in me without the picks. The tone fitted Wolf, and from then on it was a natural thing." To this day, the fingers-only approach is a hallmark of Sumlin's style.

In 1955 and '56 Hubert recorded several more sides with Wolf, among them the now classic "Forty-Four," "Don't Mess With My Baby," and "Smokestack Lightnin'." Hubert explains that oftentimes he and Wolf would get together with Willie Dixon to work out material: "We would run a number down like this — with nobody but me and Willie and Wolf. It was quiet and we didn't have nobody else, so we knew what was gonna happen when we got the rest of the group in there." Friction, however, developed between Sumlin and Wolf, which led to Sumlin's quitting the band in 1956 to go on the road with Muddy Waters. "You know how musicians is," he says. "They have their little faults. I thought I had done got good enough to play what I want to play. And so Wolf was tryin' to help me all the time by telling me, 'No, you ain't — don't think you are the greatest, don't do this and don't do that.' I just got mad and quit.

"So I joined Muddy Waters' outfit and stayed with him a little more than a year. The music was nice; I enjoyed every minute of it. I was kind of young at the time — in my twenties — and what happened was I worked 41 nights in a row. It was a job here tonight, then you had to go 400 miles to do the next job, the next night maybe 250, the next night maybe 350. Well, we was beat on some of the jobs, I'll tell you. When we got back to Chicago we thought we was gonna rest, which we didn't. This is the reason I quit — we couldn't rest. I just had my little fling and come back and told Wolf, 'Hey, man, make room.'"

Sumlin rejoined Wolf's band, and from 1957

until the '70s he almost continually worked the clubs and taverns around Chicago, as well as out-of-town venues ranging from segregated Southern roadhouses to New York's Apollo Theater. In 1957 he played on "Sitting On Top Of The World," and two years later (this time as the band's only guitarist) recorded "Howlin' Blues." His first album with Wolf, 1959's *Moanin' In The Moonlight*, was destined to become a classic.

The following year, with Otis Spann on piano, Willie Dixon on bass, and Fred Below on drums, Howlin' Wolf's band recorded three tunes that have since become blues standards, "Wang Dang Doodle," "Back Door Man," and "Spoonful." Hubert used a Gretsch electric for some records during this period, and an early model Gibson Les Paul for others ("Spoonful," he recalls, was done with the Les Paul). By this time he had developed a style of playing that was a combination of lead and rhythm, or as he describes it, "'twixt and between." His relationship with Wolf had also improved to the point where he could second-guess his leader's next musical move: "I became the only one in the group he didn't come right down on and say, 'You didn't do this right,' because I could feel the man. Like we knowed what the other was going to do, what the other one was thinking. I never would get away from him where I couldn't watch him, and we got to communicate so well that I knew what he was gonna do before he did. That's the way we were."

Sumlin and the Wolf band continued recording during the early '60s, producing "The Red Rooster" (this is one of Hubert's rare appearances on slide guitar), "Down In The Bottom," "Shake For Me," "I Ain't Superstitious," and "Goin' Down Slow" in 1961, "Do The Do" in '62, and "Tail Dragger," "Built For Comfort," and "Three Hundred Pounds Of Joy" in '63. The following year the band toured Europe as part of the American Folk Blues Festival. Once there, Hubert finally had an opportunity to record as a leader. In this context, he not only proved an expressive blues singer — with his plaintive vocal style mirroring his

> **"I** didn't know I was gonna meet all these people from famous groups, such as Charlie Watts. I thought they were the greatest; I still think they are."

bashful offstage demeanor — but also showed that his roots reached back to his rural beginnings in Mississippi. On acoustic guitar he displayed a rhythmic style recalling John Lee Hooker.

Hubert appeared on some Amiga sides with Sunnyland Slim, and then in 1966 he toured briefly with Muddy Waters and made club performances around Chicago with the Magic Sam Band. His main guitar at this time was a Rickenbacker electric. During the late '60s Chess recorded some new Howlin' Wolf material featuring Sumlin, including *More Real Blues*. In April 1969 the Cadet label released *The Howlin' Wolf Album*, which was subtitled *This is Howlin' Wolf's new album. He doesn't like it. He didn't like his electric guitar at first either.*

Howlin' Wolf, Sumlin, and other members of the band journeyed back to England in the early '70s to record *The London Howlin' Wolf Sessions* for Chess. Appearing on the LP is a host of well-known rock and rollers, among them keyboardists Stevie Winwood and Ian Stewart, Rolling Stones bassist Bill Wyman and drummer Charlie Watts, and, on lead and slide guitar, Eric Clapton. "I didn't know I was gonna meet all these people from famous groups, such as Charlie Watts," Hubert says. "It was a great thing for me to do. I thought they were the greatest; I still think they are.

"I didn't know Eric Clapton until we came in the studio together. He didn't look like I pictured. I was sittin' down, and he got him a chair and sat down by me. We recorded two numbers together before we even reached over and made names together. He said, 'My name is Eric,' and I said, 'My name's Hubert.' And he said, 'I know about you,' and I said, 'Well, man, I heard about you, too.' So we got to talking and he invited me to dinner. I went outside the studio and he had a Rolls Royce out there with a chauffeur. We went way up from London in some woods. Man, it was a big old place — I ain't been over it all yet; I've just walked through some of it. The first thing he did was take me down in the basement and show me his guitars. 'Have one,' he said. I picked out a Fender Stratocaster. He had about 140 guitars, maybe more than that. He was surrounded. In fact, I'm using that guitar right now. It's a nice instrument that plays good. I like Fenders, period. They give you a better sound. My amp is a Fender Twin Reverb. When amplifiers first came out, I had an old Wabash amp. I still got it, but it's not workin'."

During the last few years of his life, Howlin' Wolf was a sick man. In 1973 he was injured in an auto accident that caused kidney damage. Still, the veteran bluesman continued to appear in concert until just before his death in January 1976. "About four months before Wolf really got sick, I thought I had better start looking out for Hubert," Sumlin says. "The thing about it is when you love a person, you stay with him as long as I stayed with the Wolf. You say, 'He ain't gonna die; he's forever.' But you can't think like that. I don't believe the good Lord would have just taken him away from here like that for no reason. After he died, a gang of people was talking about me: 'Oh, yeah, what's he gonna do now? Wolf is gone.' And I got home one day and my wife told me people was callin', wanting to know if I would still work. I said, 'You tell them I'm gonna be working as long as there's a Hubert. I'm gonna do just like the Wolf.' He worked up until the end, so I'm gonna be working as long as I can."

Sumlin assumed leadership of the Howlin' Wolf Band in 1976, and also began working clubs around the Chicago area with Sunnyland Slim. He recorded a solo album, *Groove*, for the European Black And Blue label. In 1978 he was featured on five songs on the first volume of Alligator Records' *Living Chicago Blues* series, performing with Eddie Shaw And The Wolf Gang. By then, his original Les Paul was enshrined in a glass case in his living room, and his main stage guitars were a Gibson ES-335 and a recent-model Les Paul, both strung with light-gauge strings.

In recent years, the quiet, bespectacled guitarist has concentrated on playing under his own name.

> "After he died, a gang of people was talking about me: 'Oh, yeah, what's he gonna do now? Wolf is gone.' I said, 'You tell them I'm gonna be working as long as there's a Hubert. I'm gonna do just like the Wolf.'"

His career resurged with 1986's *Hubert Sumlin's Blues Party*, his first American recording under his own name. "I'm 55 years old," Hubert said upon its release, "and I ain't never had a record out in the United States since I been playing all these years with Wolf. This will be my first recording on any kind of major label. I'm very happy about it. It's been too long."

"Singing-wise, Hubert's most effective when he does downhome stuff," producer Hammond Scott noticed during the sessions. "He gets sort of a Lightnin' Hopkins or Jimmy Reed type of sound by himself. But I didn't want to do the whole LP like that, so I brought Mighty Sam McClain to sing songs that bring out another side of Hubert's playing. Hubert's a little absent-minded, but he's one of those on-the-spot kind of guys who's a true artist. If you can set up a framework for him to work with, then right off the cuff he'll come up with something wild that sounds really great. But if you go into a session expecting to just lay everything on him — the tunes, the arrangements, and all that — you're in trouble, because he won't do something the same way twice. You never know what to expect, and you can't rehearse his part too much. He's strongest when he can just go in there and blow." *Blues Party* was followed a couple of years later by *Heart & Soul*, featuring James Cotton and Little Mike And The Tornadoes.

For a long while Hubert was reluctant to cover Wolf tunes, but he's recently added "Down In The Bottom," "Hidden Charms," and a few others to the show. His Abilene Cafe performances a few summers ago inspired Jon Pareles to report in *The New York Times*: "Mr. Sumlin is a guitarist of few notes, masterfully placed. With his raw tone and an extraordinary variety of attacks, he mixes singing blues phrases and slashes of sheer texture—plunking out low riffs, squeezing out delicate sighs in the upper register, making single notes moan, or suddenly swooping down for a metallic shriek. Melodically, his solos are almost abstract; against the chugging rhythms of the band, they are terse and cutting."

Three years in the making, the 72-minute film *Hubert Sumlin — Livin' The Blues* was shot on location in Chicago, Boston, Texas, and Mississippi, with concert footage from the 1984 Delta Blues Festival. In addition to extensive Sumlin interviews and archival photographs and film clips, the documentary features guest appearances by Ronnie Earl, Stevie Ray Vaughan, and James Cotton.

It is interesting to note that when Sumlin looks back over a long career and encounters with most of the best-known bluesmen of the second half of the 20th century, he cites as his favorite guitarist none other than Jimi Hendrix: "I was fortunate enough to meet this guy, and I thought he was wonderful. He was already famous when I met him, and he said, 'I've been hearing about you, Hubert. They tell me you're a fine guitar player.' I said, 'Well, you know,

"You can't just say, 'I'm gonna play just like this man here; he ain't doin' nothing but making money.' If you got something of your own, you ain't got to be worried about nobody. They ain't gonna mess with you."

I try to play.' We jammed together in this club in the Village in New York. Richie Havens was there, too. Jimi played a whole set with me and Wolf's band. This was pretty close to 1970. I didn't know I liked him that much until I saw him play. This drummer, Buddy Miles, played too. Jimi was a swell guy, one of the best guitar players I've ever seen."

When talking with young guitarists, Hubert's first instinct is to advise them to find their own voice: "When you go on the bandstand, be yourself. Although you may be doing things just like other people do them, be yourself while doing them. You can't just say, 'I'm gonna play just like this man here; he ain't doin' nothing but making money.' If you got something of your own, you ain't got to be worried about nobody. They ain't gonna mess with you. Find that vibration, that feeling, that soul. If you play any instrument, that is it. If you do well, I figure it's like this: You gonna be thought of."

A SELECTED
HUBERT SUMLIN DISCOGRAPHY

Solo albums: *Groove*, Black And Blue; *My Guitar And Me* ('75), Black And Blue; *Gotta Run*, Paris; *Hubert Sumlin & Carey Bell* (Sumlin plays acoustic on most cuts), L+R; *Funky Roots*, Vogue; *Hubert Sumlin's Blues Party* ('86), Black Top; *Heart & Soul*, Blind Pig.

With Howlin' Wolf (on Chess, except as noted): *Howlin' Wolf* (a.k.a. "The Rocking Chair Album," '57-'61); *Moanin' In The Moonlight* ('59); *His Greatest Sides, Vol. 1* ('54-'63); *Change My Way* ('59-'66); *Chicago — 26 Golden Years*; *His Greatest Sides, Vol. 1*; *Muddy & The Wolf*; *The London Howlin' Wolf Sessions*; *The Real Folk Blues* ('56-'65); *More Real Folk Blues* ('53-'59); *Chester Burnett A.K.A. Howlin' Wolf*; *The Back Door Wolf*; *Howlin' Wolf, Vol. 1*, Chess U.K.; *Howlin' Wolf, Vol. 2*, Chess U.K.; *Howlin' Wolf, Vol. 3*, Chess U.K.; *From Early To Late*, Blue Night; *Live In Europe, 1964*, Sundown; *Live, 1975!*, Wolf; *The Howlin' Wolf Album*, Cadet.

Anthologies: Willie Dixon, *The Chess Box*, Chess; *Atlantic Blues: Chicago* ('72), Atlantic; *Ann Arbor Blues & Jazz Festival 1972*, Atlantic; *Anthology Of The Blues: Memphis*, Kent; *Twenty Greatest R&B Hits*, Kent.

With others: Eddie Shaw And The Wolf Gang, *Living Chicago Blues, Vol. 1*, Alligator.

On film: *Wolf* (documentary and interview with Ralph Bass, '71); *Hubert Sumlin — Livin' The Blues*.

Albert Collins

May 1988

BY DAN FORTE

ONSTAGE THE ANTONE'S HOUSE band is cranking out a shuffle in C, and the capacity crowd is buzzing with anticipation. Austin guitarist Derek O'Brien, test-driving a '50s Telecaster he acquired specifically for the gig, sounds amazingly close to Albert Collins, who is backstage playing blackjack with some Austin buddies. Albert's opponent says, "Hit me," checks his cards, and raises the stakes. Albert stares into his eyes and then slams a wad of ones onto the table.

Meanwhile, Albert's valet, Elroy, readies one of the most recognizable axes on the blues circuit, Collins' blonde Telecaster. Albert stands up but still appears to be paying more attention to the cards shuffling backstage than to the blues shuffle *onstage*. Elroy drapes the Fender over Albert's right shoulder and follows the trail of its cord out the door and towards the stage. The guitarist quietly checks his tuning and extracts a roadweary capo, wrapped with electrician's tape, from his pocket and places it at the 7th fret. He quickly twirls the volume knob to 10 and blasts a massive double-stop bend into the next room, punctuating it with stinging vibrato and a wicked smile.

Onstage O'Brien winces, as though he were just Sunday-punched, then smiles, shaking his head and shifting to rhythm guitar. The audience is now on its feet, craning to see where the tone of doom is coming from. Collins rakes the kitty of crumpled dollar bills off the table with mock politeness and stuffs it into his pocket before catapulting another volley of blues runs into the nightclub. By the time he has made his way to the stage, Albert Collins has reeled off a textbook of his patented licks — descending slide jumps, muted staccato triplets, some chicken pickin', arpeggios, octaves, double-stops, and crying bends that can only be described as painful. He strides onto the stage holding a single high note while hammering it over and over in every conceivable way — quarter-notes, eighths, muted, then sustained with shimmering vibrato.

Throughout the set O'Brien and Collins spar, with Derek shaking his head in disbelief more than a few times and Albert running through his entire

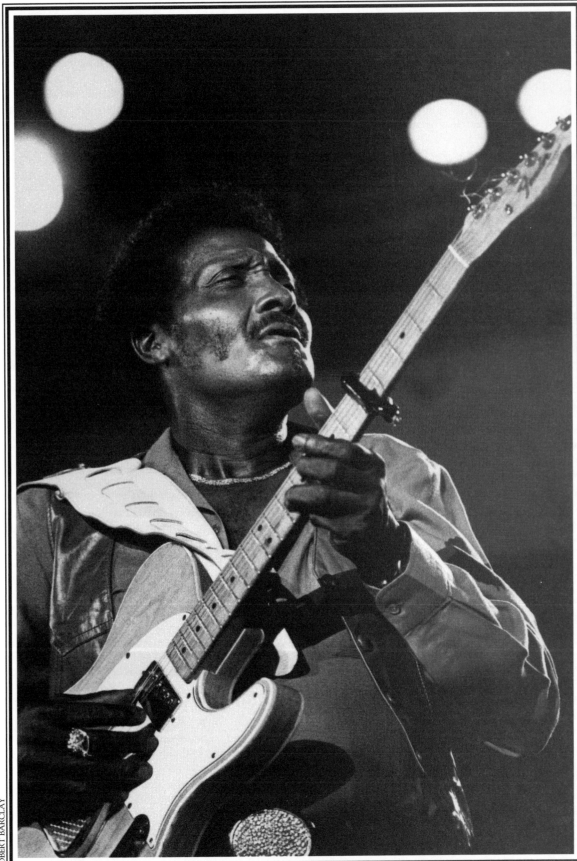

repertoire of grunts, groans, and grimaces. Other local guitarslingers line up at the side of the stage, and the next contender, David Murray of the Marcia Ball Band, plugs in a white Stratocaster. Albert gives him the floor, reading his licks like a road map before getting behind the wheel and accelerating into each turn. Murray also smiles and shakes his head.

Long after last call, David Grissom, Joe Ely's young Tele ace, is coiled in front of his Fender Bassman amp, feedback streaming into his face, while Collins fans him with a white towel. Albert does the musical equivalent of Ali's rope-a-dope before delivering a final roundhouse blow — reaching down and bending up a minor third, which hits home like a left hook that began in the next county. The guitarists at the side of the stage try to blend in with the wallpaper before the master can say, "Next?"

Albert Collins may not be the fastest blues guitarist around, or the most versatile. He is, however, the most powerful. And even though he enjoys playing at maximum volume, the power is still there when his solidbody isn't even plugged in (as evidenced during the following interview, when he repeatedly demonstrated the tricks of his trade). The fat, full tone comes from the man's hands, and the biting sting comes from the types of licks he plays — as well as knowing just *when* to unleash them.

As with many bluesmen, virtually everything about Collins' style is unorthodox. For starters, he tunes to a minor chord, instead of standard tuning. (It's an *F* minor triad, or a *Dm7♭5* without a root.) Playing essentially in first position at all times, he uses his capo to locate the song's key up and down the neck — hence, using only about a third of the fretboard at times. He picks with his bare thumb and first two fingers, often snapping and yanking up on the strings for emphasis. And while he was inspired by guitarists as diverse as Lightnin' Hopkins and George Benson, his main influences are horn and organ players.

Likewise, Albert's admirers and disciples are spread out all over the stylistic landscape. Robben

Ford, Jimmie and Stevie Ray Vaughan, Larry Carlton, Savoy Brown's Kim Simmonds, and most notably Robert Cray have all dipped into Collins' bag of tricks and incorporated his pet licks into their own styles. (Cray's traditional encore, from his days in small clubs to sold-out stadiums, is Collins' "Don't Lose Your Cool.") Still more guitarists have burned the midnight oil trying to capture that massive tone of his. As Grissom said in the video *Further On Down The Road* (which documented Collins' historic Carnegie Hall concert with Lonnie Mack and Roy Buchanan), "That tone! There's something about that tone that just kills you. I like to think of it like a Louisville Slugger, a baseball bat. Somebody hitting a home run and that bat crackin'. When Albert hits the strings, that's what it reminds me of. I've broken a lot of fingernails trying to play like Albert Collins."

When Albert's first singles — "The Freeze" and later his signature tune, "Frosty" — hit the scene almost three decades ago, his was termed the "cool sound of Albert Collins." In fact, although the gimmicky titles worked, few bluesmen sound as downright *hot*. The only thing cool about Albert's sound is the chills it can send up your spine.

Albert Collins was born 55 years ago in a log cabin in Leona, Texas, a small town about 13 miles from Normangee, where he was raised. From there, his family moved to Marquez, when he was six, and finally to Houston, when Albert was nine. After a brief period of piano lessons and a twist of fate that found his organ stolen, Albert took up guitar. After stints with an Alamo acoustic and an Epiphone, he got his first Fender, an Esquire, in 1952, the year he finally could call himself a professional. He cut his first 45, "The Freeze," in '58. Though it was a regional success, he didn't follow it up until 1962, when he recorded "Frosty," to this day his most enduring and influential tune. (Along with Freddie King, Collins was virtually the only blues guitarist to consistently record catchy instrumental sides.)

With the help of Los Angeles-based Canned Heat, Albert was introduced to the rock-ballroom circuit in 1968 and moved to California. Canned

> *The only thing cool about Albert's sound is the chills it can send up your spine.*

Heat also helped him secure a deal with Imperial Records, and although the results were uneven, many of his tunes from that period still hold up today. After six years without a new record out, the guitarist was signed to Chicago's Alligator label on the strength of his 1978 tour of Scandinavia. He has since cut seven albums for the label, including *Showdown*, his collaboration with Cray and Johnny Copeland, which won a Grammy in 1986.

While he and his band, the Icebreakers, still tour the club circuit steadily, these days Albert is at the peak of his career. He has even made such unlikely inroads as TV commercials (for Seagram's Wine Coolers with *Moonlighting*'s Bruce Willis) and movies (his scene-stealing cameo in *Adventures In Babysitting*). For the album *Spillane*, avant-garde composer John Zorn conceived a sort of "Concerto For Albert Collins," titled "Two-Lane Highway," with the bluesman playing and telling a story. The PBS documentary *Ain't Nothin' But The Blues* used Albert as its focal point, showing him in action at Antone's. His idiosyncratic style is also the subject of a revealing instructional cassette available from Hot Licks.

Typically, the guitarist is humbly taking his new-found visibility in stride. The blues is hard work, and few work harder than Albert Collins — as anyone who saw his performance at Live Aid with George Thorogood can attest. Collins is far from a purist; his brand of blues has always contained larger measures of rock and funk than most. But if the music alone doesn't win inductees over to his camp, there's always the 150' cord he uses for his entrance, and often he wades through the audience and out the front door, like a Teletoting politician stumping for supporters.

His Alligator albums show that not only has Collins gotten a lot of mileage out of his "iceman" tag, but he has gotten a lot of mileage out of a Telecaster, a capo, and his bare hands. "I was told when I started to play," he states in *Ain't Nothin' But The Blues*, "that simple music is the hardest music in the world to play. And blues is simple music." In the following interview Albert discusses

> "*I* was told when I started to play that simple music is the hardest music in the world to play. And blues is simple music."

both the inspiration and the execution of his deceptively simple craft.

What kind of music did you hear before you moved to Houston?

I heard a lot of music, but it was on radio. I wasn't into playing music, but I was around my uncle, Campbell Collins, who's a minister. He played guitar, and I used to watch him. But during that particular time I wasn't really too interested in playing — I was so young. I always liked that piano, though. I used to go to church every Sunday and see them playing piano. Guitar wasn't really of no interest to me, but I used to hear it. When I was 12 or 13, I got interested in guitar. I got a chance to hear more music when I got to the big city, you know.

Who were the first musicians who really had an effect on you?

Actually, Lightnin' Hopkins, from a long time ago. He used to go and play at family reunions — we called them "associations." He'd come to my mother's house, and I used to sit on the porch and watch him play. So I started liking guitar. I still had that thing — I wanted to play piano and organ. So I bought an organ, but it got stolen from me.

You definitely play guitar a lot like an organ.

Yeah, I try to make my chord structures like a [Hammond] B-3.

Was the organ playing you heard at that age mostly church organ?

Church organ, yeah. I didn't hear nothing about Jimmy Smith and them until around '60 and '61. That's when I really got introduced to Brother Jack McDuff and Jimmy McGriff. I really got into McGriff in 1966 because I met him when I moved to Kansas City, Missouri, and I sat in with him. That's why I wanted him on *Cold Snap*. He's always been my idol — him and Jimmy Smith. I've got two favorites, but Jimmy McGriff played more the type of thing I wanted to hear, when I met him in Kansas City. He played jazz, but he'd make it sound so bluesy. I could fit and play with him. That's around the time I met Wes Montgomery before he died. I listened to him a lot, and George Benson.

Did you ever play in those types of organ trios?

Yeah, in Kansas City, with an organist named Lawrence Wright. A bass player couldn't get a job there. That's what was in my ear when I came to California.

Besides being influenced by organists, did you pay much attention to the guitarists who played in those kinds of groups — people like Grant Green?

Oh yeah. I was around Grant Green there; that's where I first met him, too. He'd sit on a stool and play. I sure hated it when he died, because he was a real nice guy.

Who were your favorite guitarists back in Texas?

Who I was really around were T-Bone Walker, Lowell Fulson, Gatemouth Brown, Guitar Slim, and B.B. and Freddie King. The first time I met anybody from Chicago was when Jimmy Reed and Little Walter came to Texas to play. My band and I backed up Little Walter when I first met him, in the early '60s. He had a big hit then with "Juke." Then in 1966 I met up with Howlin' Wolf in Kansas City. It wasn't until the late '70s that I met Buddy Guy, Muddy Waters, and people like that. I'd heard them, but I'd never seen them. I was always into the Texas music — like horn players, instead of harps [harmonicas]. Not many harp players coming out of Texas. T-Bone Walker and Gatemouth Brown always had shows together, the Battle of the Guitars, and that really inspired me. Freddie was more like the guys out of Memphis. I think B.B. inspired him more than anybody else. You can tell by the licks he plays sometimes, and his singing.

What were the Battle of the Guitars shows like?

They were real exciting. I saw T-Bone and Gatemouth, and also T-Bone and Lowell Fulson. They had the big bands because, you know, in Texas

> *"I was always into the Texas music — like horn players, instead of harps."*

at that time the bigger the band, the better. It wasn't just a rhythm section; that was for, like, a jazz group in a small club. The big blues bands always had 13 pieces or even 18 pieces. I had 10 pieces at one time, and then 9 — and I wasn't even playing that well then. I had music teachers with me in my band — like [alto saxophonist] Henry Hayes — and they taught me how to do arrangements for horns. That's why I like brass in my band.

What was Guitar Slim like as a person?

He was a real nice guy — he just drank too much. Died when he was 33 years old. He was a tall guy, and he played the guitar down around his knees. He'd wear pink suits, red shoes — he had a hell of a show. When I saw him, he was playing a [Fender] Broadcaster, I think.

Did you get the idea for the long guitar cord from him?

No — you'd be surprised. I thought of the idea myself, before I saw Guitar Slim do that. A sax player named Big Jay McNeely used to walk out in the audience. So I went down to the music store and said, "I want a 150' cord." The guy looked at me and said, "What do you want that much guitar cable for?" "I'm gonna start playing out in the audience." He started laughing at me. That was in 1953. Then when Guitar Slim came through, he probably had been doing it all the time, but that was the first time I saw him.

Have you tried any wireless transmitters?

Yeah, I tried those, and I was going to buy one. But [record exec] Bruce Iglauer at Alligator said, "What you started out with is a tradition." I don't use no electronics.

Your style is so powerful and electric; obviously at some point you took a left turn from your early influences such as John Lee Hooker and Lightnin' Hopkins.

Well, they really inspired me when I went to guitar. I really wanted to do that, and I used to sit down and play all those guys' records. I met B.B.

when I was 20 years old, and he told me, "Man, find your own identification. That'll help you through the world." I said, "Okay." That's what I did — I tried to find my own identification. I didn't want to play like B.B. or T-Bone Walker.

When you hear younger blues players, you must hear a lot of your influence coming out in their playing.

Oh yeah, I have pretty good ears, and I can hear it. I hear when Stevie Ray Vaughan is playing like Albert King, a little B.B., then he goes into Jimi Hendrix, or me. I appreciate a musician being versatile, but I look at them and think, "Well, can he get his own identification?" I wonder about that a lot. There's so much music around, and you get one particular music in your ear, and then you start playing like this other person. I don't listen to that.

The type of power and tone you got on, say, "Frosty" in 1962 was unlike any guitarist who'd come before. Did you listen more to horn players to develop your sound and style?

Most of mine was horn players and organ players. Because the guitar players, I didn't want to sound like them. What I did was sit down with my band — I had eight pieces — and arrange the horn parts. We didn't name it "Frosty" then. We played that tune for about a year, and people started liking it. "What do you call this tune, man?" I was doing a lot of instrumentals in them days, because they were selling good. I called that tune "Diddley Dah" — because of that horn riff at the start. But that sounded so corny, so when I did the 45 for Bill Hall and Jack Clement in Beaumont, Texas, I called it "Frosty" — because my first 45 had been "The Freeze." Janis Joplin was 15 when I cut that; she used to hang around the studio all the time, and Johnny Winter. She knew Hall and Clement, because Beaumont and Port Arthur, where she was from, were right there together. Me and Johnny have some stuff that's never been released — us playing together back then. I think Hall and

Clement have it in Nashville.

When did you first start using reverb?

I started using reverb in 1965. "Frosty" was just a plain, dry amp.

If you'd given your songs titles like "The Scorcher," people would be referring to the hot sound of Albert Collins.

Well, I tried to make a little identification for my own, you know. We played in Corpus Christi one night, and on our way back to Houston, it was raining real bad and the windshield was fogged up. The bass player said, "Albert, why don't you turn your defrost on?" I thought, "Damn, 'De-frost'!" Finally I cut an album with a group of girls called the Dolls, and they had some time left over in the studio — like an hour and 40 minutes — so Henry Hayes said, "Why don't you do that tune, 'The Freeze'?" So we cut a 45 on *their* time. Sold about 150,000 copies in three weeks' time. That's what started getting my name halfway out there. But when my name really started to spread was when I cut "Frosty." I didn't follow it up until then because I had a good day job. I was playing at night and driving a truck in the daytime. And I mixed paint for automobiles for six years.

When you went to Duke/Peacock Records...

[Producer] Don Robey said I played too much like T-Bone.

Did you?

I didn't think I did, but he told me to come back in a couple of months, if I had something going. My feelings was kind of hurt, so when I cut "The Freeze," he went and got Fenton Robinson from Chicago and cut an instrumental called "Double Freeze." But I put mine out first; they had a dance called the freeze. Robey had my records stopped on the radio, by paying them to play "Double Freeze." Then he tried to get me to sign with him, but I said, "When I offered it to you

> "*I* met B.B. when I was 20 years old, and he told me, 'Man, find your own identification. That'll help you through the world.'"

before, you said no. I'm with Hall and Clement now."

You were one of the first blues players to experiment with funk-type rhythms.

Right. That's from the organ players. Also, at that time, around '59 or '60, I could have been playing with James Brown, but I couldn't read. That's the reason I didn't get the job. Everyone in my band could read, though, and that's how we played gigs like the Holiday Inn and all the white clubs. I had to lay the blues aside; I'd just comp. We got over, though, and I learned a lot from that. "Begin The Beguine," "Canadian Sunset" — my band could play all that [*plays the bass line to "Canadian Sunset"*]. They'd take care of the rest of it [*laughs*]. If I had just played blues, I'd be back on the chitlin circuit. I was trying to keep bread on the table, you know.

When you play funkier stuff, are you pretty much using the same blues licks, except with different phrasing and rhythm?

Just the rhythm is changed, that's all. It's just like playing a blues [*plays a one-chord funk pattern and then solos over the rhythm using exclusively blues licks*].

Before you cut records on your own, did you have much experience playing as a sideman?

No, I never played sideman. Always had my own group. See, I had one of the best bands in the Southwest, as far as blues bands. We could play jazz, blues, pop — like "Body And Soul," "Tennessee Waltz." Gatemouth Brown plays a lot of jazz, too.

Is it hard for you to learn a tune by watching another guitarist do it?

I have to go home and play it. I have to listen to it because my positions are different.

How did you come to use a minor tuning?

My cousin, Willow Young, played like that, but he played in his lap like he was playing a steel guitar. I just got that tuning from him.

Why did you take up guitar without using a pick?

It just came naturally because I was taking piano lessons once a week for about four months. When I did pick up a guitar, Willow didn't play with a pick, so that's how I learned. The first tune I played on a guitar was "Boogie Chillun." Took me two weeks to learn it. John Lee Hooker kind of inspired me — him and Lightnin' Hopkins. I tried to play with a pick, man, but I couldn't do it.

> **"I** tried to play with a pick, man, but I couldn't do it."

That's one of the secrets to your tone.

It's like a muffled sound, yeah. I used to play with all my fingers, and now I play like I'm playing a bass [with the thumb, index, and middle fingers].

When you get that really stinging sound, are you yanking up on the strings?

Just picking like this [*demonstrates his string-grabbing technique, pulling up on the strings*]. Freddie King used fingerpicks and a thumbpick. You know, Johnny Guitar Watson [another bare-fingers player] used to play with me, but he played piano; that's his major instrument. He's rough on piano, man — and organ.

When did you start playing Fenders?

I went to a Fender in 1952. But it wasn't a Telecaster; it was an Esquire. I got introduced to that through Gatemouth Brown. I wanted a Telecaster, but I couldn't afford it, so I went down to Parker Music Company in Houston and had them put a Telecaster neck on my Esquire body. I cut "The Freeze" and "Frosty" and all that stuff on it. Before that, I had an Alamo guitar, a hollow box, where you put a pickup on it, and I played Epiphones in 1950 and '51. I got the idea for the capo from Gatemouth, too. I started without one, but I looked at Gatemouth and said, "Man, you're using that choker." We used to call it a choker. I said, "You get a lot out of that guitar." I hung around him for a while, and his brother played with me, too — Widemouth Brown — and he used a choker, too. Now I can't play without one.

Essentially, then, you play as if you're in first

position and just move the capo up to whatever key you're in.

Well, see, I know where my B♭ and my C and my D are, but my positions are different from the way you'd play because you play in standard tuning. Mine is D minor. [*Author's note: Spelled* F C F A♭ C F, *low to high, it's an F minor triad, or a Dm7♭5 without the root.*]

So if the band is playing in C, where would you put your capo?

At the 7th fret. D is at the 9th fret, and B♭ is at the 5th fret. Up at the 12th fret is my F.

Do you actually capo it that high?

Yeah [*demonstrates, playing in a five-fret range with the capo at the 12th fret*].

Was it a dramatic change, switching from an Epiphone to a Fender Esquire?

It really changed because the Epiphone was like a Gibson, and I'd always feed back in front of the amp. In '65 I finally got a Telecaster.

So on "Frosty" and the records prior to '65 you were using the Esquire with only the rear pickup.

Yeah, with a Telecaster neck on it. When I came to California, I had a 1959 Tele. The first job I played in L.A., at the Hollywood Palladium, it got stolen. I was doing this Teenage Fair thing, and they had Gibson, Standell, and other companies, and Fender gave me another guitar. It was a Telecaster but with a hollow body, and I didn't like it, so I took it to Ace Music in Santa Monica and traded it for the one I've got now, a 1961. Been playing on it ever since. When I bought it, it had the humbucking pickup already on it.

Do you use that pickup very much?

I use both of them. I play in the middle position.

That's an unusual Tele because it's blonde with white binding on front and back.

I had that done. See, I had it refinished about nine or ten years ago, and they put the border around it. I had two guitars done like that, and one of them I gave to the Hard Rock Cafe in Chicago. I'm fixing to get mine refinished again. I tell them,

"Don't mess with nothing inside. Just leave the pickups. Just finish it."

If you had to use a different type of guitar, could you still get your tone?

Almost. I like Gibsons. I tried to buy a Gibson one time, but the neck is different — it's squarer and wider. I got so used to Telecasters, and they have a better bite than a Gibson. The only person I've seen really get down to playing on a Gibson is B.B. I've got big frets on my Telecaster, and that makes a difference, too. I get most of my sound from the amp that I use, and I always like to use my own amp. Sometimes I use an old Twin, and I can almost get the sound. My amp is a [100-watt] Quad Reverb. I've been using it since 1972.

Those are pretty loud amps.

Oh, yeah [*laughs*]. They're loud! I've got two of them. I only use one of them onstage, though.

Is your volume always set at 10?

I always play my amps that way — ever since I've been playing. I change tubes about every six months. I put the treble all the way on 10, the middle on 10, and I don't use bass, intensity, or none of that. Reverb I set at 4.

Do you record with the Quad, as well?

Right. Before they came out with the Quad in '72, I used a [Fender] Bandmaster piggyback model. I cut a lot of records with it. I've still got the bottom, with two 12s, but I lost the top. I'd sure like to find me one.

Most Tele players take the bridge plate off. Why did you leave it on?

That's just what I started out with. So now I rest my hand on it and mute with my left hand. I tried the Strat, but it felt different because I'm so used to that plate. I wound up resting my hand on the strings. And the Strat sounds different from a Tele; the Strat is for rock and roll, actually.

What's that on the cover plate?

In 1979 I was doing a TV show in Rotterdam, in Holland, and they had some lighting effects. So they got this piece of [reflective] tape and said, "This would be nice to go on your guitar." I've been using it ever since. You can buy it in stores.

Why do you play with the guitar strap over your right shoulder?

I started out with the strap across my body, but I felt too strapped in, like I couldn't move.

When you're comping, you usually play through the 12-bar changes without moving your hand on the neck. [*Author's note: Remember, Albert tunes to an Fm chord. Positioning the capo at the 2nd fret, for example, yields a Gm. The first diagram's fingering — illustrating Albert's I chord — would be G6. Next, Albert refers to the IV chord. In the key of G, the IV chord is C; however, the IV can be implied by merely lowering the 3rd of the I chord, which is what Albert does in his second example.*]

Yeah, this is how I make my "I" chord:

And this is how I make my "IV" chord:

And I mute with my ring and little fingers. I play octaves just like this:

Do you always move the capo to whatever key you're in, or do you play in more than one key in the same capo position?

I move it to the key I'm in. Only problem I ever had playing with another guitarist onstage was with Albert King — because he's left-handed, and I can't look at it when he's playing. I first met Albert in Kansas City in 1965. He tunes to a chord. I picked his guitar up onetime and said, "Man, he plays weird, too!" [*Laughs.*] The way he plays, it sounds

like a slide, to me — the way he bends.

You both bend some pretty big intervals.

Like this? [*With the capo at the 9th fret, in D, Albert bends the second string up a whole-step, from F (at his 12th fret) to G. He then drops down a fret and bends the E at the 11th fret up a minor third to G.*]

Doesn't having the capo there, with less string length, make it harder to bend?

It used to, but I guess my fingers got toughened up. Because it used to hurt my hands. They used to call this [the capo] a handicap, but that's what I've always used.

Do you fret with your little finger very often?

Not very much. You could cut that one off, it wouldn't matter.

Did you concentrate for a long time on your intonation? When you bend, it's always right on pitch — in contrast to Buddy Guy, for instance, who often bends up to notes that don't necessarily have anything to do with the key of the song.

Well, see, Buddy's been introduced to Jimi Hendrix. That's the reason why he plays like that. Buddy really don't like to play blues no more. He's into the Jimi Hendrix thing. I'm not sure, but I hope he knows what he's doing, because, like, if I wanted to play like Jimi Hendrix — I'm noted as a blues player. People say, "Hey, man, what you doin'?" *Ain't* no more Jimi Hendrix. I *try* for my intonation to be true.

Your tone and phrasing are very vocal-like, and in fact you seem to sing along with almost all of your guitar licks.

I do. That's why I used to get hoarse on the road. When I play, I'm grunting with it; it's just a habit I have. I've been doing that for years, long before I ever heard George Benson doing it — back when Ray Charles used to do it. I used to sit in high school, humming with my mouth, and then I'd go home and see if I could play it with my hands.

Your vibrato sound is quite a bit different from, say, B.B. King's or Otis Rush's.

It's in my wrist [*shakes a note with his ring finger pushing the string side to side*]. I always use my ring finger; I can't do that thing B.B. does [referring to King's fluttering index-finger vibrato technique].

How did you originally hook up with Canned Heat back in the '60s?

Canned Heat were the ones who really got my albums out. They played at the Music Hall in Houston in 1968, and Lightnin' Hopkins was on the show with them. So they said, "Man, we're lookin' for Albert Collins." And Lightnin' said, "Well, I know where he's playing at." I was playing at a place called the Ponderosa, and they came in and asked me if I wanted to come to California. They were on Imperial Records, and they wanted to get me on the label. So I left Houston in July and went to Kansas City, where my wife's from, and then she went out to Palo Alto, California, while I played some jobs. So I came out to California in November. My first job was the Fillmore West, with Fleetwood Mac and Creedence Clearwater Revival. I met a lot of them rock groups, man, in '68 and '69 — the Doors, Grand Funk, Buddy Miles, a group called the Flock with that violin player [Jerry Goodman]. We had a lot of fun together. Then I did *Love Can Be Found Anywhere*, and [Canned Heat's] Bob Hite wrote the liner notes. The Imperial records didn't get off too good, you know, so after they folded I got with this label in Denver, Colorado, called Tumbleweed and did *There's Gotta Be A Change*.

Some of your phrasing on that album sounds a little like Albert King.

You think so? It probably was, at that time, in 1972. Then Tumbleweed went out of business, and I didn't cut another record until 1979. I worked all up and down the West Coast and back in Texas. I kept working, but the money wasn't real good.

Didn't you quit for a year or so?

Yeah, I quit for about a year, around 1971. I worked with my landlord, doing construction on Neil Diamond's house. After a while he said, "Man, this is not for you. You gotta start playing." I had gotten disgusted with it because I wasn't making no money. I started to get me a truck-driving job, but my wife said, "No, you better go back to music." You just get to the point, you know, where it looks like everybody's making it but you.

Your style seems a lot closer to rock than a lot of blues players. Is that because you listen to a variety of music?

Yeah, I even listen to rap music. But I was listening to a lot of psychedelic music then, starting in 1969, when I really got introduced to it. And I was around Jimi for a minute, when he was 17. I took his place with Little Richard, when he left to play with a group called the Drifters. I worked like 15 dates with Little Richard. Me and Little Richard have been friends for years. By doing that, I got introduced to that kind of rock and roll, instead of just playing blues. I was raised up mostly around jazz musicians — horn players like Arnett Cobb, when he was real popular, and Illinois Jacquet, whose father used to play alto with me.

What was it like recording the John Zorn album? How much of that was improvised?

That was an experience for me. He just told me what was going to be happening, and I just played my stuff around their feel. But he had two drummers [Ronald Shannon Jackson and Bobby Previte]; it went into different moods. They were really good. [*Hums a jungle tom-tom rhythm and plays his patented bends over the top.*] It's a story that I check into a motel, and I go into a room and find a dead man in there. Weird. I enjoyed it, though. It was something different, but I was still playing the same thing. The organ player [Big John Patton] comes from Texas, too, so I could communicate with him real well. He knew where I was coming from.

What was it like working with Robert Cray on the *Showdown* album?

Oh, it was beautiful because Robert and I played together for three years. I played for his high-school graduation party in 1971 — that's when I first met him. The class had to pick between me and Frank Zappa [*laughs*]. I played up in the Pacific Northwest a lot, so I started using Robert and Richard Cousins, his bass player.

You're at the peak of your success right now — Grammys, movies, TV commercials. After so many years, did it hit you by surprise?

Yes. I didn't think it was ever gonna happen. I was thinking about going back home at one time, and my wife said, "Why do you want to go back?

There's nothing there. Keep on playing — somebody'll see you." One time I played at the Whisky A-Go-Go in Hollywood, in '69 — which was the last time I saw Janis Joplin. She came to my show, and the last words she said when she walked out the door were, "You're gonna make it. Keep on." That was the last time I seen her. I watched her grow, from a kid. She always wanted to sing; I was glad to see her get on with it, man.

What was the turning point that got you across to a bigger audience?

Europe really did it. I did a tour of Scandinavia in 1978, before I cut with Alligator. A lot of people over there thought I was dead. I went over there, came back, and cut an album with Bruce Iglauer in '79, and then went back again — to other countries, like England, France, and Germany. Then people back home started noticing what was happening.

What was it like playing at Live Aid?

I was excited, man [*laughs*]. That's when I really got stage-fright — about the first time in my life. I looked out and saw all those people, and George Thorogood said, "Hey, man, you scared?" I said, "Yeah!" He said, "Me, too. Let's go get 'em!"

From the beginning, were you always so animated onstage?

Oh yeah. Once I see some people out there smiling, and it looks like they're in my corner, then it's time for me to go to work.

A SELECTED
ALBERT COLLINS DISCOGRAPHY

Solo albums: *Frosty* ('62-'63), Brylen; *The Cool Sound* ('62-'63 Imperial cuts from *Love Can Be Found Anywhere* and *Trash Talkin'*), Crosscut; *Ice Cold Blues* (Liberty and Imperial sides, late '60s), Charly; *Alive & Cool*, Red Lightnin'; *Live At Fillmore East* ('69), Red Lightnin'; *The Compleat Albert Collins*, Imperial; *There's Gotta Be A Change*, Tumbleweed; *Truckin'*, Blue Thumb; *Albert Collins With The Barrelhouse Live* (Holland, '78), Munich; *Albert "Blues" Collins*, Imperial Japan; *Ice Pickin'*, Alligator; *Frostbite* ('80), Alligator; *Frozen Alive!* ('81), Alligator; *Flash Frozen* (live in Japan, '82), Yupiteru; *Don't Lose Your Cool* ('83), Alligator; *Cold Snap*, Alligator.

With others: Albert Collins, Robert Cray, and Johnny Copeland, *Showdown*, Alligator; Dave Alexander, *Oakland Blues* (credited as "Houston Twister," Albert is featured on three cuts), World Pacific; John Zorn, *Spillane*, Elektra/Nonesuch. Anthologies: *Tenth Anniversary Anthology, Vol. 1 — Live From Antone's*, Antone's; *Genuine Houserockin' Music*, Alligator.

Soundtracks: *Feds.*

On film: *Further On Down The Road*; *San Francisco Blues Festival* ('83); *Ain't Nothin' But The Blues* (live at Antone's, PBS); *Adventures In Babysitting*.

3120